SOMERSET HOUSE
The Palace of England's Queens
1551-1692

SOMERSET HOUSE

The Palace of England's Queens
1551-1692

By

SIMON THURLEY

With contributions by

Patricia Croot and Claire Gapper

Edited by

Ann Saunders and Roger Cline

London Topographical Society
Publication No. 168

2009

London Topographical Society
Hon. Editor: Ann Loreille Saunders, MBE, PhD, FSA

Publication No. 168 of the
London Topographical Society
3 Meadway Gate, London NW11 7LA

ISBN 0 902087 55 X

PRODUCED IN GREAT BRITAIN BY
OUTSET SERVICES LTD, CLIFFORD, WEST YORKSHIRE

CONTENTS

LIST OF FIGURES

ACKNOWLEDGEMENTS

The author and the London Topographical Society are most grateful to the following for permission to reproduce the illustrations below.

Ashmolean Museum, University of Oxford,
    Catalogues 1, 35, 36

His Grace the Duke of Bedford and the
Trustees of the Bedford Estates,
    Catalogue 8

The Trustees of the British Library,
    Catalogue 13

The Trustees of the British Musieum,
    Figures 10, 16. Catalogues 14, 15, 24, 25, 28

Cromwell Museum, Huntingdon,
    Catalogue 12

The Trustees of the Dulwich Picture Gallery,
    Catalogue 9

Government Art Collection, UK: Crown
Copyright,
    Catalogue 37

Guildhall Library, City of London,
    Catalogues 2a, 2b, 3, 10, 16, 18, 19a, 19b,
    20, 21, 27, 29, 39

Hatfield House: by courtesy of the Marquess
of Salisbury,
    Catalogue 5

Magdalene College, Cambridge: by courtesy
of the Master and Fellows,
    Catalogue 11

The National Archive, Kew,
    Catalogues 31, 32, 33a, 33b, 33c

Royal Institute of British Architects, RIBA
Library Drawing collection,
    Catalogues 6, 22

The Royal Collection © 2006 Her Majesty
Queen Elizabeth II,
    Catalogue 30

Sir John Soane's Museum: by courtesy of the
Trustees,
    Catalogues 7, 23a, 23b

Syon House, His Grace the Duke of
Northumberland, Syon Archive,
    Figure 1

Yale Centre for British Art, Paul Mellon
Collection,
    Catalogue 26

EDITOR'S FOREWORD

Crossing over Waterloo Bridge from the south to the north bank, the eye is held by the riverside façade of a superbly dignified eighteenth-century building – Somerset House. A road and a line of trees separate this southern face from the Thames, while the northern entrance front gives onto the Strand close to where Temple Bar once marked the boundary between Westminster and the City of London.

This palace – for it seems no less – was built between 1776 and 1801 to the designs of Sir William Chambers; it was then the largest government office block in Europe. Today, since 1989, the building has been in the care of the Somerset House Trust, with the Courtauld Institute and Gallery occupying much of the northern, Strand frontage; the magnificent courtyard is used for concerts and film showings in summer, while in winter it becomes an artificial ice-rink crowded with skaters.

All this, and even Chambers's edifice itself, is recent history. Two and a half centuries earlier, another building was under construction there. That building was a real palace, commissioned by Edward Seymour, Duke of Somerset, Protector of England during the minority of Edward VI, Henry VIII's nine-year-old son. Seymour, however, became too powerful for his own good and ended his life on the executioner's block, and

his unfinished London palace became Crown property. Eventually, it became the home of queens, both regnant and consort; this book tells its story.

The volume is arranged in two unequal parts; the first, longer section describing the medieval site, the construction and development of the building and its varying fortunes, while a shorter Catalogue reproduces and discusses all the principal illustrations of Somerset House in its changing ownerships.

While the author has recorded his gratitude to those who have contributed to the research, the editors would like to thank all those who have helped to bring this book from a first draft into a reality. Some seventeen libraries, galleries and archives have allowed material to be reproduced from their collections, often without charge; each is acknowledged in the appropriate place. Dr Sheila O'Connell of the British Museum, and John Fisher, Jeremy Smith and Michael Maglio of the Prints and Maps Department of the Guildhall Library have given immense support, as has Kim Harnetty of English Heritage. The Society cannot thank Graham Maney enough for all his care and attention. Roger Cline has compiled the index. We trust that you will be fascinated and moved by this story of a vanished palace.

ANN SAUNDERS

INTRODUCTION

Somerset House is the poor relation in terms of the major sixteenth- and seventeenth-century buildings in London. Other than the *History of the King's Works* sections, nothing utilizing primary material has been written on the seventeenth-century royal palace since Raymond Needham and Alexander Webster's book *Somerset House Past and Present* in 1905. This is surprising given the house's prominent position on the river and the Strand and its enormous influence during the seventeenth century. It was, after all, the principal residence of three Catholic queens: Anne of Denmark, Henrietta Maria and Catherine of Braganza and played a major role in the crisis of the Stuart dynasty.

In 2002 I organized a conference for the Society of Court Studies on Somerset House supported by the Somerset House Trust and inspired by recent excavations of the Stuart palace. A number of major themes emerged: the house as a centre for religious non-conformity; the house as a centre for architectural innovation; and the house as a major London landmark. The speakers reinforced the point that the role of Somerset House in the topography of seventeenth-century London had been grossly underestimated. This book sets out to put that right; to place Somerset House in its topographical context and thus to demonstrate the part it played in London's political, religious and artistic life.

At heart, much of this book is about architecture, but it is impossible to divorce architecture from topography. At every turn the building history of Somerset House illuminates the development of London itself. As a royal palace Somerset House was integrated into the city-wide topography of monarchical power; as the headquarters of royal Catholicism it was both a geographical centre for Catholic worship and the focus of hate and fear amongst Protestants; as a cultural centre it was one of the principal conduits for foreign artistic fashions into the Court and City. Royal power, religion and foreign influence were the three principal ingredients of the explosive events of mid-seventeenth-century England. Somerset House is important in understanding those events and the role that London played in them.

This book attempts to reconstruct the lost palace of Somerset House in its wider context within London. As one of the most important secular buildings in the capital, it was extensively recorded by topographical artists and mapmakers from its foundation. As a building periodically maintained by the royal Office of Works, it was measured and drawn. The Catalogue publishes, for the first time, this rich archive with a commentary explaining why it is important and what it tells us of the house and its environs. Particularly important is a fact that has escaped almost everyone. It is the only seventeenth-century royal house for which we have plans of the state and privy lodgings — that is, the lodgings on the first floor where the queen actually lived. This is because the fall of the land from the Strand to the river means that the royal lodgings at Somerset House were at ground-floor level rather than on the first floor. Thus ground plans of Somerset House uniquely show the royal apartments rather than service areas and kitchens as they do elsewhere. These allow us to get a much more detailed understanding of life at Somerset House.

Our knowledge is enriched by three inventories that have recently been discovered. One for Anne of Denmark has been published in the *Journal of the History of Collections*. A second, for Henrietta Maria, lies unpublished in the Society of Antiquaries. The Somerset House Trust has recently purchased a third, for Catherine of Braganza.

Anne of Denmark's most recent cultural biographer, Leeds Baroll, believed that in studying the court of the queen the buildings which she inhabited were 'irrelevant'.[1] This mistaken view is rarer today than it was ten years ago, but our understanding of the Duke of Somerset, of Anne of Denmark, Henrietta Maria and Catherine of Braganza is fundamentally incomplete without comprehending their principal residence. I would also contend that our understanding of London is incomplete without a deeper understanding of the influence and impact of Somerset House. This book aims to provide the foundations for that understanding.

SIMON THURLEY

1

ACKNOWLEDGEMENTS

This book has been five years in the making, and during that time I have had the benefit of help from a number of people. Esther Godfrey and Dr Olivia Smith spent many hours in libraries transcribing and checking references. Melissa Beasley drew the magnificent set of plans and sections in the text; our discussions teased out many issues that would have otherwise remained dormant. Kim Harnetty organized the rest of the illustrations. Deborah Osborne prepared the bibliography. Their time was paid for by English Heritage which also was good enough to provide a grant for the illustrations. Without support from English Heritage this book could not have been written.

I have had correspondence and discussion with several people over aspects of the text: with Helen Payne on Anne of Denmark, Luc Duerloo on confraternities, and with Anna Keay who was most generous with her material on Charles II's reign. Richard Hewlings and Gordon Higgott kindly took the time to discuss the respective roles of Inigo Jones, John Webb and Hugh May with me. Malcolm Smutts's Court Space conference at the Huntington in 2007 helped focus many thoughts, as did Malcolm Airs's Stuart Palaces conference in Oxford the previous year. I am also grateful to Alan Robson of Fielden and Mawson who kindly made his sketches of Old Somerset House available to me.

I was really delighted when Patricia Croot and Claire Gapper agreed to be my collaborators on the early topography of the site and the excavated plaster work; they have contributed two important sections to this publication. A number of people kindly read this book in draft and were good enough to make many useful suggestions, comments and corrections. I owe special thanks to Richard Hewlings, Anna Keay, Ann Saunders, Mark Girouard and Roger Cline who also compiled the index.

Finally, thank you to Ann Saunders, Roger Cline and the wonderful London Topographical Society for making a book like this possible.

SIMON THURLEY
King's Lynn
December 2008

I. EDWARD SEYMOUR:
PATRON OF ARCHITECTURE

Introduction

SOMERSET HOUSE today bears the ducal title of Edward Seymour, the man who was responsible for its existence. Until the old palace was demolished in 1776, most of what was visible was his, thrown up at breakneck speed to create a setting for his might. Although much has been written about the man who became the Duke of Somerset, most historians have confined their comments on his town house to a few factual observations. The story, though, is more complex.

Seymour's character and abilities have been the subject of considerable historical debate. The great Tudor biographer, A. F. Pollard, writing in 1900, portrayed Seymour as a social and religious reformer, a liberal champion of constitutional freedom. Later historians have seen him described in less sympathetic terms as a dogmatic and unimaginative soldier with conventional attitudes.[2] Recent scholarship has made fewer black and white judgements, but opinions remain divided about Seymour's intentions and his motivation.[3] Diarmaid MacCulloch has, however, recently pithily characterized Somerset as combining 'the reforming zeal of Thomas Cromwell, the *chutzpah* of Cardinal Wolsey and the flashy populism of Queen Elizabeth's doomed Earl of Essex'.[4] This portrait of Somerset, I believe, gets us closer to the man who commissioned a vast metropolitan palace on London's mid-sixteenth-century millionaire's row — the Strand. A man who, like Cardinal Wolsey, not only exercised the power of a king but, because that power was a personal one, wanted to create a setting for it commensurate with his status. Somerset Place, as it was called in the sixteenth century, was built on a royal scale and at a royal speed, like Wolsey's manor of the More near Rickmansworth, or indeed like Hampton Court itself. In this, Somerset is the central character, not merely as the man who paid the bills, but as an active and sophisticated patron making deliberate and careful choices about style and plan.

For a long time architectural historians shied away from regarding Somerset as an intelligent architectural patron. Nikolaus Pevsner, in his 1954 article on Old Somerset House, followed the 'bad duke' view of his character, believing him to be a soldier uninterested in architecture.[5] Recent architectural historians have taken a more sophisticated view of Seymour the patron, attempting to set his work in a wider social and political context.[6] Yet much more needs to be done to rehabilitate Somerset as an engaged and well-informed patron of architecture.

Seymour and the defence of the realm

In 1538 King Henry and his advisors became convinced that a Catholic crusade to invade England was inevitable and imminent. The response was to commission a refortification of the English coastline from Lowestoft in the east to Milford Haven in the west. This building campaign was prosecuted with a sense of purpose and determination that was bred from a genuine sense of threat. By December 1540, in the space of two years, the extraordinary number of 24 new fortifications had been completed and garrisoned. In 1542 the king changed tack; he decided to go on the offensive and thrust England back into continental warfare for the first time since 1523. This war, and its accompanying Scottish campaigns, was also accompanied by extraordinary expenditure on military engineering, at Calais, Guines, Boulogne and elsewhere. The costs at Calais alone were over £120,000 between 1538 and the king's death.[7]

In this Edward Seymour played an important and, eventually, a leading part. Before the marriage of his sister Jane to the king he had been a minor courtier, soldier and diplomat, but the marriage propelled him into a position of power and influence. For ten years after his creation as Earl of Hertford in 1537, he was at the centre of Henry VIII's military campaigns in France and Scotland. These required him not only to master field tactics but also to understand military engineering and to converse daily with master masons, architects and engineers.

Henry's determination to protect England against invasion from France and Scotland and his need to garrison towns on the French coast and Scottish borders entwined the arts of architecture and warfare with late Henrician foreign policy. The king himself was at the centre of this, visiting fortifications, examining plans and specifications and at times overruling his own architects and engineers. Henry's own interest in fortification was reflected amongst leading members of the court. An element of this was simply Tudor machismo; but knowledge of the latest innovations in military engineering was essential intelligence for a member of Henry VIII's inner circle.

The disciplines of history have tended to separate the practice of domestic architecture and military engineering in the sixteenth century, a distinction reinforced by the layout of the *History of the King's Works*. This is essentially misleading. To most members of the court, as to the king himself, there was no distinction between engineering and architecture; for most masons fortification and architecture sat hand in hand. Indeed, in April 1539 Henry gave orders for the construction of fortresses at Sandown, Deal and Walmer, and it was the master mason, master carpenter, controller and surveyor from Hampton Court who were put in charge.[8] The major English fortress designers of the age, John Rogers and Sir Richard Lee, had careers that spanned engineering and architecture. Rogers designed a new royal house for Henry VIII at Hull, and Lee started his career by designing and supervising the construction of the new outer court at Thomas Cromwell's House in Hackney. He subsequently advised Thomas Wriothesley on the conversion of Titchfield Abbey (Hampshire) and built himself a fine house, Lee Hall, at Sopwell near St Albans.[9]

Edward Seymour, as Earl of Hertford, came not only to know Rogers and Lee well, but to work with them in great detail upon the most important building projects of the 1540s. John Rogers was the junior of the pair emerging from the Hampton Court Office where he had been a mason in the 1530s. Probably on the recommendation of the Hampton Court officers, he was sent first to Guines in 1541 and then to Hull where he was responsible for the design of a new royal residence as well as the fortification of the town, working closely with Henry VIII himself. It was probably while refining the designs for Hull that Rogers won the king's trust, resulting in his promotion in the royal works and the granting of a valuable sinecure at the Board of Ordnance.

It is not clear when Rogers first met Seymour, but they went on a top secret mission to Scotland together in May 1544. Thereafter, until Seymour's death, he and Rogers had an ongoing professional relationship. They were closely involved in the fortification of Boulogne and in treaty negotia-

tions with the French in 1546. During the Protectorate Somerset used him for advice, draughtsmanship and design at Sandwich, Sheerness, Guernsey and Portsmouth, and in May 1552 entrusted him with a massive project for the fortification of the Irish coast. It was also Somerset who granted him former church lands in Folkestone and Somerset.[10]

Sir Richard Lee owed his initial advancement to Thomas Cromwell for whom he directed works at his house in Hackney in 1535. Cromwell secured him the post of Surveyor of Works at Calais, one he held with great success, transforming the run-down fortifications into what the Venetian ambassador called an 'impregnable fortress'. It was in Calais that Lee got to know Seymour when he arrived at the head of a Royal Commission to inspect the fortifications there and in Boulogne.[11]

Rogers, Lee and their contemporaries worked very closely with a group of Italian engineers or architects who were employed by the king, his ministers and commanders to advise on the design of new fortifications. England was not alone in seeking the advice of Italian experts. Courts as far apart as France, Russia and Scotland had Italians in their pay to introduce the latest form of fortress, the *trace italienne*, a system of earth angle-bastions capable of withstanding artillery fire.[12] There were probably up to a score of Italians active in England in the 1540s, from Sicily, Naples, Bergamo, Florence and elsewhere.[13]

So who was actually in charge of the design of these fortifications? Clearly there were master craftsmen and surveyors who had the task of drawing the plans and supervising the execution of the work. They had a pool of special (mostly Italian) advisors who were linked into wider European experience of military engineering. These advisors did not have executive powers like the English masons and surveyors, but worked with them on the design of the works. But it is crystal clear from the documents that royal aristocratic officers working in close collaboration with the king bore the responsibility for the design of much that was built.[14]

Right at the heart of this creative scene where avant-garde architectural ideas were being discussed and implemented with an international cast was Hertford. The State papers are filled with examples of his direct involvement in the design of new fortifications. For instance, on 1 April 1546 Lord Lisle, the Lord Deputy of Calais, wrote to Henry VIII describing the receipt by Hertford of a plan devised by the king: 'I toke occasion to shewe unto the same [Hertford] your majesty's plat with the newe addition thereof, being present, Mr Seymour, Sir Richard Leigh and Rogers, which by them was veray well commended ...'.[15] Two months later Hertford himself was writing to the king, enclosing a plan of a mole to be built at Boulogne:

> I should sende this berear [*sic*] Sir Richard candishe unto you with the platte of a mole that is to be made here. I have accordingly depeched him unto your highness with the same whiche by him, your majesties Surveyor of Bulloyne and me and sondrye others what I have spoken withal upon the sygt [sight] and view of the same place, ys thowyet the best and most easiest waye to be don.[16]

These letters sent from France to London prove that Hertford had a very hands-on attitude to the construction of the buildings, personally directing and motivating the workforce.[17]

Somerset was thus not some architectural ignoramus; he was part of a very tight-knit group of patrons, architects and engineers who were at the heart of the most exciting and innovative building projects of the last years of Henry VIII's reign. This interest clearly carried through into his period of supreme power. There is no doubt that for Somerset fortresses were an integral part of his military strategy and foreign policy,[18] and equally there is no doubt that for Edward VI fortresses were important too. In the young king's diary there are several references to fortifications, most of which he can never have seen, but must have known from maps and plans. In August 1552 his diary describes a visit to Portsmouth where he participated in a discussion about the construction of two forts.[19]

This architectural patronage was clearly exercised in the name of the king and was bankrolled by royal coffers. It could be argued that this was simply part of Seymour's job. Yet an examination of his personal patronage reveals a man equally passionately involved in architecture.

The domestic building patronage of Edward Seymour

Somerset Place is the best known of Protector Somerset's personal building projects. However, it was far from being the only one, and perhaps far from being the most ambitious. Even before assuming the role of Protector, Somerset was a considerable private patron of architecture; afterwards his patronage was royal in scale.

A sense of his outlay on building can be gained from an account of his personal expenditure for three and a half years ending January 1549.[20]

Cost of the duke's household	£8,395 6s 5¾d
Cost of works and buildings	£5,532 12s 11½d
Costs of foreign travel	£5,393 19s 2½d
Cost of the duchess's household	£2,707 16s 8d
Cost of the duke's wardrobe	£2,163 15s 3¾d
Costs of wages and liveries	£1,481 7s 3d
Costs of the duke's stables	£911 19s 9d
Cost of household implements	£437 8s 4¼d
Cost of plate, etc.	£361 11s 10d
Total expenditure	£26,935 17s 3¼d

Seymour's second largest outlay was building, amounting to about 20% of his outgoings and averaging £1,500 a year. A prominent courtier could build a fine house for less than £1,500; Sir Nicholas Bacon, while Solicitor to the Court of Augmentations, spent just over £1,250 on Redgrave Hall, Suffolk, between 1545 and 1554. For £3,500, the cost of Sir Thomas Kitson's house, Hengrave Hall in Suffolk, you could make a considerable splash.[21] Thus before work really started on Somerset Place, Seymour was spending very heavily on building.

To manage this level of architectural expenditure required a professionalized office of works. Like Wolsey before him, Somerset had a large office staffed with men of talent.[22] The man in charge was the duke's steward, John Thynne. Thynne entered Seymour's service in 1536 and was by his master's side throughout his career, ending up in the Tower after Seymour's final fall.[23] As both steward and close friend, he was intimately involved in Seymour's building projects. The correspondence to prove this still exists at Longleat amongst the Thynne papers, but only definitively links him with the duke's house at The Brails, Great Bedwyn. Few have doubted that his involvement spread to Somerset Place, but it should be noted that there is no definitive documentary proof. Indeed, when Thynne was questioned by the royal council at Somerset's fall, he denied any detailed knowledge of the financing of the duke's building works.[24] We should set this aside, for it is quite clear that Thynne was integral to the duke's property affairs and was very probably central to the conception of Somerset Place.

Under Thynne came the key financial officer, Sir Richard Fulmerston, Comptroller of the duke's household.[25] Answering to him was the man with day-to-day responsibility for financial management, John Pickarell, who was both Cofferer to the duke's household and his paymaster of works. For Somerset Place and Syon there was a clerk of works, Robert Lawes; Bryan Teshe was the clerk of works at The Brails.[26] By a lucky chance the British Library has one of Pickarell's summary accounts enrolled in May 1553 and covering the period 1 April 1548 to 7 October 1551.[27] The particular books from which the summaries came covered household expenditure as well as building work, but the roll is important as it gives us the totals for work at individual houses and the principal headings under which money was spent. In all, the roll covers 'workes and buildinges' to the value of £16,769, a sum equivalent to that which Henry VIII had, over a ten-year period, spent on remodelling Oatlands Palace in Weybridge; in other words, a great sum of money in a very short timeframe.

Somerset Place	£10,091 9s 2d
Syon House	£5,546 18s 10d
Reading	£993 0s 10d
Odiam	£254 0s 7d
Wolf Hall	£45 6s 8d
Banbury	£94 14s 1d

Moreover, Malcolm Airs has made the point that Pickarell's accounts certainly do not tell the whole story and building expenditure must have also been accounted for elsewhere.[28] Even if the £16,769 were the whole sum, it is clear that after 1549 Seymour's expenditure on building had nearly trebled to approaching £5,000 a year. This was at a time when his annual income had risen to around £13,000.[29] Not only this, but Somerset Place was now absorbing the lion's share.

Before we turn in detail to Somerset Place, it is worth asking what can be learnt of Seymour, his methods and his mind, from his family house, Wolf Hall, and his other two great architectural commissions, Syon House and The Brails, Great Bedwyn.

Wolf Hall can be despatched quickly, as we know very little about Seymour's Wiltshire family seat. It cannot have been particularly large, as when Henry VIII came to stay it had been necessary to convert an agricultural barn into a great hall large enough for the royal entertainment.[30] Miscellaneous accounts also show that there must have been an ornamental garden, as seeds were bought for it.[31]

Wolf Hall was not a suitable residence for the Lord Protector of England, and at the end of 1548 Somerset commissioned a new country house three miles to its east at The Brails, Great Bedwyn. Letters from Seymour's agents and bailiffs describe in some detail the careful siting of the new mansion and progress of its construction. It was never finished, but evidently the ground was levelled, a conduit constructed, foundations laid and a gatehouse commenced. Over two million bricks were to be used and quarries were specially opened. Bryan Teshe wrote to Thynne on 30 March 1549, explaining that he would start marking out the house on the ground 'according to the plat which my Lord's grace resolved upon the last time, and so be ready to lay the foundation'. But more decisions were required and he would go to London 'with a plat of all the levels of the courts and gardens'. In fact there was a continuous stream of information both ways from London to Wolf Hall and back. The Protector found himself approving samples of stone couriered to him and deciding whether the well-head in his new base court should be round or square. When he was too busy to reply promptly, work on the new house ground to a halt, 'for fear of offending my Lord's grace' by making the wrong choices.[32]

All this rings very true given what we know of Seymour's experience with the royal fortifications. Here was a man obsessed with the detail of the work, and having detailed knowledge of construction techniques and materials and a facility to read and amend architectural drawings.

As to the nature of the new house, we have few clues.[33] But it does seem as if Somerset was intending to employ a range of foreign workmen and experts. John Berwick, the duke's receiver general, seems to have been fairly unimpressed by the Protector's foreigners. Two miners, Foscowe and Hance, were sacked as they would only deal personally with the duke and refused to co-operate with his staff. Then the nine French masons appointed for the job proved to be a big disappointment. Berwick wrote to Thynne, saying,

Fig. 1.   Plan of Syon House at the time of the Duke of Somerset, *c.* 1548.
(His Grace the Duke of Northumberland, Syon House)

ye sent us downe suche a lewde company of Frenchmen masons as I never saw the lyke. I assure you they be the worst condicyoned people that ever I saw and the dronkenest; for they will drink more in one day than three dayes wages wyll come to, and then lyke beasts on the floor not able to stoned.

Berwick explained how he had warned them, but they had first ignored him and now left for London, unannounced, leaving debts of 30s unpaid. What the lewd and drunken French masons would have built can only be guessed at, but their presence in Wiltshire (however unwilling) demonstrates Somerset's continued interest in what foreign craftsmen and designers had to offer.

Somerset's lofty promotion in 1547 came with the requirement for him to be located, at all times, close to the young king. Henry VIII had made Hampton Court with its satellite houses, Nonsuch and Oatlands, into his principal country base. The formation of a vast hunting ground centred on Hampton Court and the consolidation of royal land holdings around it in an honour ensured that this would be Edward VI's principal country house, too.[34] Like great royal ministers before him (Wolsey, for example) it was going to be necessary for Somerset to have a house close to the king. His eye fell upon the former royal nunnery at Syon, which had been dissolved in 1539 and converted into a royal house and an armaments factory.[35] It was granted to him by letters patent on 23 July 1547.[36]

Syon was an obvious choice. Somerset would have known the house and estate well, as it was the engine that produced the equipment for his wars in Scotland and France.[37] It is not clear what works Henry VIII commissioned, but a plan from *c.* 1604, that apparently shows the first floor of the main house, suggests that the Office of Works built a standard suite of royal lodgings for him.[38] Between 1548 and 1551 Somerset spent over £5,500 on extending and embellishing these, creating a magnificent modern country house. It must have been much to his liking. The majority of his surviving correspondence is signed at Syon and his household accounts make it clear that he shuttled

between Somerset Place, Syon and 'the courte' by river.[39] In July 1550 the house was host to the king himself, who came across from Windsor to dine with his uncle.[40]

So what did Somerset build at Syon? After his fall the house had a chequered history, owned by a series of courtiers and even briefly being restored as a nunnery under Mary I.[41] But in 1594 it once more became a royal residence and its maintenance fell back to the Office of Works. There is no evidence that any major alterations or extensions were undertaken at Syon between Somerset's death and the re-adoption of the house by Queen Elizabeth. Therefore the surviving royal enrolled accounts describe the house at Somerset's death. It is clear that there was a great hall which was raised up on an undercroft and that from the great hall stairs led up to the great chamber, which, as it had lead laid on its roof, was on the top floor. From here the layout of the rooms is clear; beyond the great chamber was, as was usual, a presence chamber, which led to a privy chamber. Then came a lobby which gave access to the withdrawing chamber, and then onto a bedchamber and a coffer chamber. As far as can be made out, this led to the long gallery. The privy lodgings overlooked the 'green court' and presumably contained the queen's bedchamber which was 'over the second gate'.[42]

To the evidence provided by the royal accounts can be added two further sources. A plan of the first floor of the house that has been dated to 1604 (Fig. 1) and the dimensions provided in an early seventeenth-century 'book of measurements' in the West Sussex Record Office.[43] This shows that in plan Somerset's new house, based on the quadrangular plan of the Bridgettine nunnery, was pretty conservative; the rooms arranged round a court in the same sequence as any late Henrician royal palace. The corner towers seem to date from Somerset's time and give the building a slightly military air; if it were battlemented as today, in Somerset's time Syon would have appeared as a small four-square castle by the Thames.

II. THE STRAND BEFORE SOMERSET PLACE

by PATRICIA CROOT

SOMERSET PLACE was built on the site of several properties on the south side of the Strand, acquired at different times by Edward Seymour between 1537 and 1550: Chester Place, Worcester Inn, the small parish church and churchyard of St Mary of Strand, a chancery inn called Strand Inn and a public inn called the Goat. Seymour's activities in building Somerset Place, as it was known while in his ownership, are surrounded by a great deal of myth, based on the rather sweeping statement by John Stow in his *Survey of London* that Seymour had ordered that all the buildings comprising Worcester Inn, Chester Inn, Strand Inn, the church and churchyard, Strand Bridge, and the lane down to the Thames be 'pulled down and made level ground in the year 1549'.[44] Stow's statement has been amplified by later historians and commentators to comprise as many as four or five bishops' inns: Llandaff's Inn, omitted from Stow's list but mentioned in his description of the Strand, was added later, and perhaps some count the Bishop of Coventry, Lichfield and Chester as three bishops instead of one.

Recent detailed research on the topography and ownership of property in Westminster, including the bishops' inns along the Strand,[45] has made it possible to amend Stow's description and give a more accurate picture of Somerset's activities.

The bishops' inns

Land on the south side of the Strand was used for a number of substantial mansions or private inns created in the Middle Ages and mainly the property of various bishoprics. The location was convenient, midway between the City of London and Westminster Palace, with river access available for travel to both. In the Middle Ages many bishops served the king as his principal officers and spent considerable time in London, using their inns in Westminster. Bishops who did not have public office tended to let their inns to men who did. By the sixteenth century, therefore, the inns along the river had become accepted as quasi-official residences for crown officials. Not only that, they also had become part of the housing of

the government bureaucracy, since most of the principal officers of the Crown also housed the clerks who worked under them.[46]

At around the same time as the monasteries were dissolved, most of the bishops' inns along the Strand were taken from their bishoprics and transferred to the king's closest courtiers and officials, and this is therefore generally seen as part of Henry's attack on the Church and its influence. Although Henry was changing the nature of the Court and government, with more secular appointments, and removing churchmen from official life to a great extent, the removal of inns near Westminster from episcopal ownership, taken by exchange and not outright forfeiture, should be seen not as part of the seizure of church lands but as a redistribution of semi-official residences to the new lay officials whom Henry was appointing from among his courtiers. It was part of a tradition of housing ministers near Westminster that began when the Treasury was moved to London in the late twelfth century.

It was a matter of practicalities, since even Henry's building programme could not provide suitable accommodation for all the new men he needed around him. Furthermore, as they were new men, they needed property and residences to suit their new positions and the titles and offices conferred on them; Henry endowed them with monastic lands but accommodated them in the only buildings available in Westminster which could house aristocratic households and retinues. Although they could have simply leased the inns as in the past, the transfer of the freehold was needed in order to allow rebuilding, which was desirable to provide more suitable accommodation for secular and aristocratic families and to obtain the architectural expression of their power and influence, as well as for dynastic reasons.[47] This is the context in which Edward Seymour acquired his first property in the Strand, Chester Inn.

Properties on the site of Somerset Place

Chester Inn was the name commonly used for the property in the Strand belonging to the bishopric of Coventry, Lichfield and Chester. The bishopric had property in Strand parish by the second half of the thirteenth century, but the first indication of an episcopal residence there was under Walter Langton, Treasurer of England 1295-1307 and leading councillor of Edward I, who was Bishop of Coventry from 1296 until his death in 1321. He acquired land and buildings next to the church of St Mary of Strand in or before 1300,[48] apparently to augment the property already held by the bishopric. In 1305 he received a licence to crenellate all his buildings in Strand parish, both those held in right of his bishopric and those built by him of stone and lime on his freehold plot. He also received permission to build and crenellate a stone turret in the angle of his dwelling towards the east by the Thames.[49] Shortly before his death he added a plot 112 ft by 16 ft acquired from the Bishop of Worcester, his neighbour on the west side, to enlarge his mansion[50] and left all his property in the Strand to his bishopric. By 1358 the inn included six shops by St Mary's church, from which the bishopric received 64s a year.[51]

Given that the bishops were often referred to as the bishops of Chester, and that their inn was usually called Chester Place by themselves and others by the sixteenth century, the bishops' inn was certainly the Chester Inn to which Thomas Hoccleve, a clerk of the privy seal, referred as his dwelling in *De Regimine Principium*, completed *c.* 1412. As mentioned, the bishops of Coventry, like other bishops who were not also royal ministers, commonly let their London inns to men who were, as in 1381 when the inn was occupied by John Fordham, keeper of the privy seal. John Stow stated that the lawyers' Strand Inn was also known as Chester Inn because it belonged to the Bishop of Coventry, and because of Hoccleve's connection with a Chester Inn it is assumed that the chancery inn existed in Hoccleve's time, and that the later Strand Inn was part of the Bishop of Coventry's property. However, no other evidence for Strand Inn's existence before the early sixteenth century has been found, nor for its connection with the Bishop of Coventry.[52]

In 1535 the bishop's property in Strand parish was valued at £10 12s a year. The inn consisted of the capital messuage called Chester Place, with gardens, orchards, courts and other buildings, and also thirteen tenements called Chester Rents, which were probably at the Strand end of the inn.

In the thirteenth century the bishops of Worcester also had a small estate in the parish of St Mary of Strand comprising a house occupied by the bishop, which had a chapel in 1282,[53] and plots and houses occupied by tenants; these included a lane from the Strand to the Thames, with a chamber built over it by the river.[54] In 1373 the whole inn seems to have been occupied by the bishop, who had resumed the various plots from his tenants. By the end of the fourteenth century, the inn had a great gate to the Strand, and houses and a plot of land between the gate and its western neighbour, the Savoy: in 1398 the bishop granted keepership of the inn to Henry Cambridge, citizen and fishmonger of London, who was to build on the plot and provide vegetables from the gardens for the bishop's household when in residence. In 1435/6 the bishop also paid sums for the construction of eight houses on the property. By 1535 the bishop was receiving rents of £6 2s a year from his Strand property, as well as residing in the inn: the rented property probably comprised the houses which lined the Strand frontage either side of the gatehouse, as seven tenements there for which details are known accounted for £5 in rent.

The bishops of Worcester also held the advowson of the church of St Mary of Strand, which lay separated from their inn by Chester Place. The bishops were patrons of St Mary's by the 1240s, and continued until in 1546 they were forced to grant the advowson of the church with their inn to Henry VIII (see below).

The church was not appropriated. It stood in a churchyard and, given the site, was not large, but it did house the court of chancery on several occasions, and inquests by the Middlesex coroner. The Pope gave dispensations from penance for ten years from 1354 to those who helped repair the church; a rector who died in 1445 left goods for repair of the chancel and money for improvement of the church.

In 1355 Henry, Duke of Lancaster, granted a plot 70 ft by 30 ft to enlarge the churchyard, probably on the south side. The following year he granted a plot 7 perches square between the church and the Thames with a gateway and chamber on it to the rector, John de Branketre, to live in for life. In 1375 John of Gaunt, Duke of Lancaster, granted the plot to a subsequent rector, William of Wymondham (d. 1377), with the houses Branketre had built on it, but on condition it reverted to Lancaster when William ceased to be rector. By 1401 the rector had been leased a messuage and garden on the north side of the Strand opposite the Savoy by the king as Duke of

Lancaster, possibly as a parsonage house, and it is unclear whether the rector still occupied property between the church and the Thames, as no further references to this site have been found as yet in the duchy records.

Strand Inn, one of the chancery inns affiliated to the inns of court, is the least documented of the former properties on the site of Somerset Place, which perhaps suggests it was not in existence as the house of an incorporated society of lawyers very long. The earliest known reference to it dates from *c.* 1506, when Giles Penny, surveyor to the Dean and Chapter of Wells (Somerset), resided there.[55] Penny and the inn's principal, John Kekewiche, were among five members of the inn assessed in 1523 for the subsidy levied on the members of inns who were officials in the king's courts; for example, John Kekewiche paid on goods of £100, Giles Penny on goods of £200, John Forde on goods of £140, Thomas Hymerford on goods of £50 and Thomas Hanard on goods of £40.[56] The inn was affiliated to the Middle Temple by the early sixteenth century, and Somerset is said to have tried to get the Inner Temple to relinquish to the Middle Temple its readership in one of its chancery inns in compensation for the loss of Strand Inn, but this never took place.[57]

The lack of any reference to the inn before 1500 makes it very likely that the lawyers were using an inn in the vicinity of Strand church which had once belonged to the bishopric of Llandaff, but was no longer in the bishop's possession by 1535. Between 1280 and 1287 Prince Edmund, Earl of Leicester and of Lancaster, granted to William de Breuse, Bishop of Llandaff, a plot of land belonging to the honour of Leicester (later part of the duchy of Lancaster) near the church of St Mary of Strand, on which the bishop had built two houses, the main one north of the other, by his death in 1287. In 1311 the bishop's successor was granted a plot of land 98 ft by 12 ft on the west side of the bishop's houses and next to the church by Edmund's son, Thomas, Earl of Lancaster; the grant was referred to by Stow in his *Survey*.[58] In 1373 the bishop's property, described as his inn and garden near the Strand, was in the hands of the king for debt; in 1399 the inn was given into the keeping of Thomas, Bishop of Llandaff, for 60s a year to the Exchequer, that being the value of the property. Apart from the mention of the bishop's garden as an abutment in a deed of 1479, no further reference to the

bishop's inn in the Strand has been found and the bishopric had no property in Westminster in 1535. Its location suggests that it housed the Strand Inn in the sixteenth century: since the bishop and his successors were not royal officials and therefore had little reason to visit London, it is likely that they let the inn, and quite possibly to lawyers; the chancery inns generally seem to have developed out of the households of officers of the royal courts.[59]

Adjoining the Strand Inn was the Goat Inn leased by 1534 to Richard Yeomans, one of two properties held of the honour of Leicester and lying on the south side of the Strand at the Stone Cross, which had been granted by Henry le Waleys in 1293 to Combe Abbey (Warwickshire). The second property was in St Clement Danes, separated from the site of the Goat by another property comprising several small houses, and consisted of two tenements with gardens and a stable, leased to Nicholas Gravenor, citizen and leatherseller of London; the quitrent to the honour of Leicester was represented by 12s a year paid to the bailiff of the Savoy as receiver of the rents of the duchy of Lancaster.

Kekewiche increased the facilities of Strand Inn by setting up a conduit in the well yard or backside of the Goat Inn to supply water and began erecting new chambers 6 ft within the Goat's garden. These were completed by his successor, Richard Sherard, in 1534, who then negotiated for the use of the site with Yeomans in exchange for a lease of Strand Inn's great garden, which stretched from the Goat's garden to the Thames, when Yeomans desired it. That lease was sealed in 1538, for 35 years at 40s a year, with the lessee to manure twice a year.[60] The location again suggests that the chancery inn was using the buildings and garden which had belonged to the bishops of Llandaff.

Reconstructing the topography of the site

The topography of the site, in particular the way the properties on the east side fitted together before 1550, poses some problems since the creation of Somerset Place obliterated their boundaries (Fig. 2). Furthermore, the creation of a lane on the east side in the 1540s also seriously affected the layout of properties there. On the west side of the site, the boundary between Worcester and Chester Inns can be placed fairly well since Worcester's gatehouse and frontage to

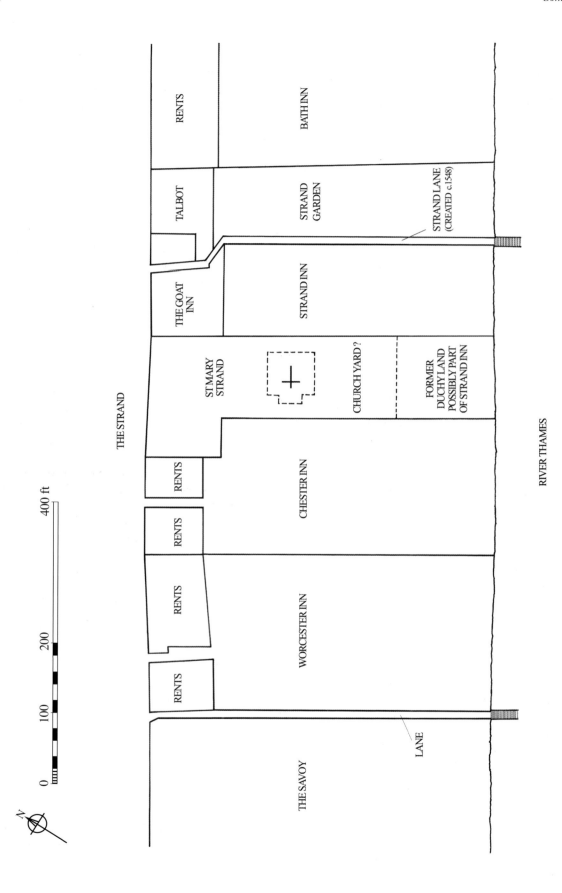

Fig. 2.   Plan of the future site of Somerset Place, *c.* 1525.
(Patricia Croot; drawing Melissa Beasley)

the Strand was unchanged in the sixteenth century. However, the exact measurement of the frontages of the two inns is not certain, nor the size of the site of the church and churchyard and the Goat to the east.

Not much research has been directed towards establishing the layout of properties in the Strand, because of too great a reliance on the *Survey* of John Stow. However, Stow's description of the Strand is in the past tense but undated and he does not indicate that he actually saw the buildings he describes; he is careful to state, when treating Llandaff's Inn, that his evidence for its existence is the grant in the reign of Edward II. In fact, his description of both the chancery inn (Strand Inn) and Llandaff Inn suggests that they lay between the church and the Thames, not fronting the Strand. Later historical works have ignored the subtleties of Stow's description, most notably the *British Atlas of Historic Towns*, where the map purporting to show London c.1520 gives somewhat inaccurate locations for several buildings in the Strand and St Clement Danes.[61]

Contemporary plans for the area are also lacking, but Anthonis van den Wyngaerde's Thames panorama of *c.* 1543 (see **cat. 1**, p. 91) shows some recognizable buildings: Bath Place with two paths to bridges on the Thames, one around the west side of the house, the other through buildings on the east, then a grouping of gables and the church of St Mary, possibly lying back from the Strand with houses in front, though Wyngaerde may have been trying to indicate the houses on the 'island' in the Strand on which St Clement Danes also stood. In front of the church tower seems to be a three-bay building with arched windows, apparently the hall of a separate building lying on the south side of the church, and south of that along the waterfront is a long gabled building of about six bays with a crenellated tower at the west end. Westwards again, along the water is a large mass of building, probably the Savoy hospital, and between the two are some smaller buildings, either Worcester's Inn or some outbuildings (if the latter, then Worcester Inn is part of the Savoy buildings). The perspective and the informality of the drawing make it difficult to be certain of the layout of the individual inns, however. Given the wording of the licence to Langton in 1305, the main part of Chester Inn seems to have been the building by the waterfront: in Wyngaerde's panorama it even appears to be closer to the river than Durham Inn, whose hall in the

early seventeenth century had an entry from the river.

The topography and ownership history of the buildings fronting the south side of the Strand is well documented for the fourteenth and fifteenth centuries, and it is clear that Llandaff's Inn did not front the Strand itself. Since it evidently had lost its identity with the bishopric and passed to other occupants by the sixteenth century, it is difficult to identify its location for certain. The earls of Leicester and of Lancaster held the land south of St Mary's Church and west of Bath Inn and made grants of several plots in the vicinity, which suggests that this is the general location of Llandaff's Inn: the first grant to the bishop describes his houses as lying near the church; the second grant of land was next to the church. In 1479 the bishop's garden lay on the south side of a tenement in the parish of St Clement Danes near the boundary with St Mary's:[62] assuming the garden adjoined the bishop's inn, this would place the inn south of part of the churchyard of St Mary and of the later Goat Inn, stretching eastward to the parish boundary, with its garden straddling both parishes. Room has also to be left for the plot granted to the rector of St Mary's in the later fourteenth century, which could not have been part of Llandaff's inn. This location strongly suggests that it became the Strand Inn of the sixteenth century. In June 1547 the Goat Inn fronted the Strand between the church of St Mary on the west and the parish boundary and tenements in St Clement Danes on the east, with the house called Strand Inn and its garden on the south. Part of Strand Inn may have lain south of St Mary's churchyard: it is not known how the inn was reached from the Strand. The land between the church and the Thames is unaccounted for; it is unlikely to have been added to Coventry's Inn without leaving a trace in official records, and the most likely explanation is that it was either granted to the church of St Mary or became part of the Strand Inn and garden in the sixteenth century. Whatever the case, it later became part of Somerset Place.

Stow also refers to Strand Bridge and a lane under it to the Thames as being part of the property demolished by Somerset. Strand Bridge is mentioned in the sixteenth century as the location in the Strand for various properties on both sides of the highway, close to the junction with Little Drury Lane; it was also mentioned in the Act of 1543 for streets requiring paving, and seems to have been approximately on the site of the modern church of St Mary-le-Strand. As part of the public highway and the principal route between Westminster and London, the bridge itself could not have been demolished by Somerset, and indeed it continued to be used as a location of property into the seventeenth century. Presumably Stow is referring to the lane under it, probably like Ivy Bridge Lane a former water-course. The problem is that no such lane is mentioned in any of the medieval or early-modern documents seen for property in the area, where it would be an obvious boundary or feature to mention. This is unfortunate since there must have been some means of access to the Llandaff's Inn and the Strand Inn, for which this lane would have been ideal. Alternatively, however, there may have been a lane through or beside the churchyard of St Mary's, which was not mentioned separately from the church, and this would have passed to Somerset and been removed with the church in 1547-8.

The lane which appears as Strand Bridge Lane on Morgan's map of 1682 (**cat. 18**) and on modern OS maps as Strand Lane, was apparently created between 1545 and 1549 by Sir Thomas Seymour across land shared between himself and his brother, Edward Seymour. Sir Thomas Seymour, Baron Seymour of Studeley from 1547, was granted the former inn of the bishops of Bath in the Strand in 1545 and retained ownership until his attainder and execution in March 1549; the inn subsequently became Arundel House. Abutments in fifteenth-century deeds indicate that land which belonged to Arundel House in the sixteenth century, lying south of houses in the Strand, was not part of Bath Inn in the fifteenth century but belonged to Llandaff Inn. The most likely opportunity to add the land to Bath Inn was when Strand Inn came into Seymour's hands *c.* 1547. The new lane, which formed the boundary between Somerset Place and Arundel House, was probably created by Thomas Seymour to replace the lane shown in Wyngaerde's panorama, which ran very close to the main hall of his inn down to a landing-stage, with one farther to the west, which similarly ended in a landing-stage used by local residents. Seymour created a new access to the Strand by acquiring a tenement and part of two gardens fronting the Strand from Nicholas Gravenor, who received property in exchange, confirmed by the Crown in September 1549 after Bath Inn had returned into its possession.

Edward Seymour's assemblage of the site

The site of Somerset Place was assembled by Seymour piecemeal over the period 1537 to 1550 (Fig. 2). It is not known precisely when he took up residence at Chester Inn, but it must have been before February 1537 when his son was baptized in the inn's chapel.[63] His residence there was presumably initially as a tenant of Rowland Lee, Bishop of Coventry, Lichfield, and Chester, who was at the time serving the king with some success as Lord President of the Council in the Marches.

Seymour secured the freehold of the inn in April 1537 when Lee was forced by the king to exchange it with Seymour for the latter's property at Kew. The bishop had every reason to feel aggrieved at the exchange and he wrote both to Henry, begging unsuccessfully to keep his inn, since Kew was rather too far to attend the Court, and to Cromwell, asking for good compensation, which his bishopric seems to have received.[64] The inn was confirmed to Seymour, by then Earl of Hertford, and his heirs in 1539 by Act of Parliament when it was described as 'gardens, orchard, court and other buildings'.[65]

In 1546 the Bishop of Worcester had been forced by Henry VIII to exchange his property in the Strand and elsewhere for the former property of the Carmelite Friars in Fleet Street, formally completed in May 1547 after the death of the king. Worcester Inn and the advowson of St Mary's church were granted at farm in 1546 to Sir Ralph Sadler, a royal administrator, and in fee to him the following year.[66] The day after the grant in fee, Sadler conveyed the property to the Duke of Somerset.[67] Worcester Place and the advowson of St Mary's were confirmed to the duke in 1550 after his rehabilitation.[68]

No instrument giving possession of Strand Inn to Somerset has come to light, but he presumably acquired it around 1547. In March 1547 Richard Sherard, who described himself as the former principal of Strand Inn, wrote a memorandum to explain how the Strand Inn's garden came to be leased to Richard Yeomans of the Goat, a document which is in the public records:[69] this may be an indication that the Strand Inn had been closed by then.

The Goat passed to the Crown on the dissolution of Combe Abbey and in 1539 Henry VIII granted the property to Mary Fitzroy, Duchess of Richmond and Somerset, widow of Henry's illegitimate son. Subject to the duchess's life interest, the rents and later the freehold were sold to Thomas Brooke, merchant tailor of London, and John Williams in 1543 and 1544. The two men, with the duchess, sold the Goat to John Skutt, merchant tailor, in 1546 to be held of the king for knight service and 8s a year.[70] The other property was sold to the lessee, Nicholas Gravenor. In 1547 Skutt sold the Goat and its garden to William Gyes of Strand and his wife Christian, who in 1550 conveyed it to the Duke of Somerset in exchange for property Somerset had acquired on the north side of the Strand: they were allowed to continue living in the Goat until they received possession of their property, which was tenanted, at which time they would also be allowed a month to take down the old stables, lofts and chambers at the back of the Goat, which were excluded from the sale.[71]

Although John Stow was in his 20s when Somerset Place was built, his account does not suggest he was an eye-witness to events in the Strand: the fact that not all the buildings on the site were demolished as stated by Stow indicates the degree of hyperbole in his account. Some buildings in Worcester Inn were presumably demolished to enable Somerset to enlarge Chester Place, perhaps forming the stable yard, but the layout of the western side of Somerset Place on Morgan's map of 1682 (**cat. 18**) seems to reflect the area occupied by Worcester Inn, and its gatehouse with the houses either side fronting the Strand remained untouched. There were at least seven of these, two with gardens, let by the Crown in the later sixteenth century: in 1559 one messuage abutted east on the gate of the late mansion called Worcester Place, and south on the said mansion towards the Thames;[72] in 1573 one abutted the former wall of the bishop's mansion on the south, and another on the bishop's garden, though this may not necessarily mean that either the wall or garden still existed in 1573.[73] Access to land and buildings in the south-east corner of the Savoy was granted by the Crown in 1574 over land formerly belonging to the Bishop of Worcester

near Somerset Place through an old gate to the Strand.[74]

While the gatehouse and any buildings along the Strand frontage of Chester Place were demolished, it is unlikely that the main hall and chambers were pulled down, since Somerset continued to live there and to run the government from there for at least part of the period 1547-9, holding privy council meetings there throughout 1547. If the main buildings of the inn were indeed by the river, as Wyngaerde's panorama seems to suggest, then Somerset would not have needed to demolish them to build the parts of Somerset Place attributed to him.

St Mary's church was still in existence in June 1547[75] but, by the time the chantry certificate was being drawn up in the first half of 1548, the church had been dissolved by the Duke of Somerset and the building demolished.[76] A century later it was stated that Somerset had promised to build another church with a minister's house on a new site, but had been executed before he could do so.[77]

Given their location, the Strand Inn buildings must have become part of the site of Somerset Place by 1550; the inn was said by Stow to have been demolished by the duke. The inn and its garden were still mentioned as abutments in Somerset's purchase of the Goat in 1550, whereas St Mary's is called the 'late' church, but it seems likely that even if still standing the inn already belonged to Somerset by 1550. In fact, the creation of Strand Lane suggests that the acquisition and demolition of Strand Inn had taken place by the end of 1548. The Goat Inn was not demolished nor the site incorporated into Somerset's new building. It remained as part of the Crown's Somerset Place estate, being let for periods of 21 years during Elizabeth's reign; by 1567 it was called The George and lay between two other tenements with the garden of Somerset Place on its south side.[78] Its garden however became part of the grounds of Somerset Place, and was later built on.

III. THE DUKE OF SOMERSET'S SOMERSET PLACE

Introduction

ON ASSUMING the title of Protector, Seymour was able to exercise the absolute power of the Tudor imperial crown. His power, like that of the king himself, was a personal one exercised directly by written order and word of mouth. The residence he would require in London needed to reflect both the practical and the iconographic significance of this. Henceforth there would be two royal households and two royal palaces; the king's and Somerset's. King Edward's household was an educational and recreational cocoon while the Protector's was more businesslike, focusing on the nuts and bolts of government. These roles were reflected in the places in which the two households resided. Although they would sometimes co-locate, more often they were housed in close proximity to each other. Thus in practical terms Syon and Somerset Place became satellites to Hampton Court and Whitehall.[79] But Somerset and his house were more ambitious than that since Somerset Place was intended to stake its own position in the iconography of power in London.

After his assumption of power Somerset resolved to continue work at Somerset Place rather than to build anew at another location in Westminster, perhaps closer to Whitehall. The reason for this was that the topography of royal power in London placed Somerset House in a pivotal location. It lay on the Strand, the key processional route between the royal palaces of Westminster and Whitehall in the west and the royal fortress of the Tower in the east. This was the great coronation route used by monarchs in procession before their coronations since at least 1377. But it also lay between Westminster and St Paul's which, during the fifteenth century, increasingly became the amphitheatre for public royal ceremonial in the city. John of Gaunt, that great promoter of royal civic ceremonial, chose to be buried in the cathedral in 1399, the same year in which Richard II's body was displayed there so that all could see that he was dead; Henry V gave thanks for his victory at Agincourt in St Paul's and on his death lay in state there; following the defeat of Lambert Simnel, a great celebration was held there by Henry VII. Prince Arthur and Katharine of Aragon were married at St Paul's; in 1518 and again in 1522 Henry VIII celebrated great diplomatic alliances there.[80]

The Lancastrians, Yorkists and Tudors used St Paul's as the public arena for the monarchy at moments of triumph or when public statements needed to be made. As often as not these occasions were accompanied by a formal entry like that at a coronation. On these occasions the buildings lining the route were dressed to impress both the bystanders and those in procession. Somerset Place was deliberately designed to play a part in this. The design of the Strand façade, as this book will argue, was specifically intended to make the Protector's house one of the pearls on the string that linked Westminster to the Tower via St Paul's.

Clearing the site and early works

Thanks to Wyngaerde's panorama (**cat. 1**), we can visualize the buildings on the site of Chester Inn in about 1544 after Seymour had owned it for about five years. Several letters survive, signed by Seymour at the house,[81] so it is certain that there was suitable accommodation for him there. Wyngaerde shows a structure on the riverfront with three gables and a low tower surmounted by a steeply pitched roof on the west. Lying between the Strand and the Inn seem to have been gardens. The backdrop is formed by the parish church of St Mary of Strand.[82] Wyngaerde's panorama is not accurate or detailed enough to show which of these structures Seymour had rebuilt or remodelled.

What we know of the construction of Somerset Place after 1547 comes from a fulsome account provided by John Hayward in *The Life and Raigne of King Edward the Sixth* published posthumously in 1630, but circulated in manuscript from about 1611-20 and written some years earlier.[83]

> many well disposed mindes conceiued a hard opinion of him [Somerset], for that a church by Strand-bridge and two Bishops houses were pulled downe to make a seat for his new building in digging the foundation whereof, the bones of many who had beene there buried were cast up and carried into the fields, and because the stones of those houses and the church did nothing suffice for his work, the steeple and most

part of the church of St. John of Jerusalem neere Smithfeild most beautifully erected and adorned not long before by Docray [Docwra] Priour of that church was mined and ouerthrowne with powder, and the stones applied to this spatious building. And because the worke could not be therewith finished, the cloister of Paules on the north side of the church in a place called Pardonne church yearde and the dance of death, very curiously wrought about the cloister, and a chapel that stood in the midst of the church yeard, also the charnel house that stood upon the south side of paules (now a carpenters yeard) with the chappell tombes and monuments therein were beaten downe, the bones of the dead carried into Finsbury fields and the stones conuerted to his building. It is constantly affirmed that for the same purpose hee intended to pull downe the church of St. Margaret in Westminster, and that the standing thereof was preserued only by his fall.[84]

In reality, the assemblage of private and episcopal lands to create a vacant site and then the plunder of church buildings to fabricate a house was not unusual. Both Cardinal Wolsey and Henry VIII had bought and exchanged land for the creation of first York Place and then Whitehall Palace; the king himself had plundered many monastic buildings for the construction of his palace.[85] Courtiers all over England were being rewarded with church property which was either cannibalized or converted for domestic buildings.[86] The criticism of the Protector came not because what he was doing was inherently unusual, but because it was so prominent.[87]

The land assembled by Seymour for his house covered an area measuring approximately 500 ft by 400 ft, but the site was not unencumbered. All along the valuable Strand frontage, taking advantage of the dense footfall of Londoners, were shops and taverns. The actual frontage available for Somerset Place on the Strand was thus limited to 135 ft. However, behind the commercial buildings on the Strand the house spread out to its full width of over 300 ft (Fig. 3). The principal entrance to the outer court was to be more or less on the site of the old gatehouse to Chester Inn, and the entrance to the stable and service yards on the site of the gate to Worcester Inn. The boundary between the two episcopal inns remained an abiding factor throughout the history of the house, effectively dividing the principal mansion and its service yards. Another fundamental point was the steep slope from the Strand to the river at this point. The Strand is 46 ft above sea level, the medieval foreshore only 20 ft. This is disguised on the present site as, to construct the present Somerset House, the ground level was raised by over 33 ft (Fig. 19, see p. 67).

The fall in ground level determined the layout of the new house. Seymour set out to build a house of two courts, similar to several of the former episcopal inns on the Strand. But like many London houses, such as Crosby Place in Bishopsgate, the disposition of the courts was constrained by the dense development in this fashionable part of London. Seymour's outer court would essentially be on the Strand, entered from the thoroughfare. But the subsidiary ones would have to lie either side of this as courts running down to the river would have necessitated either the terracing of the ground with courts on different levels, or a massive build-up of fill, as was eventually to happen in 1776 when the present building was constructed. It was cheaper and more convenient to build the courts in a line parallel with the Strand and keep the southern part of the site for a garden. The lie of the land was thus primarily responsible for the house not being built hard against the water's edge, as had been traditionally the case in the middle ages.

The progress of work

It has already been noted that very little documentary evidence survives to enable us to discern the extent of Seymour's work at Somerset Place, let alone its course. John Pickarell's enrolled account covering the period from 1 April 1548 to 7 October 1551 is the principal source, but it can be supplemented by an account taken of Seymour's 'debts and chattels' after his death.[88] The starting point, though, is Pickarell's account that covers £10,091 9s 2d of expenditure. The principal headings are:

Timber boards, planks, rafters, laths, etc.	£417 14s
Nails and ironwork	£521 13s 7d
Chalk, lime, sand, etc.	£266 17s 8d
Wainscot	£125 17s 8d
Brick and tile	£492 8s 7d
Stone and slate	£148 6s 7d
Normandy glass	£52 3s 5d
Skilled craftsmen	£4,040 12s
Other craftsmen	£510 12s 8d
Labourers and gardeners	£2,103 4s
Purveyors	£9 7s 8d
Scriveners and clerks	£101 7s 1d

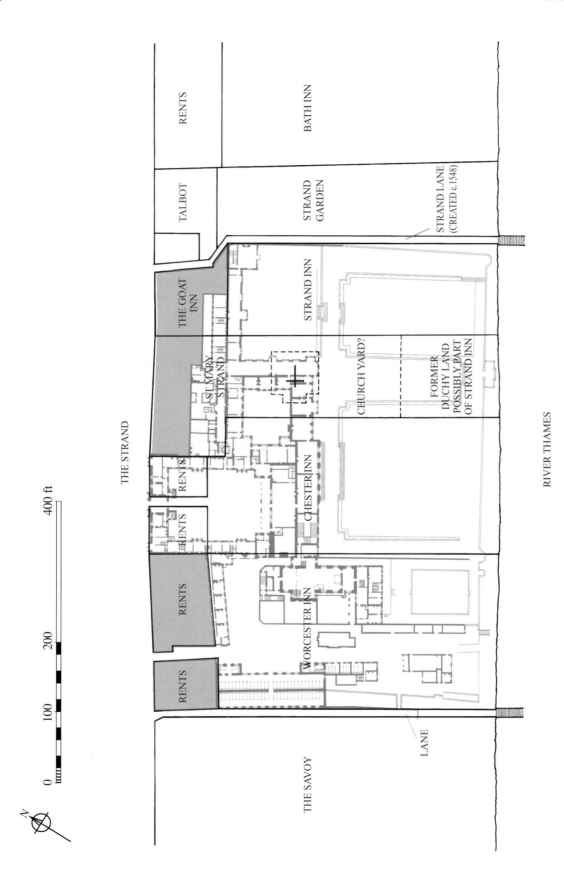

Fig. 3.   Plan of the future site of Somerset House with the palace at its final extent in 1777 overlaid. (Simon Thurley; drawing Melissa Beasley)

The breakdown makes a number of important points clear. First, it is notable that the sums for stone, brick and tile are relatively small. This can be explained by the fact that the majority of the stone for the house and presumably some of the bricks were salvaged from former ecclesiastical buildings. This would have meant that the cost of the rubble foundations, footings and all the core work was minimal. The likelihood is that some of the face stone was also salvaged as both St Paul's and St John's would have had plenty of fair faced ashlar. Second, that there is no figure for lead, the key material for setting cramps in stone, for flashing tile roofs and covering lead flats. This was also clearly salvaged: there was a glut of lead after the Suppression.[89]

Labourers were paid over £2,000 and this would have covered the digging of foundations and the transport of materials across London to the Strand. Structural timberwork and associated metalwork suggest the insertion of floors and roof structures. Some walls must have been completed as the finest window glass was imported from Normandy.[90] The figure for wainscot is comparatively low, perhaps suggesting that the fit-out of the interiors was not completed. By far the largest figure was that for skilled craftsmen, principal amongst whom must have been masons, cutting and setting the ashlar, but also carving the various external embellishments, windows, doorcases and the like.

Some of the artificers are known to us from the accounts, and the first thing to note is that many went on to achieve high office in the Elizabethan Office of Works. John Revell,[91] who was promoted under Queen Elizabeth to be Surveyor of the Royal Works (1560-3), certainly worked at Somerset Place, whether as master carpenter or not is not clear, but it is quite possible that given his seniority (he was master carpenter to the Court of Augmentations) he was in charge of the joinery. Lewis Stockett,[92] another senior joiner, also appears in the accounts. He became Surveyor of the Queen's Works after Revell from 1563 to 1579. He was close to Thynne, in whose London house he had installed panelling. Another future senior member of the royal works was Humphrey Lovell,[93] Queen Elizabeth's master mason from 1564 to 1585. William Cure, the carver, was the founder of three generations of royal carvers; his son Cornelius later worked at Somerset Place for Anne of Denmark.[94] Less lofty but almost as important was John Puncherdown[95] who was

Queen Elizabeth's Sergeant Plumber from 1545 to 1563. The transfer between Somerset's works office and Elizabeth I's shows that once again there is a close parallel with Cardinal Wolsey whose private works office contributed officials and craftsmen to the royal office after his fall in 1529. It suggests, too, that architecturally these craftsmen were building for Somerset much in the style that they were later to build for the queen.

As well as native craftsmen and administrators, several foreigners appear in Pickarell's accounts. Most, like Petre de Woolfe, are now anonymous figures, however important or skilful they may have been at the time. Two names stand out as being significant, Nicholas Bellin of Modena and Giles Gering, who were the designers and manufacturers of the stucco panels of Nonsuch Palace. It is not clear what these two figures contributed to Somerset's building operations, or even if Somerset Place fell into their remit, but their presence on the list is important none the less.

Josephine Turquet has argued that the iconography of Nonsuch was conceived as an educational tool for Edward, Prince of Wales.[96] Based on a broad view of Henry VIII's last years gleaned from a close look at Hampton Court and Oatlands, I have further argued that Nonsuch was actually built for Edward VI rather than being yet another residence for Henry VIII.[97] Thus for two reasons Somerset would have been very closely involved in discussions about the form and decoration of the house. It must have been there that Seymour got to know the two foreign craftsmen, and after Henry VIII's death they seem to have been heavily involved in his works. Gering, in particular, must have been very active; between April and September 1548 he presented five bills totalling £246 13s 4d, and after Somerset's fall he was still owed £151 13s 3d. Bellin of Modena was paid the lesser amount of £42.

The list of 'debts and chattels' also tells us a little more about materials purchased for the house. Certain fine timberwork items had clearly been amassed ready for installation. 'Shell timber of Walnuttree' worth 30s is listed,[98] as are 50 wainscots worth 100s. But most interestingly two of the Churchwardens of St Bride's purchased a 'Streame of wayneskotte late the said dukes framed for his halle on stronde Place' for the substantial sum of £26 8s 4d. This wainscot turns out, according to Stow, to have been a screen:

> [the parish church of St Bridges, or Bride, of which the choir is old, the nave and aisles new, built at the

Fig. 4.   Anon., traditionally identified as the Earl of Arundel, but recently suggested as being
Edward Seymour, Duke of Somerset.

(His Grace the Duke of Norfolk, Arundel Castle)

charge of William Venor, Warden of the Fleet, *c.* 1480.] The partition between the olde worke and the new, sometime prepared as a screne to be set up in the hall of the Duke of Somersets house at Strand, was bought for eight score pound, and set up in the yeare 1557.[99]

Clearly the great hall, at least, was nearing completion, possibly because it had been reused from Chester Place, or because it had been started soon after 1537. A small number of other fine materials are listed, such as 'marble pyllers bought in [Flaunders] by Willm [Safill]', costing the huge sum of £13 11s 8d. What these would have been for can only be guessed.

Harrison in his *Description of England* is one of a number of chroniclers who tell us that, at the time of his death in 1552, Seymour's great house was incomplete:

Of Summerset place I speake not, yet if the fist beginnner therof (I meane the lord Edward, the learned and godlie duke of Summerset) had lived, I doubt not but it should have beene well finished and brought to a sumptuous end: but as untimely death tooke him from that house and from us all, so it prooved the staie of such proceeding as was intended about it. Whereby it commeth to passe that it standeth as he left it.

An important question is what was standing in 1552? The Elizabethan royal building accounts, which will be referred to below, give us enough information to deduce the layout of the principal rooms. Figure 5 is a conjectural plan of the house in 1600. First, it is clear that, at first-floor level, galleries occupied two sides of the outer court. One overlooked the Strand ('the prevey gallery towards the stronde') and the other leading to it ('the longe gallerie') ran along the east side of the courtyard from the Great Chamber. On the Strand front there was a 'great chamber', possibly in the middle.[100] The west side of the first courtyard was incomplete. The work had probably been carried up to the first floor, and it remained like that throughout the Elizabethan era. Facing the entrance on the Strand was the great hall and kitchen; these were complete, and may have predated Somerset's rise to the Protectorship.

The second court to the east must have been well advanced, as suggested by Elizabethan works accounts. In May 1549 we know that Somerset spoke to Nicholas Ridley, Bishop of Rochester, in the long gallery at Somerset Place. This must have been the gallery on the Strand front or the east side of the outer court.[101] During Elizabeth's reign there are a number of views of the incomplete house. The woodcut map of 1561-70 (**cat. 2**) appears to show the south front of the house much as we see it in later, more accurate, depictions. The main block of the hall and privy apartments are discernible, as is the eastern long gallery. There is an attempt to show the outer court and the Strand range. Significantly, although there appears to be a garden on the riverfront, there also appears to be a huge pile of rubble or building material by the waterfront. John Norden's remarkable view of Westminster from around 1600 shows us more (**cat. 3**). As the elevation is higher in this view, it is possible to see the outer court clearly from above and, more indistinctly, the inner court to its right.

The architecture of Somerset Place, radicalism and tradition

Building coursed in Somerset's blood, whether it was fortresses in France and Scotland or his own projects in London and Wiltshire. Architecture was not merely a function of his military responsibilities and his quasi-royal status; it was an absorbing interest and a personal talent which he wished to exercise. He was intimately involved in matters of design and engineering, discussing schemes with everyone from the king himself to master craftsmen on site. He mixed with the most influential and skilful designers and architects from England and abroad and his craftsmen came from France, Italy and the Low Countries as well as from home. Seymour was a man with an international cultural perspective; he had accompanied Wolsey to France in the late 1520s, and the king and Anne Boleyn in 1532. His diplomatic and military postings took him to the Continent and France and threw him together with men better travelled than himself. He was not only interested in streams of new thought — he swam in them.[102] This interest in the avant-garde is a hallmark of his life and particularly his regime after 1547. His reign was accompanied by a hyperactive social and religious programme of reform and an energetic architectural renaissance.

During the period that Somerset conceived Somerset Place, his circle included three of the most interesting figures in the development of mid-sixteenth-century architecture in England; Sir John Thynne has already been mentioned. He was the builder of Longleat House, Wiltshire, the first and most sophisticated of the Elizabethan great houses; a restrained and refined essay in French-inspired classicism that was at once entirely original and English in form. Somerset's kitchen cabinet also included Sir Thomas Smith, builder of Hill Hall, Essex, and Sir William Cecil, builder of Burghley House, near Stamford. For these men, as for Seymour, architecture was a passion. Smith was appointed Clerk of the Privy Council and Master of Somerset's Court of Requests. Both bodies met at Somerset House. Cecil succeeded Smith at Somerset's Court of Requests and both became Secretaries of State. It is inconceivable that Thynne, Smith, Cecil and Seymour would not have discussed details of the house as it rose on the Strand.[103] This house was designed to stand out, be radical, and be ahead of its time; it was an expression in stone of Somerset's wider world picture, of his political, religious and economic programme of reform.

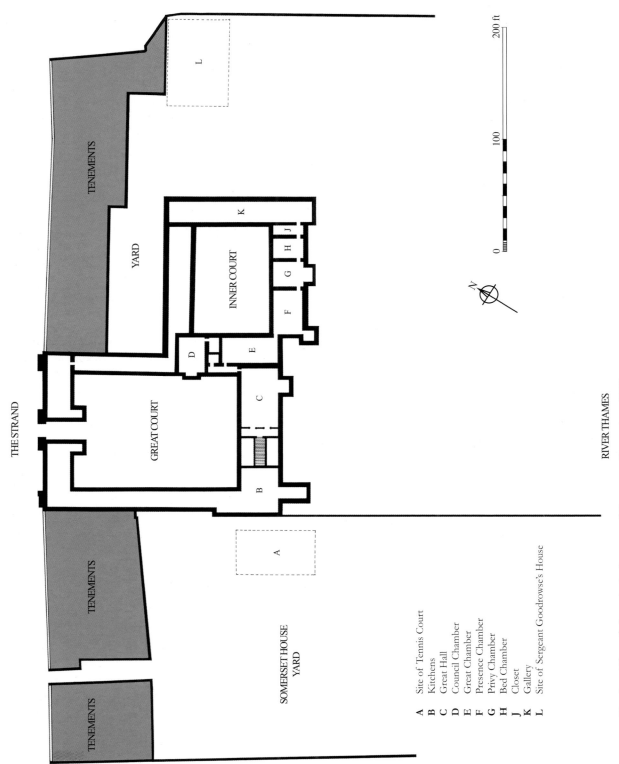

THE STRAND

TENEMENTS

TENEMENTS

TENEMENTS

SOMERSET HOUSE
YARD

GREAT COURT

YARD

INNER COURT

A

B

C

D

E

F

G

H

J

K

L

RIVER THAMES

N

0   100   200 ft

A Site of Tennis Court
B Kitchens
C Great Hall
D Council Chamber
E Great Chamber
F Presence Chamber
G Privy Chamber
H Bed Chamber
J Closet
K Gallery
L Site of Sergeant Goodrowse's House

Fig. 5.   Plan of the principal rooms of Somerset House in *c.* 1600.
(Simon Thurley; drawing Melissa Beasley)

The greatest obstacle to a proper assessment of the architecture of Somerset Place is the almost complete lack of any architectural context. It has been all too easy in the past to claim that it was the first building in England to display a range of features loosely identifiable as 'renaissance',[104] but this position is becoming less and less tenable as archaeology reveals more of its contemporaries.

Twenty years before Somerset House, Wolsey was using applied classical architectural mouldings in terracotta at Hampton Court where excavated fragments of fluted pilasters have been attributed to his phase of work.[105] Wolsey was not alone. Recent archaeological discoveries at Southwark Place, the London house of Charles Brandon, Duke of Suffolk, are if anything more remarkable than the finds from Hampton Court, comprising the whole vocabulary of classical architecture in terracotta.[106] Finds from the Priory of St John Clerkenwell, although more decorative in nature, include a round-headed arch, possibly part of a screen or triumphal archway.[107] Terracotta is, of course, different from stone, and Somerset House had a monumentality to it borne of a unity of materials. Yet most of the terracotta-decorated buildings of the 1520s were painted so as to unify terracotta and brick to give an illusion of stone, so the effect cannot have been very different from Somerset House.

Somerset Place must be seen in this context of increasing use of renaissance architectural elements beginning around 1515. In the 1510s and 1520s this was driven by the availability of northern European craftsmen working in terracotta and in technological advances in moulding and firing. During the 1530s and 1540s the impetus was maintained by an increasing flow of prints and books providing a rich new seam of inspiration. The portrait at Arundel Castle, previously believed to be of Henry Howard, Earl of Surrey, but recently claimed to be of Somerset, is a case in point (Fig. 4). The elaborate architectural setting in which Seymour stands is based on a print by an unknown artist of the School of Fontainebleau published in 1540. If the painting is indeed of Seymour, this reinforces his interest in and knowledge of contemporary continental decorative and architectural prints.[108] Such new renaissance decorative forms were grafted onto traditional structures and mixed with native decorative traditions. This is what happened at Somerset Place. But before this can be properly addressed it is necessary to ask, what did the Strand façade originally look like?

This book argues that the earliest drawn elevation of the house, that by John Thorpe of 1610-11, is in fact not a record drawing but a proposal for the completion and remodelling of Somerset's original façade. So to discover the appearance of the elevation intended by the Protector requires the removal of the parts that we know were added under Anne of Denmark. At the very least the balustrade and the cresting above the windows should be eliminated leaving a flat parapet; it is likely that the balcony in the upper part of the frontispiece is also part of the proposal (**cat. 7**).

The chimneys, however, are likely to be part of the original design; they would have been needed the moment the building came into use. The form of some of them is minutely recorded in a series of drawings undertaken immediately before the demolition of the house (**cat. 32**). Each is a Doric column with its drum decorated with geometrical designs either copied from Serlio's fourth book or influenced by it. These handsome features demonstrate that the roof of the Strand range was designed to be a terrace for viewing processions along the Strand. The chimneys would not have been visible from the street, but from the lead flats they would have been a source of delight (**cats 2, 3, 10**).

During Somerset's life, and possibly up until the end of the first decade of the seventeenth century, Somerset Place either had a flat parapet, or possibly was finished with crenellations like the garden façades. It is also possible that the projections at either end of the façade were originally higher than the walls either side, giving the impression of corner towers. The principal roofline element shown by Thorpe would have been the chimneys.

The elevation (**cat. 7**) is carefully proportioned — the centrepiece was 28 ft wide flanked by curtain walls of 35 ft and terminated at either end by shallow projections 14 ft wide. The whole is, in block form, like Syon, the silhouette of a castle, with a gatehouse and corner towers. The 'corner towers' are not bay windows; they are frontispieces to a 3 ft deep projection. On Thorpe's drawing the effect of the façade is strengthened by the prominence of the ashlar coursing. This must have been the existing appearance of the masonry — this treatment is not found on any of the other drawings in Thorpe's book of drawings. Later elevations of the façade, such as William Moss's drawing in the Ashmolean (**cat. 36**) confirm the façade as being of carefully cut blocks of stone.

Fig. 6.   The English arch for the *Joyeuse Entrée* of Charles V and Philip of Spain into Antwerp in 1547 designed by Lambert van Noort and published in Cornelius Grapheus, *Spectaculorum in Susceptione Philippi Hispaniae Principis Divi Caroli V Caesaris Filii Anno M.D.XLIX. Antverpiae Aeditorium Mirificus Apparatus.* (Antwerp, 1550)

This was lavish. Whitehall and St James's were of brick, so was Hampton Court; Nonsuch was of timber, slate and plaster. The stonework of the walls and windows would have been one, unlike the earlier attempts at classical detailing in terra-cotta.

This façade probably represented, at the time, a new departure for English architecture. It introduced a treatment that, as bay windows, would be taken up at Longleat House and elsewhere as a core component of Elizabethan design. These windows, we now know, were furnished with a rare type of mullion known as a tramline mullion. In the excavations in the inner court of New Somerset House in 2000, a number of window fragments with characteristic tramline mullions were excavated. It is uncertain where exactly these came from, but they seem to have formed part of the Protector's building. Mullions with these profiles later appeared at Longleat House, and Wollaton Hall, Nottinghamshire. Longleat was, of course, the house of Sir John Thynne, providing a direct link with Somerset House. The form of the mullions is French and had only once before appeared in England, in a smaller and fussier form, at Nonsuch. The Protector's French masons must have been responsible for the detail.[109]

The most novel element was unquestionably the centrepiece, based on a triumphal arch. Triumphal arches were a fundamental ingredient of early renaissance architecture, based on an easily understandable antique concept and well-preserved originals. One of the earliest and most influential Italian examples was the triumphal gateway to the Castel Nuovo in Naples built between 1452 and 1466. This structure was influential in inspiring a number of French imitators, including the entrance to Anne de Montmorency's Château de Écouen (1530-8) and most prominently the Porte Dorée at Fontainebleau (1528-40). Although ephemeral arches had been built for pageants, the closest the English had got to building a permanent triumphal arch by the death of Henry VIII was the King Street gate at Whitehall. Unlike the frontispiece to Somerset Place it had three openings, the central one of which was square-headed rather than rounded. But the centrepiece at Somerset Place was something different, much more closely modelled on Roman examples. Several publications became available in the 1540s that would have made this possible: Serlio's third *Book of Architecture*, published in Venice 1540 and translated into Dutch in 1546, was the most influ-

ential, but Jacques Androuet Du Cerceau's book of his own and antique triumphal arches was published in 1549.[110]

These arches quickly entered the mainstream of northern European architecture. In common with their compatriots from Spain and Germany, the English merchants of Antwerp wanted to impress Charles V and Philip of Spain as they made their *Joyeuse Entrée* into the town in 1549. They commissioned a triumphal arch from the painter and architect Lambert van Noort (b. *c.* 1520) at the entrance to the market place (Fig. 6).[116] Lambert's arch was based on Serlio's depiction of the arch of Constantine, but made taller and deeper. Lambert added a second order above the first and a balustrade and attic above that. In fact, the archway, exactly contemporary with the front of Somerset House, contained all the elements of Somerset's gatehouse. The vocabulary of the triumphal arch was thus in the mainstream of fashionable architectural design in the 1540s and its use by Somerset is not really surprising.

The question that has tantalized historians is: who was it who actually composed the Strand elevation? Two of Somerset's craftsmen, John Revell and Lewis Stockett, were clearly designers later in their careers, but they do not seem to occupy a major position in the surviving accounts and it must be doubted whether they were responsible for the Strand elevations. Neither Gering nor Bellin of Modena is known to have been involved in this sort of architectural design; their speciality was the design and manufacture of stucco panels. The portrait now thought to represent Seymour (Fig. 4) shows precisely this sort of stucco work directly inspired by the Fontainebleau school. Indeed, it is possible that the portrait may even have the hand of Bellin in it, particularly in the grisaille setting which, it can be argued, is in a different hand from the portrait itself. Pushing the argument further, it may be that the painting was intended to fit into an architectural framework which incorporated real three-dimensional stucco, possibly in Somerset Place itself.

Thus the foreign stucco makers are ruled out as designers of the main façade. At The Brails Thynne seems to have taken a major role, possibly even directing the design. What we know of his architectural taste and abilities largely comes from Longleat. A satire written against Thynne by a critical and perhaps envious neighbour there in 1575 suggested that Thynne filled Seymour's head 'with plattes and forms and many a subtle thing'.[111]

But who was the master and who was the pupil? Seymour's mind was full enough of 'subtle things' without Thynne. It is much more likely that Somerset was filling Thynne's mind with overblown architectural ambitions than vice versa. Yet Thynne was certainly capable of drawing plans[112] and was deeply involved with the drunken French masons at The Brails.

Thynne, Sir Thomas Smith and Seymour had, between them, enough experience and knowledge of architecture to design the front of Somerset Place themselves, particularly with a gang of French masons and some drafting and structural talent from the English Office of Works. It is unlikely that a single mind, other than Somerset's own, was responsible for the design. This fits what we know of the man. The Strand façade set out Somerset's political programme; Seymour was a soldier and the triumphal arch would have been seen as eminently suitable as an entrance to his town palace. Like the Castel Nuovo and Écouen, the Somerset Place frontispiece probably had a viewing balcony or loggia allowing it to be used to address the populace, which is what Somerset did at Hampton Court in 1549. The roof was a huge terrace from which invited guests could view processions winding their way to and from St Paul's. It was also a vehicle for sculpture, with winged victories over the archway and possibly figures in panels either side of the loggia (**cat. 31**). Most important of all was a niche centrally placed over the gate intended for a statue, but never filled.

Somerset Place was conceived from the start as a quasi-royal palace with a dynamic relationship with the City iconographically reinforcing Somerset's position, but also responding to the ceremonial liquidity of the Strand as grandstand and if necessary pulpit. Yet this was all skin deep. On its inner side the gatehouse had massive tapering stone pylons containing vice stairs and capped with what the accounts call 'types', the Tudor term for lead cupolas (**cat. 38**).[113] There was a frontispiece over the archway with columns,

although these were possibly added in the early seventeenth century. Three clumsily placed windows with pediments looked on to the inner court. Could these be from 1550, or were they added to the composition later? Likewise there are two roundels on the top floor; these could be for terracotta emperors' heads as at Hampton Court and Whitehall or more originally they could be oculi. The whole of the south side of the gate was born of military engineering. As Somerset left his courtyard to enter the Strand, he would have been reminded of his position as a military hero. As he came home again he would be seen as a forward-thinking reformer in touch with the latest in design returning, victorious, through his triumphal arch.

The courtyard itself was unfinished at Seymour's death and was reconstructed by Anne of Denmark in 1611-12. Both the window frontispieces and the loggia shown on Thorpe's plan were added for her and so it is not really possible to make an assessment of the impact or the quality of Somerset's architecture. The river front, however, is shown on early views of the house (**cats 9, 10, 11**) and can be seen to be of a less avant-garde style than the Strand façade. This must tell us something about how Somerset wanted the house to be viewed from the river. From a barge, looking at the house across the garden, it would have looked much like the venerable battlemented inns of the bishops lining the riverfront. This strongly suggests that Somerset was eager to reinforce the traditional appearance of a riverside mansion as a way of demonstrating gravitas and pedigree. Seen from a barge, this was a house with deep architectural and historical roots, not the house of a parvenu duke.

In this way Somerset Place is like its creator, an enigmatic mix of radicalism and tradition, a house at once looking forward to the prodigy houses of Elizabeth's reign, yet still rooted in the chivalric mould of Henry VIII's later years. Seymour was above all a soldier, and Somerset Place was a soldier's house.

IV. ELIZABETHAN INTERLUDE

A house for the princess

IN 1553 Somerset Place became the official residence of Princess Elizabeth. The decision to settle Somerset Place on Elizabeth, taken by her brother the king's advisors, solved the problem of where the 20-year-old princess's official London residence would be. Henry VIII had resolved that she should have Durham Place which he had obtained from Cuthbert Tunstal, Bishop of Durham, in July 1536. The king had at first used the house for official royal functions, including the accommodation of ambassadors, but he ultimately designated it as a residence for the Prince of Wales. In his will, however, Henry VIII bequeathed Durham Place to Elizabeth.

Henry VIII's will made handsome provision for both his daughters and the details of Princess Mary's inheritance were confirmed in early 1548. Princess Elizabeth's took longer to resolve, not because it was more complicated but because of latent suspicion of Elizabeth by Edward Seymour. However, in March 1550, after his fall, Elizabeth was granted her dues by letters patent and Durham House became her official London seat. The grant was a valuable one. Durham House was the finest of all the bishops' residences along the Strand and would make an entirely appropriate home for the third in line to the throne.[114]

There is no evidence that Elizabeth used the house, and by early 1553 the covetous eyes of John Dudley, Duke of Northumberland, had fallen on it. Dudley, now Lord Protector in the stead of Seymour, wanted to assemble a vast northern landholding based on the great historic northern estates, and saw Durham Place, the former London seat of the prince bishops of Durham, as central to his ambitions. Using the Chancellor of the Court of Augmentations as his negotiator, he engineered a swap of Durham Place for the half-completed Somerset Place which had fallen to the Crown after Somerset's death.[115]

In this way Elizabeth came into the possession of the most modern and striking town house in London, sited strategically on the Strand. The only problem was that much of it was uninhabitable. Most of the interior fittings installed before Seymour's death had been removed and sold to pay his debts; much of the rest of the house was incomplete. Some expenditure had been incurred at the house by the Crown after Somerset's fall, but to what effect it is unclear.[116] To make up for this, and probably as part of the swap, the Office of Works was instructed to finish the half-built palace. It is not clear whether Elizabeth had seen the house at this juncture or whether the work was simply commissioned by Northumberland. Either way, the considerable sum of £900 was spent on the princess's new home.

Work can hardly have started when King Edward, who had been very ill for some months, died. Northumberland, from his base at Durham House, attempted to install Lady Jane Grey on the throne, while at Kenninghall Mary proclaimed herself queen. Elizabeth, loyal to her sister, was at Hatfield House in Hertfordshire and on 29 July entered London with an escort of two thousand mounted and armed retainers dressed in striking green and white Tudor livery. They entered Somerset Place where Elizabeth was to remain on and off for about six months.[117]

The building works were probably initially supervised by the keeper of Somerset Place, Robert Dudley, Northumberland's son and Elizabeth's future favourite, but he joined the rest of his family in the Tower of London with the failure of the plot. After Elizabeth's arrival in July, it is likely that responsibility passed to her household, and she may have even expressed her own preferences for how the house should be finished. The craftsman in charge of the project was John Revell, Somerset's master carpenter; over a period of 23 weeks he spent about £200 on the wages of craftsmen and labourers:[118]

Freemasons	£20 17s 8d
Carpenters	£21 12s 9d
Joiners	£26 14s 6d
Bricklayers	£18 0s 22d
Plumbers	£18 12s 5d
Plasterers	£9 6s 8d
Sawyers	£15 19s 0d
Scaffolders	53s 2d
Painters	23s 2d
Tilers	7s 4d
Labourers helping the masons, carpenters, bricklayers and plasterers	£60 4s 6d
Founder	2s 8d

Matt makers	10s 6d
Clerk	£6 0s 16d
Purveyor	40s 8d
Porter	£4 2s 6d

These figures show that, whilst work was clearly still underway on the external shell of the building (plumbers for roofing, masons and bricklayers feature prominently), much of the work was finishing and fitting out the house. The bills for materials confirm this. The largest (about £150) was for timber, some for rafters but mostly for boards and wainscot. The metalwork bill was the next largest outlay at £73, mainly for casement windows, locks and keys. There was also a bill of £16 for glazing. In addition to all this there were a number of large individual contracts, the most important of which were panelling the 'greate gallorye' with wainscot at a cost of £90 and 'paynting and trymmyng the roofe of the withedrawing chamber' by the sergeant painter at a cost of £132 12s 11d.

This is all very important as it confirms that, while Somerset may have completed most of the principal external elevations and the great hall, the residential parts, the great chamber, gallery and closets were panelled and decorated by Richard Pye, master joiner, Ralph Hills, master mason, and Anthony Toto, the sergeant painter. This suggests that in essence there was little difference in architectural style between the works of Somerset and the Office of Works.

By the end of 1553 Elizabeth had left Court and left London; she was to return to Somerset Place occasionally over the next three years amidst the twists and turns of conspiracy politics in which she was implicated. In November 1556, after much lobbying of her sister, Elizabeth received an invitation to come to Court for Christmas. As three years previously, she set out from Hatfield and processed to London with a retinue of about two hundred in livery. At Somerset Place she received many courtiers and visited the queen at Court herself.[119] Just over two years later on 5 December 1558 Elizabeth finally came to Somerset Place as queen. She arrived by river from the Tower where she had been since 28 November and stayed for eighteen days, holding fifteen meetings of her council.[120]

Life in Elizabethan Somerset Place

In 1558 Somerset Place thus became, for the first time, a royal palace in actuality, not merely in function. The accession of Elizabeth did not, however, catapult the house into the royal limelight. The queen's principal residence was Whitehall and nearby St James's had precedence over Somerset Place as a secondary London residence.[121] Despite the fact that in her first year over £130 was spent there,[122] the palace was to become a vehicle for patronage and base for diplomatic and state ceremonial rather than a regular residence.

Elizabeth rewarded her closest courtiers with the great London houses that she had no direct use for. Thus Durham House was given to Essex; Baynard's Castle to Pembroke; the Charterhouse to Lord North, then the Duke of Norfolk and the Earl of Rutland; Somerset Place in the meantime went to Henry Carey, Lord Hunsdon. Carey was Elizabeth's first cousin, created Baron Hunsdon in 1559, given a variety of courtly diplomatic and military appointments and appointed Lord Chamberlain of the Household in 1583.[123] Somerset House became his London seat, the venue, for instance, for his daughter's wedding. It is not clear where his private apartments were, but it is known that Lady Hunsdon had a lodging over the gate.[124] Hunsdon gave up the house after buying his own residence at Blackfriars in 1585.[125]

Hunsdon's quarters occupied only a portion of the mansion and other courtiers had chambers there too. From 1570 the Earl of Leicester had a room, which is interesting considering his earlier brief role as keeper.[126] The principal royal lodgings were used to accommodate ambassadors and suitors during great embassies. On 28 March 1560 the Duke of Holstein, the King of Denmark's nephew, arrived in London and was lodged at Somerset Place. In 1571/2 the Duke of Montmorency stayed at the house while negotiating a possible marriage between the queen and the Duke of Alençon, and alterations were made for their comfort;[127] in 1578/9 John Cassimir, son of Elector Palatine, stayed during his visit, and others came too.[128] It must have been partly to service these distinguished guests that improvements were made to the domestic infrastructure, especially work in 1570/1 to build a new kitchen with attendant offices: a boiling house, larder, rush house and chaundry.[129]

On occasion the queen herself would stay; in fact she stayed at least once in each of fourteen years of her reign.[130] In 1585, for instance, she decided to spend Lent at the house. The reason for this is not immediately clear, but the Whitehall accounts suggest that the Preaching Place may have been encumbered with scaffolding as the Lord Chamberlain's lodgings and other structures were being re-roofed and their walls painted.[131] Barnaby Penethorne wrote to Earl of Hertford in March, reporting, 'there is a new preaching place made at Somerset Place and a great many other building expenses because the queen will spend Lent there'; this is confirmed in the works accounts.[132] The queen heard her Lenten sermons sitting at a window in the outer court where she could be seen by the public who thronged into the courtyard to hear. Her own private services were held in the Savoy chapel next door.[133]

More often, in Elizabethan London, Somerset Place played the very role that its founder had intended for it, as a pearl on the great string of royal monuments strung between Whitehall and the Tower. By the reign of Elizabeth the relationship between the City of London and the monarchy was at its height. The Crown secured international peace and good trading conditions for the merchants and they, in exchange, lent money to the Crown and kept the unruly population in order. It was a cosy club, a neat and mutually beneficial arrangement.

Elizabeth nurtured this relationship, travelling along the processional route from Whitehall, past Somerset Place to St Paul's to celebrate the great events of her reign.[134] In June 1561 a bolt of lightning struck the cathedral's spire, turning the crowing pinnacle of the City into a burning pyre. The destruction of the spire and the damage it caused to the crossing and to the interior was a national disaster. The queen herself instructed the Lord Mayor and the Archbishop of Canterbury to raise money for rebuilding. She offered a thousand marks, a thousand loads of timber from royal forests and her own surveyor of the works to rebuild it. Work to re-roof and rebuild the spire was slow and after years of nagging in 1582 she appointed one of her most senior courtiers to enquire why 'the principal ornament of the chief city of the kingdom was still in decay'. Elizabeth failed to solve the problem, and in 1608 James I was still writing to the mayor and the Bishop of London, calling the state of the cathedral a scandal.[135]

Royal interest in St Paul's was matched by interest in another building on the route from Westminster to the Tower, the Royal Exchange. The Exchange was built not by the Crown, nor even by the City Corporation, but from the personal wealth of Sir Thomas Gresham. After the death of his son and heir, this merchant-cum-royal-servant decided to devote part of his vast fortune to the construction of a stock exchange on Cornhill, on the processional route from Westminster to the Tower. In January 1571 Queen Elizabeth attended what was effectively the opening party, leaving Somerset Place, where she was staying, and processing to the new building which she christened the 'Royal Exchange'. The epithet was apposite. The building was furnished with 26 life-size statues of English monarchs ranged in niches round the inner courtyard. Such pantheons had appeared before in royal buildings and cathedrals, but such a thing had not been seen in a public building outside a church before. This new building was of symbolic importance on the monarchical spine of London and an extraordinary public expression of the mutual interests of trade and the Crown.[136]

On 24 November 1588, after the defeat of the Spanish Armada, Queen Elizabeth knelt before the west doors of St Paul's Cathedral giving thanks to God, before being escorted inside by 50 clergy in full vestments to hear a sermon. After dinner at the bishop's palace the torchlit procession ended triumphantly at Somerset Place.[137] For an occasion such as this, in the midst of national rejoicing, the ability of the queen to stay amongst her people rather than out west was part of theatre of majesty.

The Tudor manipulation of the hearts and wallets of the City by magnificent and magisterial display is strongly within the tradition of the English monarchy which concentrated expenditure on entourage rather than architecture. Queen Elizabeth did not build palaces, but she knew how to stage a royal entry or grace a festival. The strength of her monarchy lay not in massive architectural display, but in silk and pearls, swords and chargers, banners and litters. In this way she wove Somerset Place into the pageantry of London life, using it as royal hotel, conference centre, grandstand, assembly point and crucially as one of the monarchical punctuation points of her capital city.

The plan of Elizabethan Somerset Place

The Elizabethan building accounts give us enough information to deduce the layout of the principal rooms (Fig. 5). At first-floor level galleries still occupied the east and north sides of the outer court, and on the Strand front there was a 'great chamber' probably on the second floor, incorporating a balcony facing the street. It was from here that royal guests could watch the pageantry of the queen's processions to the City.[138] The west side of the court was incomplete, probably only single-storeyed, and it remained that way throughout the Elizabethan era. Facing the entrance was the great hall and to the west of this was the kitchen.[139]

John Thorpe's plan of 1603 (**cat. 7**), which shows the hall and screens passage, demonstrates that there was a second court to the east containing the state rooms and closed on the east side by another long gallery. These must have included the standard sequence of chambers leading off the upper end of the hall. We also know that there was a council chamber on the east side of the outer court.[140] In addition the house had a tennis court and a bowling alley.[141] Somerset's house did not have a household chapel, whether through design or simply because it was not completed, but Elizabethan accounts mention a chapel near the great stair. We know that while Elizabeth used the house the great hall was set up for communal worship or the nearby Savoy Chapel was brought into use. Elizabeth, her ambassadorial guests and

possibly the Duke of Somerset had a private chapel, but where this was located we do not know.[142]

An important feature of the house was its garden. Whitehall presented to the river an uninterrupted wall of building, some of the most important royal rooms being literally at the water's edge. The same applied to the old Palace of Westminster or the much newer Bridewell Palace. At Somerset Place the buildings were set well back from the waterfront and between it and the house were gardens much admired by foreign travellers.[143] Stairs led down from the privy lodgings and the great hall into the garden, whose privacy was assured by a heightened wall to keep prying eyes from the queen. At the bottom of the garden was a new landing stage or 'privy bridge' with its own porter's lodge. And somewhere was a banqueting house.[144]

Somerset had presumably intended to provide lodgings for his duchess and these may have been on the north side of the inner court. There is a stray reference to a 'queen's side' and this may, in the sixteenth century, have been it.

V. DENMARK HOUSE:
PALACE OF THE FIRST STUART QUEEN

Introduction

THERE is no doubt that it was Anne of Denmark who transformed Somerset House into one of the great buildings of seventeenth-century England: great architecturally, but also important as a cultural centre and as one of the pivots upon which royal London turned. The transformation was not immediate; she waited six years before she commissioned any new work. Reconstruction works started in 1609 and continued for nearly five years. Ultimately the cost of completing and furnishing her palace was well over £45,000, making it the single most important and expensive royal domestic architectural work of the early Stuart period. In comparison the cost of the new palace at Newmarket was £4,600, alterations at Theobalds £8,000 and Inigo Jones's Banqueting House at Whitehall £15,000. The scale and importance of the queen's work should not be underestimated. Neither James I nor Charles I built for themselves on this scale. Therefore, and this is an important fact, the queen's lodgings at Somerset House are the only specially commissioned and coherently designed suite of royal lodgings of the early Stuart period, and so the first major reconstruction of an English royal palace since the death of Henry VIII.

In 1603 James I inherited a large pool of royal residences for himself, Queen Anne, the nine-year-old Prince Henry, his three-year-old brother Charles, and Elizabeth, their sister, aged seven. He seems to have been in no hurry to assign permanently the former Elizabethan palaces to his wife and children. While Henry was immediately lodged at St James's, the palace built by Henry VIII for the heir to the throne, the principal focus of the Office of Works was the renovation of the queen's lodgings at Whitehall and Eltham. Eltham seems to have been James's first choice as an eastern country house rather than Greenwich, probably because the hunting there was superior. Two small hunting lodges were also planned, at Bagshot and Ampthill, but it was not until 1607 that James was sure enough of his preferences to commission major new country residences at Newmarket and Royston and to purchase a great new country house at Theobalds. Meanwhile, new lodgings were commissioned for the queen at Greenwich as Eltham had, in practice, proved to be inconvenient. In 1607 expenditure at the Office of Works hit a high of £23,000, double its total in 1604. In 1609-10 a series of further major decisions were made that were to fix the pattern of royal occupation and residence for the remainder of the reign. In 1610 Henry was created Prince of Wales and was granted Richmond, Woodstock and Byfleet; new work was commissioned at Richmond almost immediately. It was at this point that it was decided to bring Somerset House into use as a regular residence.

In 1603 Sir Robert Cecil was asked to look into the rights and privileges of a queen of England. He proposed that Anne's jointure should be modelled on that of Katharine of Aragon, the last royal princess to marry an English king. In all, Anne's settlement was worth £6,376 a year, from which the direct costs of the queen's household were to be met. The cost of building and maintaining the queen's palaces would be covered by the Crown. None of the estates held by Katharine was available and the clutch of houses, castles and lands held by Anne were therefore a new assemblage. Most importantly the Tudor queens' London residence, Baynard's Castle, had fallen out of royal use before the end of Henry VIII's reign; Cecil had therefore to propose an alternative metropolitan seat. Somerset House was the obvious choice, even if it was incomplete and now rather old-fashioned.[145]

From James's accession to 1609, Somerset House had been used very much as it had been under Elizabeth — as lodgings for important state visitors.[146] In April 1604 the Venetian ambassador overheard the Spanish ambassador asking James if he could use the house to lodge the Constable of Castile; he reported to the Doge,

> It is the most splendid house in London, after the royal palace. Somerset House, by ancient usage, belongs to the queen, and so his majesty replied laughing, 'The ambassador must ask my wife, who is my mistress'. The ambassador did so, and the queen readily assented.[147]

Before 1613 Anne had barely, if ever, stayed there and the property had been principally a source of

31

income; the tenements on the Strand frontage were worth £24 8s 4d a year to her, and two other rented plots annually brought in an additional 13s 8d.[148]

Somerset House and the Strand in the early seventeenth century

PATRICIA CROOT

The tenements were a very lucrative part of Anne's estate. Their extent is shown on Figures 7 and 11 (see pp. 37 and 48) and they were probably all retail premises and taverns, each with a shop (workshop) on the ground floor and living quarters above, occupied by a range of tradesmen. They were all of two or three storeys plus garrets, and built of timber and Flemish wall unless indicated below, and most were identified by signs. When in 1650 an Act of Parliament was passed for the sale of 'several tenements in the Strand, parcel of the possession of Charles Stuart and Henrietta Maria', a survey was made of the Crown properties attached to Denmark House, which not only gives an idea of the range of occupations, but also indicates the amount of division of properties and multi-occupation, which took place in the course of the first half of the seventeenth century, turning the 24 tenements into 35.[149] These were:

> The Three Bells, in the Parish of Mary-le-Savoy, occupied by a saddler;
> Another part of the Three Bells, including garden and yard, occupied by a milliner;
> The Sugar Loaf, in the same parish, occupied by a sempster;
> The Gun, with front and rear parts, occupied by a shoemaker;
> A tenement (Mrs Peele's house) next to Somerset House on the south;
> The Prince's Arms, three storeys in front and two at the rear, occupied by a cutler;
> The Golden Lion;
> Tenement adjoining Three Pigeons and Mrs Peele's house standing behind, with a long narrow entry from the street, occupied by Dr Nisbet;
> The Three Pigeons, with another workshop and chamber on the second floor;
> The Feathers, adjoining Somerset House on the north;
> Tenement adjoining Somerset House on the north, occupied by a milliner;
> Cellar under the above tenement and under part of Somerset House, occupied by a heel-maker;
> The White Horse, occupied by a saddler;
> The Golden Fleece, in the Strand, with a shop next

> to the street and another behind, occupied by a cutler, and with a tailor's shop on the 2nd floor;
> The Pied Bull, built of brick and flemish wall;
> The Goat, formerly one tenement but divided into three (four?) separate properties, probably by 1610, one described as 'new built', and another part of 3 storeys in the front with the rear part occupied by a tailor.
> The Mitre tavern;
> A mean tenement in disrepair, called the Red Lion, and occupied by a spectacle-maker;
> The Jackanapes, part brick and part timber, occupied by a confectioner;
> Mortar and Pestle, of brick, probably a tavern;
> The Chequer, built on former waste ground in Strand Lane, leased to William Goodrouse, esquire, in 1603, and including drinking rooms;
> A tavern called the Kings Head;
> The Sugar Loaf in the Strand;
> The Three Pattens, of brick;
> The Golden Ball, or house next to it;
> The Golden Ball, occupied by Mrs Susan Bradford;
> A tenement in Strand Lane adjoining the Chequer, in St Clement Danes parish;
> Another Sugar Loaf in the Strand, occupied by an apothecary;
> A tenement adjoining the Sugar Loaf;
> The Plough in the Strand, occupied by a chandler;
> The Bird in Hand in the Strand adjoining the Mitre, occupied by a chandler.

All these properties were fairly snug: the Three Bells, occupied by two different tenants, was 28½ ft wide on the street front and 31 ft deep and, with the yard behind with a back-house built on it, the site measured 81 ft from the street to brick buildings in Somerset Yard belonging to Somerset House.[150]

In addition to the properties held on Crown leases, some small yards or backsides were also surveyed, which lay between tenements fronting the Strand and the wall of Somerset House, but which had not been included in the leases: one was used by the Bird in Hand and had a cellar under it, one was used with the Mitre and included a shed with four drinking rooms, coal-house, and other outhouses; four separate backsides adjoining Somerset House wall were used with the various tenements of the Goat, and included on one a house of two mean rooms.[151] These yards were still evident on Morgan's map of 1682.

It is not now possible to identify the precise locations of most of these properties, although Hollar's view (**cat. 10**) shows the yards and plot divisions quite clearly. Yet the list makes the very important point that Somerset House was, from the start, sited hugger-mugger amongst one of London's most popular retail districts. The walls of the palace directly abutted the rear walls of taverns and workshops with all the noise, smell, risk of disease and lack of privacy that came with such close proximity. However, in the early seventeenth century such a crowded urban environment was the norm in London and Westminster,[152] and with a lack of choice for living quarters at that time, the Strand, despite being a main thoroughfare between London and Westminster and one of the capital's most commercial streets, remained in demand for aristocratic residences. However, most mansions, rather than having their principal rooms looking out onto the street, maintained the medieval style of inward-looking accommodation facing a courtyard, gardens, or the river Thames, and most, like Somerset House, were also hidden from the street by the rows of shops and houses.

The later sixteenth and early seventeenth centuries saw the apogee of aristocratic living in the Strand, with most of the leading political families having their London residences there.[153] Somerset House's most important neighbour was Arundel House, the former inn of the bishops of Bath, which lay on the east side of Strand Lane. From the mid-sixteenth century various owners had added to the main buildings and laid out gardens. Under the ownership from 1607 of Thomas Howard, Earl of Arundel, and his wife Alatheia Talbot, the house became renowned for their collections of classical antiquities, sculpture, and paintings, as well as drawings and manuscripts, which they with Inigo Jones and their agents brought back from Italy and elsewhere. Lord Arundel made his collection available both for scholars to study and for aristocrats and artisans to learn from. With a shortage of space inside, most of the sculptures were set out in the gardens, in the Italian style: they later formed the basis of the Ashmolean Museum's collection.

A little further east lay Leicester or Essex House, formerly the inn of the bishops of Exeter. In the mid-sixteenth century it belonged to Robert Dudley, Earl of Leicester, who added a storey to the house and a banqueting house by the Thames, *c.* 1575; he was another early collector renowned for his collection of paintings. After his death his widow, Lettice, and then his stepson, Robert Devereux, second Earl of Essex, owned the house, and various family members had apartments there.

West of Somerset House and the Savoy hospital lay Russell House, renamed Worcester House when it passed to the Herbert family, earls of Worcester, in 1601. Dacre House, next to it, was sold to Robert Cecil, first Earl of Salisbury, in 1601, on which he built Salisbury House and Little Salisbury House, acquiring part of the garden of Durham Place to enlarge the site.

On the north side of the Strand Thomas Cecil, Lord Burghley, built Burghley House in the 1560s, known as Exeter House from 1605, and added a smaller house to the north-east on the garden, used by Robert Cecil until he built Salisbury House. Another house was built on the east side fronting the Strand, occupied in the 1620s by Edward Cecil, Viscount Wimbledon. On the west side of Burghley House the Russell family built a new residence, Bedford House, in the 1580s.

This was the architectural and topographical context of early Jacobean Somerset House. By 1603 Somerset House was certainly still a royal palace, but not a very impressive one. Despite minor Elizabethan improvements it was looking old-fashioned next to more up-to-date houses like Burghley House and Salisbury House, and of course anyone entering the outer court could see that it was unfinished. Whoever was going to live in it next would inevitably have to spend significant sums completing and modernizing it. That is exactly what Anne of Denmark did.

Anne of Denmark's architectural patronage

Anne had been only fourteen when she arrived in Scotland from Denmark but had soon become a powerful figure in Scottish politics, building herself a political and social network as well as a royal palace of her own at Dunfermline.[154] Anne's architect was William Schaw, the king's master mason and Anne's own chamberlain. He had been amongst the Scottish party that sailed to Denmark to bring the queen to Scotland and had subsequently travelled in France and elsewhere. Thus he was not only part of the queen's inner circle, but was a cosmopolitan force at her court.[155] At Dunfermline, Schaw designed Anne a block of lodgings on top of the gateway to the abbey precinct. Sadly, it is not clear how this was arranged, but we do know that it contained a dining room, 'dais' room and a wardrobe amongst others.[156] Stylistically the entire enterprise was wholly in the mainstream of traditional Scottish design, with no suggestion of Italianate features or influences from the court of her father Fredrick II.[157]

There were, however, Danish influences on the structure and behaviour of her court. Danish queens did not have a separate household as in Scotland and England, and when Anne arrived at Holyroodhouse there was no recent memory of a consort's court. Thus Anne had to create a new type of household for herself with its own etiquette. Scottish observers believed that what they saw as a more restrained way of royal life at Dunfermline was influenced by her upbringing. William Dundas, writing to Archibald Douglas in June 1590, observed that 'things are beginnand to be greatly altered here; the court wondrous solitary, & ye patron of the court of Denmark is greatly before the king's eye, & ye eye of our reformatours'.[158]

Anne's life was transformed, not entirely for the better, by her move to England. Her influence in the small and incestuous Scottish court may have been significant, but in the tumult of Whitehall her voice was lost. Meanwhile the court which she created in Scotland was now scrutinized and moulded to create a new type of English consort's household.[159] This, too, was perhaps more restrained and dignified than the English expected. Jane Drummond, one of Anne's closest Ladies of the Bedchamber, wrote to Cecil in November 1611,

> I acquented her Majestie with what your lordship wrote of her loving no body, bot dead pictures in a paltry gallery: her majestie commanded me to return the ansur, that she is more contented amongst those hermits pictures in Hir paltry Gallery, then your lordship is with your great Imployments in fair roumes all things considderd.[160]

To house her new Anglo-Scots household, Anne had to rely on the English Office of Works as her architectural mentor, Schaw, had died in 1602. The man in charge of the Office was Simon Basil, the king's Surveyor of Works appointed in 1606 in the stead of James I's Scottish master mason, David Cunningham. Basil was an Office of Works veteran and a client of the Cecils whose talents were largely managerial and administrative rather than artistic. He presided over an astronomical increase in royal building expenditure and the largest series of royal construction projects since the 1540s. It was he who was responsible for interpreting the queen's wishes and producing a scheme for Somerset House.[161]

His brief was to complete the unfinished parts of the house, modernize its appearance and provide a suite of up-to-date state and privy lodgings suitable for the queen and her household. The functional brief for this work may have been issued by Anne herself. Two plans survive of the scheme, probably from within a year of each other, each showing aspects of the work. The more comprehensive is Robert Smythson's copy of a plan of the whole scheme (**cat. 6**). It is incomplete and some parts have incised lines ready for inking that were never marked up. The second (**cat. 7**) may well be a copy of a presentation plan for Anne herself drawn by John Thorpe. The surviving designs are thus in two different hands and were the responsibility of a third. There is strong evidence that yet another hand may have been involved, too — that of Inigo Jones.

Inigo Jones's early career was deeply indebted to Anne's patronage. While he had several wealthy and influential patrons, it was royal patronage that transformed both his status and his creative opportunities. Jones was introduced into the court of Queen Anne through the recommendation of her brother Christian IV of Denmark who had employed Jones to design an allegorical pageant celebrating the homage of Hamburg to the Danish monarch in 1603.[162] Anne immediately took Jones into her circle, commissioning him to design *The Masque of Blackness* in 1604, the first of more than 50 entertainments designed for the early Stuart court. The transition from the queen's masque designer to the queen's architect was a gradual one, but it will be argued here it was one in which Denmark House was a crucial stepping stone.

The documentation recording Anne's reconstruction of Somerset House into Denmark House is prolific. As well as a complete run of enrolled accounts from the Office of Works there are estimates and bills in the State Papers, three plans and a full inventory.[163] Letters and diaries supplement these and allow us to interpret how many of the rooms were intended to be used. This account will attempt to avoid duplicating the full chronological analysis of the house in *The History of the King's Works*[164] and Roy Strong's account of the gardens in *The Renaissance Garden in England*.[165] It takes a thematic and topographical approach to the development and significance of Somerset House, concentrating on what alternations and extensions to the Tudor structure tell us about the court of the Stuart queens and their influence and the place of Somerset House in the metropolis.

Acquisition of the land

A prerequisite for the start of work was the consolidation of land ownership on the site. The land to the west of the house had, during the Elizabethan period, been let out to a variety of people. One Arthur Bromfield had a tennis court, and a man called Walter Kirby rented a house next to it that he had converted into an 'eating house' which was patronized, according to Kirby, by noblemen, knights and gentlemen, although some of Kirby's detractors thought that there were loose women in the establishment.[166] More land to the north and south of the tennis court was leased to the occupants of buildings known as the upper house and the lower house. These houses were held on a lease dated 1630 by John Villiers, Viscount Purbeck, elder brother of James I's favourite and Groom of the Bedchamber to Prince Charles.[167]

The story of the gardens to the south-east of the house is more complicated. Sir Robert Cecil was granted the keepership of Somerset House in October 1603, together with the position of High Steward of the queen's courts. However the queen, probably on Cecil's recommendation, resolved to grant part of the gardens to the king's surgeon and herbalist, John Gerard. Gerard had been Superintendent of the Cecil family gardens at Theobalds and in London and took the lease in August 1604 on the condition that he provide the queen with seasonal herbs, flowers and fruit. His land is described as being

> adjoining on the east part to the mansion house called Somerset House or Strand House, abutting on the West upon the lane commonly called Strand Lane, upon the south upon the bank or wall of the river Thames, and on the north upon the back side of the house standing in the high street called the Strand containing by estimation two acres or there about.

At the same time it was decided to regularize the tenure of the tennis court and other tenanted buildings in Somerset House yard to the west. To make this possible Cecil's patent had to be revoked and re-granted, less the tennis court and garden. This was achieved on 10 October 1606.[168]

While the tennis court and eating house remained for the time being, Gerard gave up his garden, surrendering the head lease to Cecil in 1605. It is not clear why he gave up this prestigious plot of land; perhaps the veteran gardener, now in his 60s, found it too much on top of his own garden in Holborn and Cecil's in the Strand. At least some of the land now seems to have passed to William Goodrowse, one of the king's Sergeant Surgeons who, in 1609, was paid for landscaping the ground broadly on the site of Gerard's plot.[169] We know nothing of Goodrowse except that he would have known Gerard well, as Gerard was, by 1609, one of the most senior members of the Barber Surgeons' Company of which Goodrowse was also a member. With Goodrowse's work completed, the Crown bought his part of the land and the house he had on it for 500 marks in March 1611.[170] Three months later Cecil himself gave up his interest to the queen.[171] By this circuitous route Queen Anne had secured most of the land she required to extend her house eastwards.

The scope of work

Until his death in 1612 Robert Cecil, the queen's Lord High Steward, was the most powerful influence on Somerset House. At the start of work in September 1609 Sir Robert Aston, one of the king's boon hunting companions, wrote to Cecil telling him that the king was pleased that the queen was at Somerset House with her court, and that she had reminded him that he was paying for all the work there.[172] This reminder was probably timely, given her extravagance in Scotland and the ambition and scale of works proposed at Somerset House.[173] James seems to have regarded Cecil's prominent position in the queen's household affairs as a means of restraining her extravagance. Godfrey Goodman, observer of James's court and later Bishop of Gloucester, noted that James used Cecil on at least one occasion to rein in his wife's expenditure on the project.[174]

Cecil was, of course, himself a considerable architectural patron. The second son of William Cecil, Lord Burghley, Queen Elizabeth's great minister and builder of both Burghley House and Theobalds, Cecil was his father's son in architectural patronage as in so much else. Robert Cecil swapped Theobalds for Hatfield where he built himself another great country palace, and in London he built himself a town house in the aristocratic quarter on the Strand to be called Salisbury House after his title.[175]

In 1609 work started in earnest with the demolition of the privy gallery and the rooms adjacent to it, and their immediate reconstruction with a three-storey tower containing closets or cabinets at its south end (V on fig. 7). At its north end was another new gallery, two storeys high, running east (X on fig. 7) and terminating in a stack of cabinets including a library (Y on fig. 7). This was built on the site of Sergeant Goodrowse's former house. The principal lodgings were substantially remodelled, but remained, largely, in their former locations.[176] To facilitate easy communication between the old lodgings and the new gallery a passage (Q on fig. 7) was constructed on the south elevation between one of the Tudor towers and the end of the gallery. Built up on arches, pilasters and columns, it linked the privy chamber and the privy gallery circumventing the withdrawing room (Fig. 8 and **cats 10, 15, 24, 26**).[177]

On the west side of the privy gallery (U on fig. 7), overlooking the inner court (or square court), were three new rooms: two with bow (or cant) windows and the central one with a large chimney breast. These were the queen's great and little bedchambers separated by two closets, her coffer chamber and her diet chamber — probably a breakfast room.[178] The council chamber, bedchamber, presence and privy chambers which originally had their windows looking out onto the inner court (see fig. 5) had them filled in, and new windows were made looking out south onto the gardens and, in the case of the council chamber, onto the outer court. With the northern windows blocked, the state rooms were rearranged to have their magnificent new painted and gilded fireplaces on the inner walls of the court to allow for throne canopies on the walls facing the doors. They were also given new geometric design plaster ceilings with hanging pendants. Several of the innermost rooms were panelled as well as the virtuoso panelling in the two galleries. The sergeant painter later decorated them with gold leaf and oil paint.

Remodelling in the entrance court was no less extensive. Other than the Strand frontage much of the courtyard was either incomplete or only temporary. The west range was therefore completed and the east range, that had contained a gallery, virtually rebuilt three storeys high to match the west range, although with a pitched roof rather than a lead flat. Finally the hall itself was modernized, primarily by removing the central hearth and installing a black marble fireplace on the south wall.[179]

Denmark House: form and function

Denmark House, as completed for Anne of Denmark, was used like no English royal palace since the first half of the reign of Henry VIII. Because of James's virtual abandonment of London for much of the year, Anne's household acquired an independence that had not been enjoyed, for instance, by Henry VIII's later queens and was not reflected in the household of her successor Henrietta Maria. The last truly independent consort's household had been that of Katharine of Aragon based, in the City of London, at Baynard's Castle. Denmark House expressed this independence from the monarch in its form and its function, and in 1614 it was given literary expression in a masque.

By 1614 Denmark House was more or less completed and Anne decided to throw a joint party; half-housewarming and half-celebration of the marriage of her favoured lady-in-waiting, Jane Drummond, to the Earl of Roxburghe. The centrepiece of the celebration was the performance of a masque by Samuel Daniel, *Hymen's Triumph*.[180] A strong theme running through the text is the 'feminine commonwealth' in which 'no wild, no rude, no antique sport' is allowed. There is no doubt that the physical location of this commonwealth was the 'faire structure' of Denmark House whose 'roofs you reared of late', a domain 'sacred to integrity' were 'honour keeps the doore'.[181] The sense of Denmark House being a private world apart from the raucous climate of the king's household was further emphasized by a change in name. On Shrove Tuesday 1617 the queen entertained James to see the completed splendours of her house. The king, in her honour, declared that its nickname 'Denmark House' should henceforth become its official title.[182] This change emphasized the foreignness of the building and its independent existence from the king.

Did this mean that James rarely visited Denmark House? References in letters and official papers generally only refer to the house when the king was involved in something specific there, such as knighting someone or listening to a sermon with the queen and Prince Charles.[183] It is possible that these public occasions conceal a more regular pattern of visits by the king, but this seems unlikely. With Anne unwell in early 1618, the king sent messengers from Whitehall to persuade her to come to see the tilting there. Eventually, Buckingham was sent to coax her out. When it became clear that she really was unwell, James himself went to see her at Denmark House on his way to Theobalds, probably a rare visit.[184]

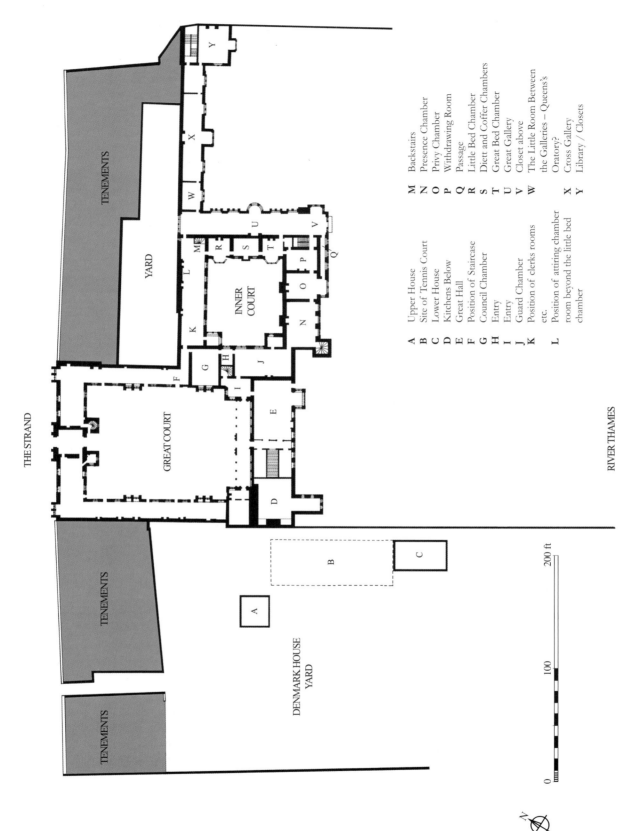

A Upper House
B Site of Tennis Court
C Lower House
D Kitchens Below
E Great Hall
F Position of Staircase
G Council Chamber
H Entry
I Entry
J Guard Chamber
K Position of clerks rooms etc.
L Position of attiring chamber room beyond the little bed chamber

M Backstairs
N Presence Chamber
O Privy Chamber
P Withdrawing Room
Q Passage
R Little Bed Chamber
S Diett and Coffer Chambers
T Great Bed Chamber
U Great Gallery
V Closet above
W The Little Room Between the Galleries – Queens's Oratory?
X Cross Gallery
Y Library / Closets

Fig. 7. Plan of the ground floor of Somerset House in *c*. 1620. (Simon Thurley; drawing Melissa Beasley)

The entrance range

For most people in seventeenth-century London, the entrance façade of Denmark House would have been the only part they ever saw. Its great doors would have been normally closed and the shops and inns either side of the entrance would have concealed the bulk of the building behind.

An analysis of John Thorpe's survey of the house of 1610/11 (**cat. 7**) demonstrates that Anne was responsible for modifying the Strand façade with the addition of a balustrade, open-work cresting and other carved stone refinements. The lead down-pipes carefully recorded by James Hunter in 1775 (**cat. 31**) are dated 1612 and bear the initials I*R and A*R, confirming that the façade as shown by Thorpe owed its appearance to Anne of Denmark's architect. This embellishment transformed the building's public face, possibly even replacing a battlemented roofline facing the Strand. The frontispiece, that had hitherto been an isolated feature in the centre of the façade, was brought into harmony with the rest by the unifying action of a balustrade and the balancing effect of the end fretwork crests. The additions created a façade which now looked modern, not just unfinished.

The components of this design (the flat balustraded roofline, the finials, the open-work cresting) were hardly avant-garde in 1613. Considering the Strand façade as modified for Anne of Denmark in the light of contemporary houses such as Charlton House, Greenwich (1607-12), Audley End House, Essex (1603-16), Bramshill House, Hampshire (1605-12) or Northumberland House nearby at Charing Cross, it can be seen that the works completed in 1613 made Denmark House look modern again. Protector Somerset's triumphal arch, which was undoubtedly a novel feature in 1550, had been, by the early Jacobean period, assimilated into the mainstream of courtier design. What happened in 1612-13 was a reversal of the process as early Jacobean courtier design influenced the completion of the façade. This is most clearly seen in the design of the open-work crests which are direct copies of those erected in *c.* 1570 in the central courtyard of Burghley House (Fig. 9).[185] In 1612-13 Denmark House was not leading architectural style: it was following it.

Equally telling is the relationship of Anne of Denmark's modifications to Sir Robert Cecil's New Exchange built in 1608-9, a hundred yards away on the site of Durham House.[186] The façades

of the two buildings, completed within a very short time of each other, were symbiotic: the Exchange having elements of Somerset House — particularly the high niches between the coupled columns and the triumphal arch frontispiece, and Somerset House having the skyline of the New Exchange. Thorpe's drawing even has pencilled finials. Were both façades designed by Simon Basil? Most scholars believe that the façade for the New Exchange was influenced in some way by Inigo Jones. Jones had toured France with William Cecil, Viscount Cranborne, Robert Cecil's son, in 1609 and on their return Jones probably had had a hand in the design of the south front of Hatfield House. A drawing for the New Exchange exists in Jones's hand, suggesting that Cecil had asked him to advise on this new building, too.[187] Was Jones also asked to advise on the Strand façade of Somerset House?

The earliest plan of part of the house can be found in the Cecil papers at Hatfield (**cat. 5**). It is a plan of the rooms over the gatehouse on the Strand front. These had been, in Queen Elizabeth's time, part of the royal lodgings. They were not only exposed to the noise and smell of London's primary artery, but the Lord Chamberlain's lodgings on the ground floor had been robbed in 1600 and the windows on both floors had been given stout iron bars.[188] In 1605-6 the first-floor gallery and great room were subdivided to make lodgings for Cecil in accordance with the surviving plan.[189] As Cecil had a magnificent house a matter of yards away, these lodgings were presumably an administrative base from which to supervise the queen's works at close quarters.

The outer court

The state of the outer court on Somerset's death is not clear in detail. Although the east and north elevations of the court were probably largely complete, the south and west elevations were not. It has usually been assumed that the loggia on the south side of the first court shown in Thorpe's drawing (**cat. 7**) was, in some way, a rendering into stone of an earlier structure built by Protector Somerset.[190] There is slim evidence for this, although in its position was a 'tarris before the hall' with an 'old shed' above it which could have referred to a timber cloister.[191]

The accounts for 1611/12 describe a new terrace being built in front of the hall, 78 ft long and 13 ft high and two shallow full-height returns

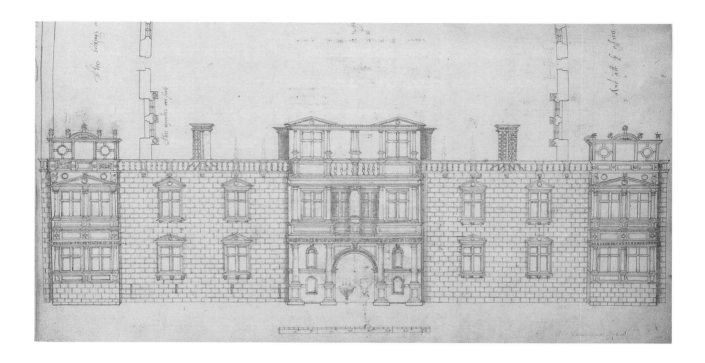

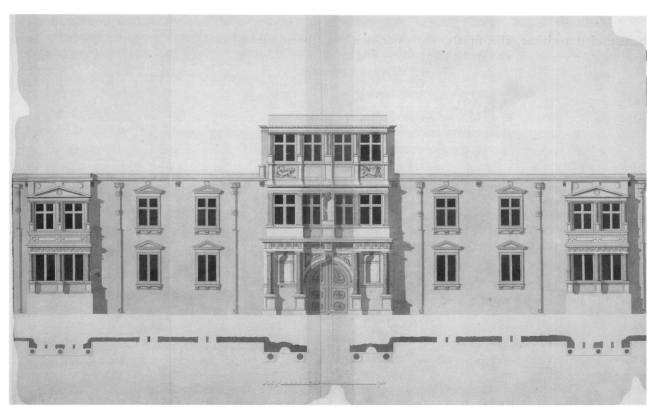

Fig. 8.   Thorpe's Strand elevation and Hunter's measured drawing compared (see **cats 7** and **31**).

Fig. 9.   A perspective view of the Inner Court of Burghley House from the west, J. Haynes, 1755.

being constructed to frame it on the east and west (**cat. 35**). Columns, pedestals, bases, cornice, architrave and frieze were erected by John Benson and John Recorde at a cost of £153 10s. The following year the door into the hall was constructed with two three-quarter columns with capitals on pedestals. By 1611 a loggia was a fashionable, not an avant-garde, addition although Inigo Jones, having seen the great houses of Genoa, believed that a loggia at the entrance to a house was 'ye greatest ornament a house cann haaue'.[192] The central courtyard at Burghley House contained loggias as, by 1612-13, did most contemporary courtier mansions.[193] Smythson's plan (**cat. 6**) shows a loggia of ten columns and two returns at the east and west ends. Thorpe shows eight columns with returns and a projecting porch in the central bay (**cat. 7**). The two plans agree that there were to be square piers with engaged half-round columns (although Smythson only shows them in the centre). The exactly

contemporary parallels for this are two loggias both designed by Jones for Robert Cecil: the south front of Hatfield House, where the piers are square in section but the pilasters are flat and not half-round, and a design for the New Exchange which has half-columns on square piers like Somerset House.

The columnation on Thorpe's plan agrees with the plans of 1706 and 1775 (**cats 19, 33**), but on these the arcade rested on freestanding columns on square bases. The earliest elevation of the loggia drawn right at the end of the building's life, in 1776 (**cat. 35**), shows just such an arrangement. Thus, although Thorpe shows a scheme similar to Jones's proposals for Cecil at Hatfield and the New Exchange, what was built was more akin to the earlier loggia at Burghley House (for Lord Burghley 1577-85) or the near contemporary loggia at Knole House, Kent (for the first Earl of Dorset after 1608). Thus, as on the entrance front, the principal architectural influence on

Anne's rebuilding seems to be Burghley House (Fig. 9).

The great hall stood behind the loggia topped by a lantern containing a clock erected in 1617-18.[194] The hall shown by Thorpe (**cat. 7**) was a highly traditional structure with central hearth, screens passage and a great bay window. A privy stair led down from beside the bay window to the garden. It was also possible to move from the hall through a lobby to the state lodgings, but a door in the return of the east range made it possible to enter the state lodgings via the lobby directly from the loggia, an essential refinement while the hall was set up for a masque. The kitchens were on the ground floor and above was the queen's wardrobe of the beds.[195]

For the other elevations of the courtyard a key piece of evidence is the painting of the 1604 Somerset House Conference (**cat. 4**). If the painter accurately recorded the view from the window of the queen's council chamber, it is possible to see the unfinished west range of the outer court. This tells us something very important, which is that Somerset's outer court was a conventional piece of Tudor architecture. There were little dormer windows with pitched roofs lighting attics in a pitched roof covered with red tiles. Brick chimneys can be seen on the skyline and a single four-light transom and mullioned window is depicted in the wall. This accords with what is known from the accounts. The west side was virtually rebuilt by Anne of Denmark, including new bay windows, the east side had two new bay windows and a new balustraded parapet, and the east, west and north sides were given a lead-covered 'platform' instead of a pitched roof.[196] Hollar's bird's-eye view of the house (**cat. 10**) shows this in general terms, but Knyff and Kip (**cat. 20**) show the earlier roof structures surviving on the east side. The balustrade had been replaced by a solid parapet by 1777 (**cat. 35**). Blue and gold sundials were placed on the entrance gate and on the east and west elevations.[197]

The inner court

Round the inner (or paved) court were grouped the most important rooms of the house. The internal elevations of the court were not designed to be shown off. On the south was a blank brick wall containing the great chimney stacks of the presence and privy chambers and the clerestory window of the withdrawing chamber. The presence and privy chambers looked out over the

gardens towards the river and were the public rooms of state.[198] The presence chamber, with its overmantle containing the arms of Denmark supported by wild men, was used for public dining and the reception of ambassadors.[199] In 1617, for instance, Anne received both the French ambassador's wife and the Venetian ambassador in the presence chamber.[200] The privy chamber was used for more intimate receptions. Denmark House was unusual because a small gallery joined the privy chamber and the great gallery, allowing the gallery to be used for public occasions without traversing the much more private withdrawing room (Fig. 7). The drawing room was where the queen could enjoy private discourse with her ladies and eat in private, served from the backstairs behind.[201]

The great gallery had a throne canopy with the arms of Denmark with three 'high' chairs beneath it; other than this the only furniture was a billiard table. The panelled walls were hung with 56 paintings of all types, ranging from landscapes and portraits to devotional subjects and still lives.[202] This vast room was the setting for private, but magnificent, audiences. The first time it was used was probably during the marriage party of Jane Drummond to the Earl of Roxburghe in February 1613, when a great banquet was held with a table running the entire length of the gallery and the queen sitting at its head.[203] This was an exceptional occasion; more usually it would have been used for ambassadorial and diplomatic occasions. In November 1617 the Venetian ambassador had a private audience with Anne in her long gallery at Greenwich. His account of the occasion describes her sitting under her throne canopy while speaking with him at length. The audience over, he took his leave and his secretary kissed the queen's hand.[204] We have no similar report of Denmark House but know that Charles I, early in his reign, gave an audience in the gallery there to a deputy from the United Provinces.[205] So it is very likely that the Somerset House gallery often acted as an audience chamber.

On the north side of the inner court was a series of inner and service rooms, looking out onto the courtyard; these are illustrated by Hollar (**cat. 10**). They were the queen's back stair, her attiring chamber and the 'room beyond the bedchamber', and the 'old narrow gallery on the backside towards the tenements', later called the pages' gallery, which ran on its north side.[206] The attiring chamber had a staircase which led down to the wardrobe below. There was the 'first wardrobe' of three rooms with its lodging and the 'second wardrobe' also with a lodging.[207]

On the west of the court were the windows of the guard chamber and the 'entry'[208] to the council chamber, but the eastern aspect was the most important. Along this side Anne had built two new bedchambers and her diet and coffer chambers (Fig. 7). This range of rooms is particularly important as they are the first known royal bedchamber suite built in a single architectural campaign and to a coherent design since the time of Henry VIII.

The fact that Anne required two bedchambers requires some explanation. In France by this date it had been the practice for 70 years or more for the monarch to have two bedchambers: a *chambre de parade* containing a raised platform or parquet on which, behind a rail, stood a *lit de parade* or state bed, and the king's chamber, the room in which he slept in a more modest bed and in a more private fashion. In England there was no such tradition, although Henry VIII (but not Elizabeth I) had two bedchambers at Whitehall, for instance; the rooms were off limits to all but the most favoured. Under James I a new department of the royal household had been created, called the Bedchamber. It was effectively a replacement for the former innermost group of the king's attendants centred on the privy chamber and known as the Privy Chamber. The creation of the Bedchamber did create new patterns of access to the king's innermost rooms but did not create a French-style ceremonial outer bedchamber or a more private inner one. Indeed, at Whitehall it seems as if James had only a single bedroom off the privy gallery.[209]

The structure of the queen's household mirrored that of the king. There was a Bedchamber staffed by the queen's closest ladies and they alone had access to the bedchambers and closets. As the Earl of Worcester explained to the Earl of Shrewsbury in 1603, 'we have ladys of divers degrees of favour; some for the privat [i.e. privy] chamber, some for the drawing chamber, some for the bedchamber'; he noted that those who were of the private or privy chamber were often 'shut owt' of the inner rooms where 'many tymes the dores are lokt'.[210] A set of household regulations dating from 1627, drawn up for Henrietta Maria, sets out these access patterns in detail and justifies them as being those which were used in Anne of Denmark's time.[211] These regulations make it clear that access to the queen's bedchamber was very restricted; however, she did eat privately in the great bedchamber from time to time, implying that it was a slightly more public room than the regulations suggest.[212] Only on one exceptional occasion in 1615 is there any record of a semi-public event taking place in the bedchamber. This was the knighting of George Villiers there by the king in front of the Prince of Wales. Others were present, including the Archbishop of Canterbury, but they were 'at the door'. This was not a typical event; the queen was convalescing and the occasion was carefully staged by the archbishop.[213] Anne's insistence on dignity and privacy enhanced her regality in comparison with that of her husband which was undermined by his free and easy ways. No wonder she could be 'terrible, proud and unendurable' when she wanted.[214]

Despite some evidence that the queen was becoming more interested in France in the 1610s,[215] there is no suggestion that the creation of a great and little bedchamber was anything other than a device to reinforce privacy and control access. It was the architectural expression of Samuel Daniels's 'feminine commonwealth' where order and dignity reigned.

The south-eastern gallery

The largest new additions undertaken for Anne were two galleries and their associated closets, the great or privy gallery facing east and the cross or library gallery facing south. Smythson's plan (**cat. 6**) shows that the original intention was to build a third gallery on the east alongside Strand Lane with a bow window and stack of closets to match the great gallery on the west. This was never built, presumably as an economy. Instead, a little after the cross gallery, a new two-storey library and closet were built.

The appearance of the great gallery's eastern elevation is unclear as almost all views of the house are from the river or the street. Kenton Couse's survey (**cat. 33**) shows the plan of the gallery at both ground and first-floor levels and from this it is possible to deduce the essentials of the design. In the middle of the gallery was a great double-height bow window and this was flanked, on either side, by two projecting features with small windows at ground level and three light windows at first-floor level with what could either be deep frames and mullions, or more likely columns. These may have resembled the bay windows in the outer court. At the south end there was an emphatic end to the gallery provided by the three-storey queen's closet or cabinet projecting eastwards as far as the bow window (most clearly seen on **cat. 9**).

The cross gallery can be seen on a number of views (**cats 9, 10, 11, 20, 24, 26**). It was two storeys high, the first floor supported on a loggia of six stone arches with a square bay window in the middle. At the principal level the gallery was divided into three — ante-rooms at either end and the gallery proper in the middle with a central fireplace and a great square projecting window. From the great gallery, the cross gallery was approached by an ante-room described in the accounts and inventory as simply 'the room between the galleries'. This room may have been used by Anne as a chapel.

It is very noticeable that in the building and repair accounts and in the 1619 inventory of Denmark House there is no mention of a chapel or even a private closet or oratory. Anne was, of course, a secret Catholic and this fact complicates any attempt to understand the geography of her faith at Denmark House. At Oatlands there was an oratory near her bedchamber,[216] but the Spanish ambassador, Gondomar, reported that at Denmark House the queen worshipped secretly in a garret.[217] This is very unlikely, as the queen could have easily concealed her devotions in her main lodgings had she so wished. Indeed, the 1619 inventory suggests that she did just that.

Apart from a couple of religious paintings in the long gallery, only one room was furnished with devotional pictures. The 'little room between the two galleries' was hung with pictures of Christ, Mary and Martha; Christ bearing his Cross; the Virgin Mary and a Pietà. It was also furnished with a 'Crucifix in a case of Ebony with fower evangelists in the leaves'. Only one other painting was in the room: a portrait of Queen Elizabeth. Both pictures of the Virgin were covered with green taffeta curtains fringed with gold lace and hung from silver rods. Where paintings elsewhere in the house were provided with curtains, they were of much lesser quality and the rods were not mentioned. Moreover, although there was no throne canopy in the room, there was a chair of state with a footstool suggesting that the queen used the room for a formal purpose.[218] Was this room, easily reached from Anne's innermost lodgings, in fact her secret oratory filled with devotional pictures? It would seem the obvious conclusion to draw from its furnishings and its location.[219]

The cross gallery was set up with a throne and throne canopy just like the great gallery, but its walls were hung with cloth of gold and gold curtains. There were cabinets, some tables and chairs, lots of mirrors and a selection of dynastic portraits.[220] This was truly part of the queen's private domain leading to her innermost library, but whom she saw in this room and how she used the throne and canopy can only be a matter for speculation.

Although a gallery leading to a private closet was not the original intention, the arrangement of gallery with closets at its end had an important English precedent. The queen's western country seat was at Oatlands, a former palace of Henry VIII used by Elizabeth and granted by James I to Anne. There on the north front were two galleries joining the royal privy lodgings at one end and at the other leading to a closet set in the privy gardens.[221] It is possible that the arrangement finally adopted at Denmark House owed something to the precedent of Oatlands, which the king and queen evidently liked. Perhaps even more intriguing is the possibility that Christian IV of Denmark saw the gallery and closet tower at Denmark House and ordered it copied at Frederiksborg. Work at Christian's principal residence there was nearing completion when he made his second visit to England.[222] While in London he resided at Denmark House with the queen and on his return he ordered a series of alterations to the plan of Frederiksborg, including the addition of a gallery from the inner lodgings ending in a closet.[223]

The south front and gardens

Due to the steep fall from the Strand to the river, still appreciated today by pedestrians walking up Arundel Street, the south front of Denmark House was a full three storeys high with attics and would have appeared dominant from both the gardens and the Thames. It was a hotchpotch of periods, probably including parts of old Chester Inn, some of Protector Somerset's work, Elizabethan additions and now Queen Anne's rebuilding. The queen's new works were either in brick with stone dressings, such as the great gallery (**cat. 9**) or in stone, like the loggia carrying the gallery linking the privy chamber and great gallery (**cat. 26**).

The issue for Anne's designers was how to make sense of this mixture of styles. It was decided to retain the medieval aspect of the house, and

Anne's new work was given battlements and the old battlements repaired (**cat. 9**).[224] The patchwork of brick was rendered over and lined out to look like stone (**cat. 28**).[225] Denmark House, from the south, thus looked like many of the other medieval palaces along the Strand. The retention of battlements and other features gave the house an air of venerability which, like the gallery and closet, was admired by Christian IV who subsequently incorporated gothic windows into his chapel at Frederiksborg.

The gardens, as originally proposed, are shown by Smythson (**cat. 6**), but it is clear that, as with so much else on his plan, the design was modified in execution. Many of the principal features remained, such as the terraces and the extraordinary grotto fountain depicting Mount Parnassus designed by Salomon de Caus, but the details of the knots and paths were refined on site. A view of the garden in the background of a portrait of Queen Anne probably represents the final appearance of the parterre (**cat. 8**).[226]

The death of Anne and after

Anne died at Hampton Court on 2 March 1619 and her body was brought to Denmark House for her lying-in-state. Three rooms were prepared and her body was placed in the great bedchamber watched over by her ladies. This was an opportunity for the public not only to see the queen but visit the palace, and crowds of Londoners flocked to see the queen's catafalque and effigy.[227]

This lying-in-state was the first at Denmark House and started a royal tradition. After James I's death in March 1625 his body was removed from Theobalds to Denmark House where it was placed on a large frame in the privy chamber; his body and effigy were followed by his entire household who moved to Denmark House to attend the late king. Meanwhile Charles I moved from St James's to Whitehall. The use of Denmark House was expedient — Whitehall was required by the new king already preparing for his marriage, St James's

had just been vacated and Somerset House lay empty.[228] However, James set a precedent that was to be followed later.

James I had commissioned an inventory of the queen's goods on 19 April (1619).[229] By the time an inventory was made, much of the furniture had been packed up, granted to Anne's servants or moved for her lying-in-state. She had died at Hampton Court and so Denmark House was, anyway, shut up and some of the most important items were stored in the wardrobe. Thus while the inventory gives a good idea of the way in which the house was furnished, it cannot be used to reconstruct the appearance of the state rooms in particular.

On 5 October 1619 James granted Denmark House to the Prince of Wales, together with much of its contents. The new keeper was the Duke of Buckingham who took lodgings in the house with his wife. His brother John, Viscount Purbeck, received the rents from 24 messuages (tenements) for life. Prince Charles used the house on occasion, at least once for a ball and a banquet[230] but, with St James's Palace as his principal London residence, Denmark House gradually slipped back into its former usage as lodgings for ambassadors.[231]

In 1623 Denmark House came back into focus as the future London residence of the Spanish Infanta, once she became Queen of England. The Spanish ambassador inspected the house and requested a chapel to be built there and at St James's for Catholic worship. Inigo Jones provided designs for both chapels, but for the time being work started only on that at St James's; presumably it was felt that, as Princess of Wales, the Infanta would live with the prince there and only later move to Denmark House as queen. Nevertheless in May orders were given to clear Denmark House of its current occupants in preparation for improvements there.[232] These improvements were not to come to fruition, but the house was, within three years, to be occupied by another Catholic princess, the daughter of a king of France, Henrietta Maria.

VI. HENRIETTA MARIA:
DENMARK HOUSE, FRANCE AND CATHOLICISM

Introduction

IN recent years there has been much interest in Henrietta Maria and her influence on the events leading up to the Civil War. There has also been an acknowledgement, especially amongst literary historians, that she was an important cultural patron.[233] Although only fifteen when she arrived in England, Henrietta Maria was not a silly little girl; she was, like Anne before her, the daughter of a monarch, and no less a one than King Henry IV of France. She had been brought up in the most fashionable court and buildings in Europe and, although what little education she had concentrated on religion and etiquette, these instilled in her a clear perception of her rank and the deference due to it.

It has often been stated that this young French princess set out with a mission to bring England back into the Roman Catholic fold; it is less widely appreciated that she also determinedly set out to bring French fashions and etiquette to the English court. Architecture was absolutely central to this and her patronage in this sphere far outstripped that of the king. Her taste was imposed on all the major royal houses: Denmark House, of course, but also Whitehall, Greenwich, Hampton Court, Oatlands and Wimbledon. Her taste was not only expressed in bricks and mortar but painting, tapestry, furniture, textiles, upholstery, plate and domestic utensils. To this has to be added the influence of Catholic France on ceremonies and festivals at her palaces, the masques, the pastorals, the dancing, music, food at her table and above all liturgy in her chapel. Most daily discourse was in French, at least until the mid-1630s. Thus, in every area of her existence the influence of France and of Catholic Europe prevailed.[234]

This was a very different sort of court to that of Anne of Denmark; Anne's court was essentially a private one, independent of the king's, moving in its own orbit. Her successor's court was almost indistinguishable from the king's. After 1628, the king and queen were closely entwined in all they did and this style of royal life affected Denmark House. Under Anne it had been a female refuge rarely visited by James, and then only briefly,[235] but

Charles, his children and courtiers were regular visitors, the king often staying the night despite the proximity of Whitehall. The contrast between the two queens was even stronger in matters of religion. While for Anne the practice of her Roman Catholic faith had been a personal and clandestine activity, for Henrietta Maria it was a communal and public display, nothing short of the mainspring of her court. It is against these contrasting styles and priorities that Denmark House should be understood in the years 1625 to 1641.

The queen was granted Denmark House and its valuable tenements on St Valentine's Day 1626. The grant stipulated that the king would also 'grant to her all the ornaments and household stuff therein remaining so soon as an inventory thereof can be made'.[236] A copy of the 1627 inventory is in the Society of Antiquaries of London. It gives a picture of the house when the queen first arrived in London, still filled with furniture bearing the arms of Anne of Denmark.[237] Charles and Henrietta Maria were too poor and too badly acquainted in the first years of their marriage to make any significant alterations to Denmark House, but during the 1630s there was a stream of changes; most were internal redecoration and reordering, but there was also the construction of a new chapel and convent.

The queen's privy lodgings 1625-32

Henrietta moved quickly and decisively to bring French fashions into her court and palaces.[238] On the simplest level her trousseau was enormous and hugely valuable, containing all the princess would need for her new life in England, from napkins and ball gowns to paintings and chamber pots.[239] Simply unpacking this vast train of trunks and packing cases was to introduce into Denmark House the cream of contemporary French design. Admittedly, some of what Henrietta brought with her would have been available in London which already had a significant number of shops and craftsmen supplying luxury goods in the French fashion. Yet the sheer scale and quality of the trousseau and the hundreds of staff, attendants and religious that formed it made an enormous impact.

At the heart of the trousseau was a complete set of French royal bedchamber furnishings of red velvet with gold and silver trimmings. The bed itself was magnificently hung, sitting on a red-covered dais and crowned with four great plumes of white ostrich feather. Three chairs and six coffers of matching velvet and three large Turkish carpets were also provided, as was 'Une grande Toilette de velours en broderie d'or et d'argent'.[240] This bedroom suite was similar to that which her mother had in her great bedchamber at the Louvre sited behind a great silvered rail. In the French court the bedchamber occupied a central position in the ceremonial life of the monarch; it was the room in which the most important audiences would be held, treaties signed and proclamations made; the monarch standing by the bed, frequently behind a gilded or silvered balustrade. Thus the bed and its furniture had a vitally important role and symbolic value, quite unlike the bedchamber furnishings of Queen Anne. As has been suggested, her bedchamber had no public function at all.

For Henrietta Maria the bedchamber and its furnishings were of the utmost importance in establishing her status, while for the English the bedroom was simply a rich and comfortable private room. Although the memoirs of the queen's attendants are often biased and sometimes malicious, they reveal that the queen's bedchamber was a flashpoint. Comte Leveneur de Tillières complained that, when Henrietta arrived at Dover, the 'queen was lodged in the castle ... an old building in the antique style where the queen's rooms were bad and her furniture worse'. In his view things did not improve at Canterbury where she consummated her marriage. He tells us that 'She arrived in Canterbury, where she slept with the king of England, her husband, in a bed which normally served extraordinary ambassadors, which was however, less dreadful than the one in Dover'.[241] The French entourage perhaps expected the improvement to continue as the party reached London, but they were to be disappointed. Two separate French observers describe the queen's eventual arrival at Denmark House where she was presented with the apartments of Anne of Denmark in which she expected to see a ceremonial bed reserved for her use. But 'she found as her ceremonial bed [*lit de parade*], one from the reign of Queen Elizabeth, which was so

ancient that not even the oldest people could remember ever having seen one in that style in their lives'.[242] Perhaps Charles and his advisors believed that Elizabeth's rich bed would be an honour for the new queen. They were badly mistaken or misled.

There is no doubt that Henrietta would have liked to remodel Anne's bedchamber along French lines immediately. However, the king's appalling financial situation, coupled with the painful dispute over the size and composition of Henrietta's household, meant that little or nothing was done in the bedchamber or in any of her other apartments at Denmark House. Yet within the modest means at her disposal she did begin to make some changes. Her first task was to appoint a new upholsterer. She had originally arrived from France with Gilles Alix, her personal upholsterer and interior decorator, but he had been expelled with the rest of her French household in 1626.[243] Therefore she made a new appointment, Ralph Grynder. Little is known of him personally, but his rather strange surname was almost certainly an Anglicization of a French one. He immediately began to supply the queen with furnishings in the French style. The French bed in her trousseau had presumably gone to Whitehall and there was no way in her first years in England that Henrietta could order the sort of bed that she wanted for Denmark House. At first the queen used the green damask bed that can be identified in Anne of Denmark's 1619 inventory, but within a year this 'faire field bed of green velvet' was 'translated into the French Fashion by order of the queen's majesty'.[244] This was clearly only make do and mend and, according to the Venetian ambassador, as late as June 1630 Henrietta Maria was so ashamed of the furniture in her bedchamber that she would only receive the Duchesse de Tremouille when the shutters were closed and the room was candlelit.[245]

It was only in 1632 that the queen's bedchamber was finally redecorated. Inigo Jones designed a new white marble chimneypiece for the room that was installed by Nicholas Stone in April.[246] The following month a 10 ft square platform 6 in. high was built in the queen's great bedchamber and a remarkable green and white satin bed delivered.[247] The 'large rich French Bed of sattine richly embroydered' was accompanied by 'A Rayle and Ballaster to incompasse round ye bedd silvered and varnished over'. The ensemble also included a second bed, a *lit d'ange* known in the later seven-

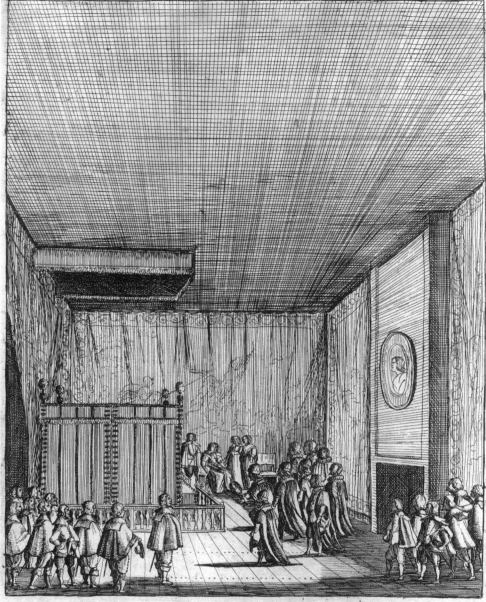

Fig. 10. Marie de Medici's bedchamber at St James's Palace.

COMME LE MY LORD MAIOR ACOMPAIGNEDE SES COLLEGVES
VIENT SALVER LA REYNE LVY FAIRE SES PRESENS

teenth century as an angel bed as the canopy was suspended from above by chains rather than supported by posts at the feet. This, too, was of green without and white within. Both the French bed and the angel bed had matching embroidered counterpanes. Finally there was also a pallet bed, a small bed designed for use by body servants at the foot of a state bed. Matching the beds were two very rich carpets for them to stand on, 'embroydered suitable of ye French Fashion', and two matching window curtains.

There is no trace of payment for this vastly expensive bedroom suite and so it is almost certain that it was sent to the queen as a gift from France.[248] It is also almost certain that these were the most magnificent furnishings of their kind in London at the time. Henrietta Maria had furnished her bedroom as a state room, capable of being used in the French manner for receptions. Payments in her privy accounts two years later show that further French bedroom suites were being purchased. In July 1634 the queen made a

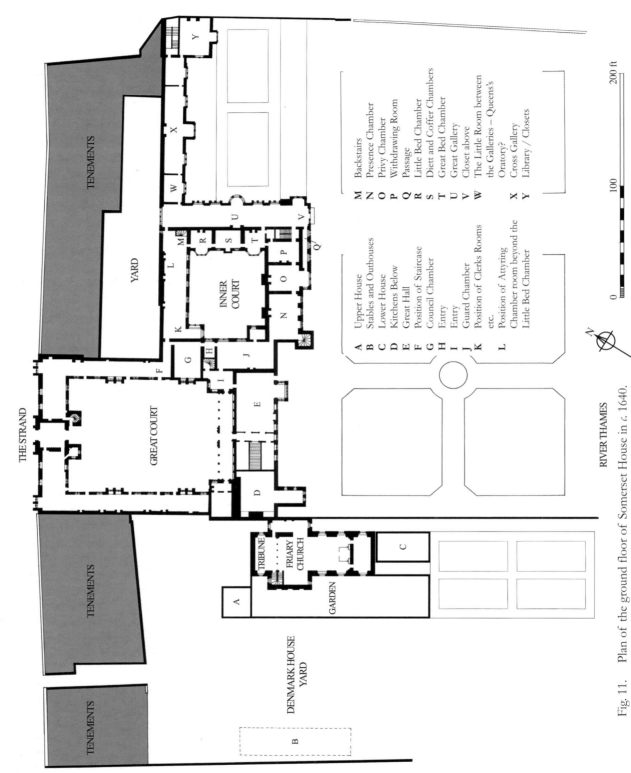

THE STRAND

TENEMENTS

TENEMENTS

YARD

TENEMENTS

TENEMENTS

GREAT COURT

INNER COURT

F

G H

I

E

D

K L M

R S

T U

N O P

Q

V

W X Y

J

TRIBUNE

FRIARY CHURCH

A

GARDEN

C

DENMARK HOUSE YARD

B

RIVER THAMES

N

0   100   200 ft

A Upper House
B Stables and Outhouses
C Lower House
D Kitchens Below
E Great Hall
F Position of Staircase
G Council Chamber
H Entry
I Entry
J Guard Chamber
K Position of Clerks Rooms etc.
L Position of Attyring Chamber room beyond the Little Bed Chamber

M Backstairs
N Presence Chamber
O Privy Chamber
P Withdrawing Room
Q Passage
R Little Bed Chamber
S Diett and Coffer Chambers
T Great Bed Chamber
U Great Gallery
V Closet above
W The Little Room between the Galleries – Queens's Oratory?
X Cross Gallery
Y Library / Closets

Fig. 11.   Plan of the ground floor of Somerset House in *c*. 1640.
(Simon Thurley; drawing Melissa Beasley)

payment of £600 to the Marquis of Sourdiar for a rich bed and matching hangings in July 1634.[249]

The timing of the alterations to the queen's bedchamber raises a further point. The work was executed in April 1632, the date set for Charles I's coronation in Scotland. Plans had been long in the making for Charles to undertake a journey north to be crowned in Edinburgh, and in November 1631 the Privy Council there was informed that the king would be arriving in April 1632. Henrietta Maria was to remain in London and, while not granted any formal powers of regency, was at least nominally in charge and responsible for state ceremonial during the king's absence. She was also to hold a formal weekly audience with the Privy Council.[250] It is possible that the queen, anticipating a temporary increase in her ceremonial role, commissioned this upgrading of her bedchambers. In fact the king delayed his journey north, only going to Edinburgh the following year, but when the Denmark House work was ordered nobody knew that was to be the case.

It is very unlikely that any of Charles I's bedrooms was ever furnished along these lines. In around 1635 the king rearranged his lodgings in the privy gallery at Whitehall, but there is no evidence that his bedchamber was a room of state or that it was furnished after the French fashion. Indeed, the parliamentary surveyors valued the king's bed there at only £80, less than a tenth of the value of the queen's ensemble.[251] Henrietta Maria's remodelling of her Denmark House bedroom in 1632 can be more closely compared with the work she commissioned at Hampton Court in 1641. That year, again, the king went to Scotland, leaving the queen with slightly more formalized powers. She resided first at Oatlands, then at Hampton Court where she had her state bedchamber rebuilt and redecorated, probably to a French style too.[252]

Unfortunately, it is very difficult to find direct evidence for the queen's use of these rooms. This might, of course, suggest that use was entirely private, particularly as one of the queen's Catholic advisers wrote in a letter to the Pope that 'no one is admitted in her bedrooms except ladies'. This is surely a pious communication. Her little bedchamber was certainly a female preserve but the whole point of a great bedchamber, decorated with the arms of France, and with a bed raised on a lavishly covered dais behind a rail, was that it should be a public room. Indeed, a contemporary engraving of her mother Marie de Medici in her bedchamber at

St James's Palace shows the French bed with its rail and the queen mother receiving guests in a formalized setting (Fig. 10). It seems a fair assumption that, if Marie was using her great bedchamber in the French fashion, her daughter, less than a mile away, was doing likewise.

Other than the queen's bedchamber, various of the queen's inner rooms were redecorated during the late 1620s and into the mid-1630s. These decorative changes are chronicled in the *History of the King's Works*.

The chapel

The marriage of Charles and Henrietta Maria was about international politics and diplomacy, not religion. Yet for it to take place the Pope himself had to grant a dispensation and papal requirements were thus built into the marriage treaty of 1624, guaranteeing not only religious rights for the queen but, in a secret appendix, wider toleration for Catholics. Henrietta Maria's family and the Vatican had intended from the first that the queen's household should be a Trojan Horse, introducing the shock troops of the Counter-Reformation into a rabidly anti-Catholic country and into the very heart of the English court.

Early seventeenth-century Paris was alight with enthusiasm for the Counter-Reformation, a zeal that blazed brightly at the court of Henrietta Maria's mother, Marie de Medici. Marie became the patroness of the first Carmelite convent in Paris in 1603, and in 1611 her confessor and confidant Pierre Bérulle founded the French Oratory there. Bérulle was also the Director of the Carmelite convent and Henrietta Maria was sent there with other young ladies from the French Court for religious instruction. It is, then, no surprise that Father Bérulle was appointed as emissary to go to Rome to facilitate Henrietta Maria's marriage and was subsequently appointed her confessor.

Thus when the new Queen of England arrived at Dover in June 1626 she was accompanied by twelve Oratorian priests led by Father Bérulle, their Superior-General and one of the most influential religious figures of his day. Her trousseau was laden with liturgical equipment — the Oratorians had their own chapel furnishings in all worth nearly 10,000 livres. In addition there were four sets of altar frontals, vestments, napery and furniture for four different liturgical settings, not valued in the inventory but hardly worth less than

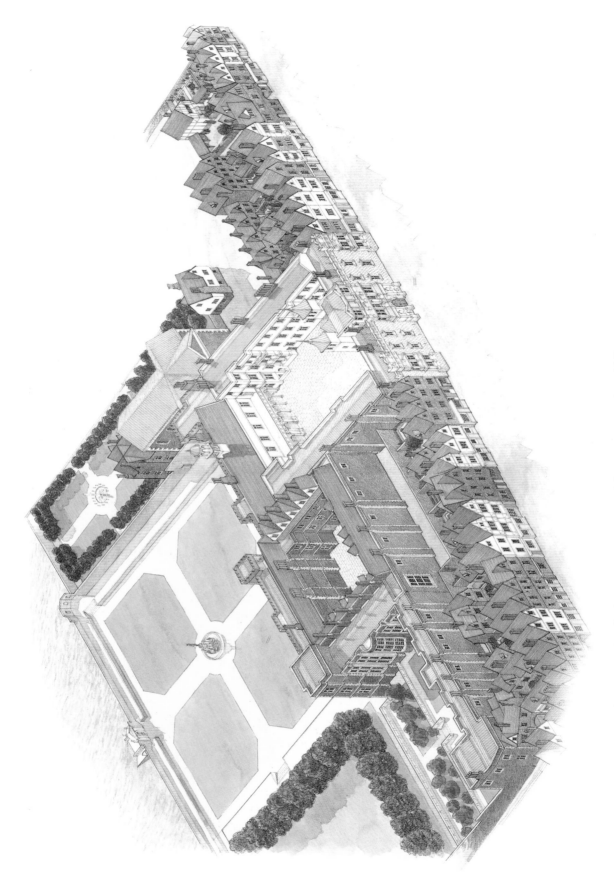

Fig. 12.   Simon Thurley's bird's-eye reconstruction of Somerset House in *c.* 1640 from the north-east drawn by Stephen Conlin. *Courtesy of* Country Life.

the Oratorians' furniture. The queen's ladies were also provided with equipment for two complete chapels.[253] The emphasis of Oratorian worship was the pursuit of sacerdotal perfection and in this the beauty of holiness was central, and so these valuable Mass sets were vital.

The Oratorians and their equipment arrived at Denmark House where there was seemingly no chapel to receive them. 1626 had been declared by Pope Urban VIII to be a holy 'Jubilee' year and Henrietta Maria was determined to celebrate this with full rites and honours. On 10 April she retired from court for a week to the cross gallery which had been 'divided and fitted up with cells, and a refectory, and an oratory, in the manner of a monastery', there the queen and her ladies 'sang the hours of the virgin, and lied [*sic*] together like nuns'. Soon more permanent provision was made for the queen, and in October it was reported that a chapel was being fitted up on the ground floor of Denmark House; we do not know where, but the Office of Works supplied it with an altar and rail with balusters painted stone colour, a large tabernacle on eight pillars and tall candlesticks. Here she heard Mass and sermons every day.[254]

It was not these private devotions in the queen's gallery or even in her oratory that caused a problem. It was the ostentatious public celebration of Mass by her Oratorians at St James's Palace that caused uproar. After a series of furious rows with the king, the Oratorians and majority of the queen's French household were expelled. It was not until November 1627 when there was a formal rapprochement and it was agreed that she should have a new ecclesiastical establishment comprising a bishop, Capuchin friars, a confessor and musicians for her chapel. It was also resolved that the Catholic chapel at St James's be completed and that a new chapel be built at Denmark House.[255] As a result, in 1630, twelve Capuchin friars arrived at Denmark House. The Capuchins were a reformed Franciscan order noted for their abnegation and proselytizing zeal. They had been in France since the late 1560s and were favoured by the French court; they were thus logical successors to the Oratorians.

The Oratorians were a congregation of priests bound by no vows other than their priestly ones; the Capuchins were different, they were a religious order bound by the Franciscan rule sharing a conventual life. For this to be possible they needed a permanent establishment. At first they were given temporary accommodation in the old Tudor tennis court in Denmark House Yard (Fig. 5, see p. 22), but in 1632 it was finally agreed that a new chapel and friary should be built for them. It is important to stress that this was not a personal chapel for the queen, it was a friary and chapel in the tradition of pre-Reformation attached friaries, like that built at Greenwich by Edward IV or Richmond by Henry VII.[256] The Capuchins were classed as Observant friars so Henrietta Maria was, in fact, reviving a long-standing pre-Reformation royal religious tradition. The dedication service for the laying of the chapel corner stone took place on 24 September 1632 in the old tennis court chapel, richly hung with tapestries and lit by silver chandeliers.[257] Two thousand people watched as the queen laid, with her own hands, the first two corner stones of her new Capuchin chapel with a silver plate between them with a picture of the king and queen engraved on it.[258]

There is much about the new chapel that will remain unclear as few of Jones's designs survive and apart from Hollar's and Kip's bird's-eye views (**cats 11, 20**) and oblique views of its eastern flank (**cat. 9**) there is no external depiction of the chapel as a whole, and later internal views only record it after the ravages of the Commonwealth (**cats 22, 23**). On the basis of what we have it is clear that in general terms it was similar in style to the chapel at St James's, but with shallow transepts. The whole was raised up on a vaulted brick undercroft, at the south (liturgical east) end there was a vestry and at the north end at second-floor level was the royal pew. Further north still were the buildings of the friary described by Clarendon as a 'small but convenient habitation'.[259]

In the absence of drawings we shall never know whether the chapel started in September 1632 was the same as that designed by Jones in 1623, but it seems very unlikely. The St James's chapel was designed by Jones in anticipation of the arrival of a Catholic princess without, as far as we know, detailed discussion with the priests that were to use it. As a result it is in its essentials a rendering into classical form of a traditional English royal chapel, and as such drew from established models available to the Office of Works.[260] In 1632, however, Jones must have been closely involved in design discussions with the Superior of the Capuchins and the queen herself. They would not only have specified in detail the functional requirements of the chapel and friary, but would have furnished Jones with details of suitable models.

It has long been known that, through the French ambassador, Henrietta Maria provided Jones with a design for a French chimneypiece for Denmark House.[261] It can likewise be demonstrated that elements of the chapel design were taken from engravings. Harris and Higgott have pointed out that the design for a window surround for the chapel was taken from a design for a Doric doorway published by Domenico Fontana in 1590. The window, which cannot have been one of the great side windows shown on Bol's painting (**cat. 9**), was probably one for the queen's closet.[262] It is perhaps significant that the design of the doorway is from the Vatican itself, but more significant is an elevation of a niche with a Christ as Salvator Mundi in it. This is undoubtedly a Jesuit feature of the type popularized on the west front of St Paul and St Louis in Paris (François Derand, 1634). I have discussed elsewhere the probable Jesuit influence on the Somerset House chapel at the Restoration (and see below),[263] but it is very likely that Jones's model in 1632 was also a Jesuit one, conveyed to him in the form of prints by the queen or her priests.

To consider properly the implications of this, it is necessary to examine the plan of the chapel in more detail. The chapel's sizeable congregation approached it from Denmark House Yard and must have entered the chapel from beneath the queen's tribune at its north end. As it was raised up on a brick undercroft, there would have to have been a staircase to provide access. Due to alterations undertaken after 1641 eighteenth-century plans of the chapel show a building drastically changed from its original form (**cats 19, 30, 33**). However, the 1702 plan does show doors into the antechapel beneath the tribune and a confusing array of steps up to it. That public access to the chapel was from a door on its west side suggests that the principal external façade of the building must have been its western one. Jones handles this brilliantly. The transepts by themselves are architecturally slight, and so he increased the width of the western transept by adding a stair to it creating a wall wide enough to present a magnificent frontispiece. This had three niches on it, one of which must have been the 'Neece with out the chappell So: Ho:' for which we have a drawing (Fig. 13). This clever device gave the illusion of a chapel correctly oriented, entered from the west, although once inside worshippers turned 90 degrees to face south. It also presented to Catholics familiar with Jesuit churches in France

and Italy a façade that was recognizably a product of the Counter-Reformation, combining austerity with iconographic emphasis.

There is no documentary evidence to show where the original friary was as it was demolished in the early 1640s and replaced with a private house (see below). The normal location for such friary buildings would have been at the east end of the chapel.[264] Hollar's bird's-eye view (**cat. 10**) and Bol's painting (**cat. 9**) show a substantial building in this location that looks much like a private house of the mid-century and not at all like a friary built at the same time as the chapel. Hollar also shows the 'new brickwall to enclose the ffryers lodgings and a place for a garden'[265] constructed in 1630-5 and converted into a private garden in the 1640s and 1650s. Thus the location of the friary is clear, but the original appearance and layout of it is lost.

All this demonstrates that the Capuchin friary, always misleadingly referred to as the 'queen's chapel', was physically very separate from the rest of the house. Although early documents suggested that a direct link from the queen's privy lodgings was intended, this was not possible with the chapel being in Somerset House Yard and the point where the chapel abutted the main building being the kitchens. When the chapel and friary were built, there was a 'passage to the queen's new chapel', presumably cutting through from the outer court.[266] The chapel was thus architecturally as well as functionally like a pre-Reformation royal collegiate chapel such as Windsor or Westminster or the friaries at Greenwich or Richmond. This was never acknowledged in England where the structure is always referred to as a 'chapel', but contemporary French documents normally refer to it as a friary, not a chapel.[267]

Although the external appearance of the chapel can now only be reconstructed from diffuse pieces of evidence, the interior is unusually well recorded. Two drawings survive; one made by Henry Flitcroft in the early 1730s for the Earl of Burlington shows the reflected plan of the ceiling (**cat. 22**) and the other is a drawing of *c.* 1731 for Isaac Ware's *Designs of Inigo Jones*, showing an elevation of the frontal of the royal pew or tribune (**cat. 23**). The ceiling is of the beamed type used in the Banqueting House, Whitehall, with a central rectangle and flanking circles and ovals for canvasses. Over the presbytery was a coffered Roman ceiling. This, together with an elevation of the tribune, gives an idea of the

Fig. 13.   Inigo Jones's design for a niche above the west door of Somerset House Chapel.
(Royal Institute of British Architects)

richness of the original interior, but perhaps more importantly the sources of his designs. Here Jones is not bound only by influences from Jesuit Paris; his inspiration is directly from antique (pagan) models, specifically from the Arundel marbles at Arundel House next door on the Strand.[268] So what was the effect of the completed interior? Was it recognizably influenced by French Jesuit churches, or did Jones design a chapel within the vocabulary that he used elsewhere at court? Without images of the side chapels or the reredos it is hard to be certain, but accounts of the first Mass would suggest that the interior stood out as being very different from what the English expected to see.

The first Mass performed there was a spectacle not seen in England for a century. Its setting was a fashionable type of Roman liturgical theatre designed and executed by the Roman-trained Flemish sculptor François Dieussart (1600-61).[269] He created a 40 ft high monstrance over the high altar in which a Host was held in a large oval flanked by prophets and supported by two pillars that soared through seven layers of 'clouds' amongst which nestled two hundred angels, seraphim and cherubim. Behind this structure hid

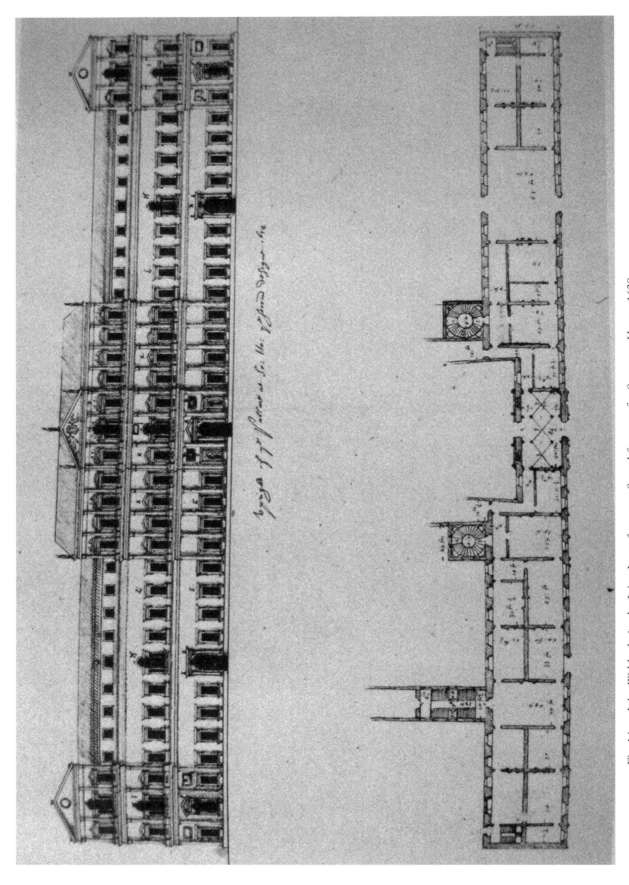

Fig. 14. John Webb, design by Inigo Jones for a new Strand frontage for Somerset House, 1638. (Worcester College, Oxford)

a choir so that its singing would appear to come from the massed heavenly host on the clouds. The whole contraption, lit by four hundred lights, was hidden behind curtains when the congregation entered and at the crucial moment Dieussart drew them aside. The queen, reportedly, wept with joy and Charles was so fascinated that he spent an hour and a half examining it after Mass was over.[270]

Unlike her chapels at Oatlands and Whitehall, which would remain empty when the queen was not present, the Somerset House chapel was staffed throughout the year. Unlike the other royal chapels, it had its own congregation of outsiders who had nothing to do with the queen's household and who could enter the chapel through the gatehouse to Somerset House Yard without crossing the domestic precincts.[271] There were services every day and on feasts and festivals the chapel was so crowded that people queued to get in. After sung vespers a Capuchin preacher would preach for an hour, and there was teaching on Thursdays in French and on Wednesdays and Saturdays in English.[272]

The congregation was enormously strengthened when the Capuchin Superior gained permission for the formation of an Arch Confraternity of the Holy Rosary at the chapel. This was an international fraternity of lay people under the Dominicans devoted to the Virgin and saying the rosary. Membership was by a small fee and many confraternities comprised a thousand people or more. We do not know the size of the Denmark House confraternity and the numbers quoted for outsiders attending Mass there were often inflated by hostile observers, but it would be safe to say that the chapel had a congregation of several hundred people by 1640.[273]

This is fundamental to the understanding of Denmark House and the impact it had on London. Henrietta Maria wanted the friary to become the parish church of Catholics in London. Denmark House was perfectly placed for this, right in the heart of where most Catholics lived. The Parishes of St Giles-in-the-Fields, St Martin-in-the-Fields and St Andrew Holborn contained large numbers of Catholics, as did St Dunstan in the West which contained a Catholic community in Fetter Lane. Other such communities existed in Drury Lane, Chancery Lane and Gray's Inn Lane. There were a number of inns owned by Catholics, one in Gray's Inn Lane and another somewhere in St Giles-in-the-Fields; these acted as meeting points and places to exchange gossip.[274] The fact that the friary became London's centre for Catholic worship is thus not surprising; it was its *raison d'être*.

It was in this way that Denmark House and particularly its chapel became a focus for both for the hopes of English Catholics and the fears of Puritans — a fact that scandalized the court, including the king and Archbishop Laud himself. It led to frequent, unsuccessful attempts to curtail attendance at the chapel for all but the queen's closest entourage. What made the scandal worse is that during the later 1630s there were a number of high profile conversions to Catholicism in the queen's circle, embarrassing the king who was powerless to stop them. For the London crowd the Denmark House scandal could be easily linked with Laud's reform of the parishes and the king's own beautification of the royal chapels.[275] Soon the Catholic chapels at St James's and Denmark House were said to be sheltering the 'Pope and the devil'.[276] Denmark House became a focus of anti-popery and anti-Henrietta Maria sentiment. In 1640 apprentices threatened to pull down St James's and Denmark House chapels because they were houses of popery.[277]

Plans for rebuilding the principal lodgings

In 1636, with the chapel completed, a new phase of work began at Denmark House that is difficult to interpret. It seems as if a new suite of state rooms was being constructed. The accounts mention a 'new' presence chamber, privy chamber, withdrawing chamber, bedchamber, attiring room and closet.[278]

The rooms seem to have been set up on the ground floor as we know of new pillars in the cellar to support the floor of the new presence chamber.[279] But the work cannot have been very lavish, the new walls were all internal and executed in timber,[280] they were also done as economically as possible — panelling and a chimneypiece were taken down in the queen's closet and stool room and re-erected in her new closet and attiring room.[281] The queen's bedchamber was probably provided with a new suite of furniture, a lady called Magdalen Russell was paid £1,000 for this in March 1637.[282] In 1649 the Parliamentary surveyors valued the suite at £1,000, by far the most valuable in the kingdom.[283] It is possible that this rearrangement was in part to make space for a bedroom and dressing room for the king, both of which are mentioned for the first time in 1637-8. This speculation is reinforced by the fact that in 1638 the king's blue satin bed and canopy was moved from Whitehall to Denmark House.[284]

Another interpretation could be that these works were preliminary to a much grander scheme that was planned. In 1638 Henry Weeks, the clerk of works, received a warrant for £500 to buy timber for 'the advancement of her majesties intended buildings' at Denmark House.[285] The 'intended building' was a rebuilding of the entire Strand frontage.

Two designs for this scheme survive, one marked 'not taken'; in other words it was presented to the king and queen and rejected. The one that was accepted, dated 1638 in the hand of John Webb, shows a new range of buildings along the Strand (Fig. 14).[286] The concept was to demolish the tenements along the road and replace them, and Somerset's entrance front, with a new façade. The intention was to keep the old courtyard behind, the two spiral stairs being in the location of the east and west return wings. The most interesting aspect of this plan is that it proposed a new entrance into Denmark House Yard through a portal in the centre of the right-hand part of the façade. This through-way would have aligned exactly with the north front of the chapel, allowing an axial route from the street to what might possibly have been intended to be a redesigned north façade. The entry contained a large porch or vestibule giving worshippers somewhere to congregate on their way into the chapel.

Although plans were prepared and approved, timber laid up and lodgings reorganized possibly in anticipation, the plan came to nothing; the royal finances were simply unable to bear a work on this scale.

Theatrical events

The staging of plays, pastorals and masques at Denmark House by the two early Stuart queens has attracted a huge amount of scholarly atten-tion.[287] Anne of Denmark used the great hall and the great chamber on the south front as a setting for plays and masques from about 1613. In 1616, for the first time, Inigo Jones built scenery in the great hall for a masque, and from that date until Anne's death masques and plays in the great hall were a central feature of her court's life.[288] After 1626, however, Henrietta Maria made the Denmark House hall the centre of scenic drama in England. In the first performance of her reign in February 1626 she caused a near scandal by taking part herself. It is likely that Inigo Jones's construction of 'a stage and scene' in the great hall three years later marked the introduction of a permanent infrastructure for theatrical entertainments.[289] Denmark House was thus the first royal palace in England to be permanently equipped with a modern theatre, predating the Whitehall court theatre by 36 years.

Performances were sometimes held elsewhere in the palace, occasionally in the presence chamber and on one occasion, the presence chamber not being sufficient, it was decided to set up the privy chamber next door for the dancing.[290] In 1633 the queen's most ambitious theatre was constructed in the inner or paved court. This was specially designed for the staging of the marathon (eight-hour) pastoral, *The Shepherd's Paradise*, written by Walter Montagu, designed by Inigo Jones and performed twice, in January and February 1633. It was accessed from a lobby just off the Guard Chamber (Fig. 11).[291]

The gardens

Henrietta Maria did not neglect the gardens at Denmark House. In many ways they were the finest royal gardens in London; the Whitehall gardens were separated from the river by a range of buildings — at Somerset House they ran down to the water's edge. *The History of the King's Works* has covered the development of the gardens, their waterworks and statuary. Their appearance during the Commonwealth, after the removal of the portable statuary, is recorded by Hollar (**cat. 10**).[292]

VII. COMMONWEALTH INTERLUDE 1642-60

AFTER Henrietta Maria left London in January 1642, Denmark House was locked up under the care of its keeper. The friary next door, at least for the time being, continued to function and the friars celebrated Mass daily much as before. No longer was this famous building known as Denmark House. Deliberately and consciously the new government, and soon the population at large, called it Somerset House, erasing its connection with the Stuart dynasty. No other royal palace was consciously renamed in this way, perhaps reflecting the special dislike attached to the London centre of Catholicism.

During the Commonwealth, Somerset House suffered a very low level of maintenance and repair and no architectural alterations were made to the building. The only significant change was Cromwell's removal of the 'Diana' fountain from the garden which was taken to Hampton Court in 1656.[293] This chapter does not therefore cover a significant period in the house's architectural or topographical development. However, it is necessary briefly to set out what took place there between 1642 and 1660.[294]

The chapel and friary

In the spring of 1643 the House of Commons finally ordered the Sheriffs of London and Middlesex to remove the Capuchin friars from Somerset House and hold them in preparation for deportation. Meanwhile four members of Parliament, accompanied by a small troop of infantry, were instructed to deface the altars and images in the chapel. This they did, smashing the confessionals, 'scourging' a crucifix and piercing another with a halberd, and allegedly tossing an altarpiece by Rubens into the Thames.[295] The chapel doors were then locked and the buildings left desecrated and deserted for nearly four years.

In January 1647 the chapel was opened up again, its last remaining fittings sold and the revenue used to fund its conversion into a Protestant preaching house. John Embree, the Surveyor of Works, set his men about dismantling the stone and brickwork of Inigo Jones's original altar and concealing the scar on the floor with 304 ft of black and white marble paving. All the internal timberwork was taken apart and removed to store; this certainly included Jones's reredos. Next it was decided to create two galleries, one over the vestry and the other in the organ loft. There is no account for the removal of the organ and it must be assumed that this had already been demolished. The cupboards in the vestry were taken apart and the furniture in the room above it removed. Part of the black and white marble floor was taken up in the transepts and two new timber staircases with plastered white interiors were inserted providing access to the new galleries. Low brick foundations were laid for new pews built on a low wooden floor in the two transepts. Pews were also installed in the galleries in the upper parts of the transepts. The great rectangular ceiling painting was removed and the void boarded over and painted plain blue. By the completion of the works all the original decorative elements except the frontal of the former royal pew had been stripped away. A plain white preaching box with galleries, wooden benches and a rather incongruous marble floor was created. The whole cost £178 8s 3d.[296] Soon after the king's execution, permission was given for public services to be held at Somerset House chapel. Mr Masterson, the minister of St Clement Danes, was licensed to use it on Thursday afternoons, presumably for preaching.[297]

The friary met an even worse fate. According to Father Cyprien de Gamache, the house in which he lived was pulled down and 'Some private person obtained permission from the Parliament to build another there in its stead'.[298]

The sale of the king's goods

Despite attacks on the chapel and friary and their subsequent conversion into a non-conformist chapel it is very likely that, in January 1649, Somerset House itself remained much as Henrietta Maria had left it.[299] The execution of the king, however, changed all that. Within a month there was concern in the Council of State for the safekeeping of the contents of the palaces which was now, with the abolition of the monarchy, property of the State. Security was increased at Somerset House and elsewhere to prevent the gradual embezzlement of the furnishings.

On 4 July an Act of Parliament resolved the future of the royal estate. Trustees were appointed to inventory royal possessions, ascertain which were to be kept by the Council of State and pass the rest on to contractors who were to sell the goods for the best price achievable. Inventories were fairly rapidly compiled and items started to be sold as early as the autumn. Some were sold directly from the palaces where they were found; many others were to be taken to a centralized saleroom located at Somerset House. During November cartloads of furniture, pictures, tapestry and household goods were delivered to Somerset House where they were arranged in the state rooms.[300]

The sale contractors thus had a central London showroom where they could display not only the rich haul of artworks and furnishings from Somerset House but also a selection of items from palaces elsewhere. What appears at first sight to have been a version of a Sotheby's showroom was, in reality, nothing of the sort. Many goods had been damaged by not being packed properly and moved in bumpy carts. Most were shown carelessly and tapestries and hangings were piled, torn and dusty on the floor.[301] Yet despite the chaos nobody could deny that Somerset House was host to the sale of the century. The showrooms were visited in December 1649 by the Spanish ambassador, Alonso de Cárdenas, who had been instructed to buy paintings for King Philip IV of Spain, but without revealing the identity of the purchaser. A letter home written after his visit survives listing over 60 paintings suitable for Philip IV at Somerset House and St James's.[302]

However, the sale did not go as fast or as profitably as Parliament had hoped and by May 1650 only a quarter of the pictures had been sold. This was not only an embarrassment, it was a crisis. The sale proceeds were intended to pay a large pool of creditors who were now angry at the inability of Parliament to pay. So the Commons changed tack. Creditors were now to be given artworks in lieu of payment, an expediency that worked. Groups of creditors formed themselves in to syndicates or 'dividends', as they called them. After receiving royal artworks, they set up their own showrooms and themselves sold the goods on to third parties for the best price they could get. By mid-October 1651 former royal goods began to leave Somerset House by the cartload and a year later, although sales spasmodically continued, the focus had moved from Somerset House.[303]

After the sale

During the summer of 1649 Parliament set forth its plans not only for the sale of the contents of the palaces but for the buildings, too. Most were to be sold for the value of their materials and their sites. At Somerset House the plan was for the chapel and friary, in particular, to be levelled and a new roadway made from the Strand to the river.[304] Yet the sale of the royal estate was a contentious issue and was delayed by long debate and procrastination by the Council of State. While its long-term fate was in the balance, Somerset House had a variety of uses. At first three great rooms were reserved and kept furnished for state use, while other rooms were set aside to accommodate members of the government and as lodgings for visiting dignitaries. In 1649, in an attempt to demilitarize Whitehall, Somerset House was made the headquarters of the army in London, while reserving the five rooms of state on the king's side, the queen's closet and the great hall for state use.[305] The rest became a barracks and lodgings for various MPs.[306] On 23 January 1652 Lodewijck Huygens saw the chapel and observed that all the paintings on the ceiling had been covered over with blue paint and that soldiers often preached there.[307] Cromwell himself was wont to visit the house every Thursday evening for supper with his captains. Now the location of Somerset House that had been so attractive to Henrietta Maria as she built her Catholic chapel was to be of benefit to Cromwell's army as it imposed itself upon London.

As the Commonwealth became more established, it found that it had need for many of the functions of the old monarchy. Thus in 1655 it was decided to set aside a suite of rooms at Somerset House for the use of ambassadors.[308] But its most monarchical use came in 1658 when, on Cromwell's death, it was the venue for his lying-in-state. Several other Parliamentary generals and admirals had been accorded this honour, one in Somerset House, but Cromwell's lying-in-state was entirely regal. Over the gatehouse facing the Strand was a great escutcheon bearing Cromwell's arms, inside the Presence, Privy and withdrawing chambers were hung in black, just as they had been for James I. In the withdrawing room lay

Cromwell's effigy under a canopy (**cat. 12**). This display, with various variations, was maintained for 81 days until his funeral was held at Westminster.[309]

Even after Cromwell's lying-in-state, it was the intention of Parliament to sell Somerset House, and as late as May 1659 the House of Commons agreed that, in order to pay the arrears of the army, it should be put on the market immediately. Two months later, as a result of lobbying by the French congregation in the chapel, the sale was restricted to the palace buildings and not the chapel.[310] On 8 July an agreement was drawn up for the sale of the house and the tenements for £9,663 but, before the transaction could be effected, rapidly moving political events halted the sale in its tracks.[311] At one point it was thought that Richard Cromwell could be offered Somerset House as he stood down from power[312] but, in the end, more prosaically, it was again taken over by the army for housing a regiment of foot soldiers. They were still installed when, in 1660, Charles II returned to London as king.[313]

VIII. THE STUART DOWER HOUSE

The Restoration

IN 1625 Somerset House had been granted to Henrietta Maria for life, and in 1660 both Parliament and Charles II confirmed that the dowager queen would have her London house and her dowry restored to her.[314] Not surprisingly, given the variety of uses to which the house had been put, much was in poor condition and the Office of Works was ordered to make preparations for the queen's return to her former home.

Makeshift privies had been erected round the house by the army; these had to be taken away. Partitions had been made to create smaller rooms; panelling which had been dismantled and sometimes burned needed reinstating. All the ceilings and cornices needed painting white and the stone chimneypieces and marble hearthstones scouring. The backstairs and passages were all cleaned and painted. Holes in the roof were patched. The hall cupola was scaffolded to allow the clock dial to be painted and gilded and the dome to be re-leaded. New furniture was made for the council chamber and the room was taken over by the Committee for the Receipt of the Queen's Goods. To receive both returned royal property and new items, the standing and privy wardrobes were overhauled and enlarged.[315] Gradually paintings and throne canopies were hung, while in the chapel an altar and pulpit were made. In the garden labourers worked to remove rubble and other debris.[316]

While the house was being prepared, as much of it as was serviceable was set aside for the king's youngest brother, Henry, Duke of Gloucester. He moved out for the Dutch ambassador for whom a tall buffet for plate was set up in the presence chamber and for whose retinue tables were erected in the hall. Gloucester's tenure of the house was short-lived as in September he contracted smallpox and died. His body was carried to Somerset House where it lay in state, just like Oliver Cromwell's two years before.[317]

When she had left England in 1642, Henrietta Maria had probably been the most unpopular woman in the country, and in her exile she had not been helpful to Charles or popular with her hosts. Despite this, there was no question that the tactless and bitter dowager would return to London for the great Stuart family reunion. Henrietta Maria arrived at Dover in November 1660 with her youngest daughter, Henrietta Anne, to be greeted by her eldest son, the king, his brother James and their sister Mary, Princess of Orange; by their side was their cousin, Prince Rupert of the Rhine. After a short stay in Dover the royal party returned to London and Henrietta Maria was installed in her former apartments at Whitehall.

The happiness that attended their reunion had been tempered by the impetuous secret marriage of James to Anne Hyde, a union of which the dowager queen strongly disapproved, but this woe was to be overshadowed by one much larger. On Christmas Eve, Mary of Orange also died of smallpox, plunging the family into deep mourning again. Like her brother's, Mary's body was conveyed to Somerset House for the second lying-in-state within a year of the Restoration.[318]

Tension over the Duke of York's marriage and the death of her daughter, combined with the necessity of celebrating the marriage of Henrietta Anne to Philip Duke of Orléans, caused Henrietta Maria to leave London for Paris after Christmas. Before she went, however, arrangements were made for the rebuilding of her palace of Somerset House.

Although the royal Office of Works was reconstituted in 1660, in the early years of the Restoration there was an architectural vacuum at the heart of it. The Surveyor of the King's Works was a royalist gentleman, Sir John Denham, who was interested in architecture but was no architect himself, rather a soldier and poet. He had distinguished himself in the king's cause during the Civil War, attempting to hold Farnham Castle against the Parliamentarians and then assisting in the escape of the young Dukes of York and Gloucester to Holland. Like many Royalists he went into exile, and in September 1649, as Charles was leaving France for Jersey, he dispatched Denham and William Crofts to the Baltic to drum up support for his claim to the throne. It was an important mission, and, as Denham left Charles, he was promised the post of Surveyor of Works when he was restored. Charles II's experiences in exile were crucial in determining the distribution of the offices of state in 1660. Denham remem-

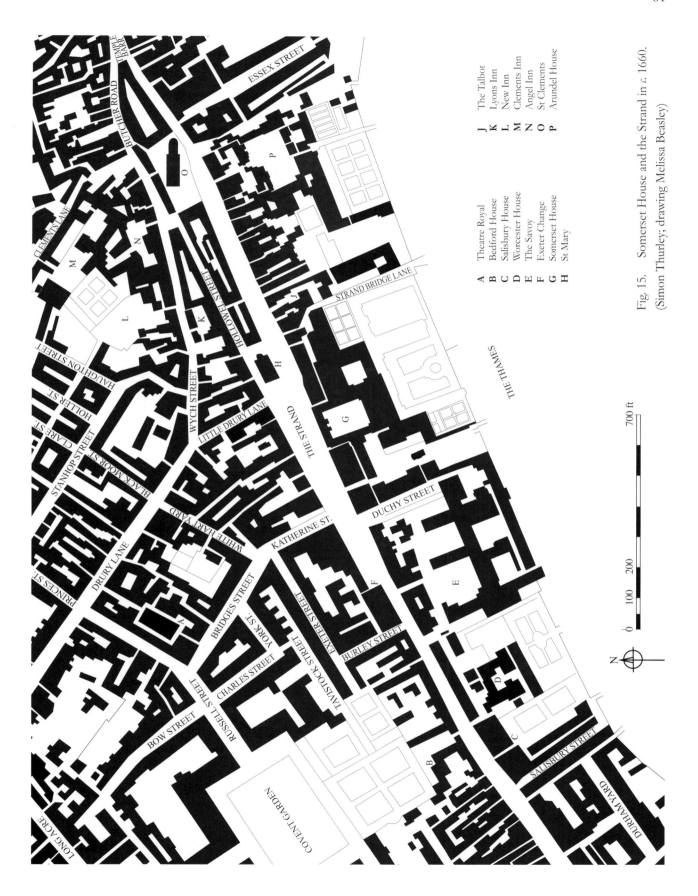

A   Theatre Royal
B   Bedford House
C   Salisbury House
D   Worcester House
E   The Savoy
F   Exeter Change
G   Somerset House
H   St Mary

J   The Talbot
K   Lyons Inn
L   New Inn
M   Clements Inn
N   Angel Inn
O   St Clements
P   Arundel House

Fig. 15.   Somerset House and the Strand in *c.* 1660.
(Simon Thurley; drawing Melissa Beasley)

Fig. 16.   Marie de Medici hosting her Circle at St James's Palace.

LE CERCLE DE LEVRS MAGESTES DANS LA CHAMBRE DE
PRESENCE A S. IAMES

bered the king's promise of 1649 and claimed his prize, kneeling at the king's feet at Breda in spring 1660.[319]

The man who felt most aggrieved by the appointment of Denham as Surveyor was John Webb, Inigo Jones's deputy and draughtsman, and the most accomplished architect working in England at the Restoration. Webb's credentials were no less royal than Denham's. Not only had Webb had a close personal working relationship with Charles I, visiting him at Hampton Court while he was imprisoned, but he had acted as a royalist spy and courier in the early stages of the Civil War. Despite continuing his architectural practice, working for a number of prominent Parliamentarians, Webb obtained a pass to travel to France in July 1656. His reasons for travel are not specified, but a Mr John Webb appears in a list of Charles II's household in the Bruges archives dating to *c.* 1657.[320] There are other contemporary John Webbs who were connected to the royal household in the early 1660s: a messenger of the household, a cook in the privy kitchen and, more significantly, the former Master of the Royal

Tennis Courts. Yet the strong balance of probability is that it was the architect who is listed as part of the king's exiled household.[321]

Thus Webb, like Denham and many others, was one of the Royalists who did a stint at the exiled court during the 1650s. He cannot have known that Denham had already been promised the top job and did not travel to Breda when the Restoration was announced. In fact Webb was already at work,[322] having been appointed architect for the rehabilitation of Whitehall, a task he probably imagined would have landed him the Surveyorship when the king returned. He was not to know that, by the time Charles took up residence, hundreds of household positions had already been awarded to other equally deserving loyalists.

Although Webb was not appointed to the lucrative and prestigious post which he craved, he scooped every important royal architectural commission at the Restoration. Denham needed an architect of talent and one who had the confidence of the king. Webb was both. Soon he was designing a new palace at Whitehall and was working on the practicalities of the new palace at Greenwich.[323] At Greenwich he would have been potentially in close contact with Henrietta Maria who was staying there in 1662 while Somerset House was being prepared. Henrietta Maria and John Webb would already have known each other. With Inigo Jones, Webb had worked closely with the queen in the late 1630s on a remodelling of the Strand range of Somerset House; he had also worked on masques and other court entertainments. In the RIBA drawings collection is a drawing by Webb undertaken at this time for the queen, proposing a new landing stage and water gate at Somerset House.[324] This demonstrates that Webb was perhaps hoping to be commissioned by the dowager queen as her architect. It was not to be.

Although it is tempting to attribute the queen's new works at Somerset House to John Webb, Webb himself never claimed them. In 1669, on the death of Sir John Denham, he wrote a detailed petition to Charles II, setting out his credentials for assuming the role of Surveyor of the King's Works. In it he listed the architectural commissions he had undertaken since the Restoration and in his list there is no mention of any work at Somerset House. It is inconceivable that Webb, in his last ditch attempt to gain the post he so craved, would have omitted the fact that he had designed the largest and most prominent architectural

commission actually to be completed in the first nine years of the Restoration.[325] In the queen's Privy Purse accounts there are two other names that could provide a clue to the architect she employed, William de Keyser and Hugh May.[326] De Keyser is listed as a sculptor and was paid £40. He is known to have made architectural drawings for Greenwich, but whether any of his architectural schemes were executed is uncertain. Hugh May, like Denham and Webb, was a Royalist who had been in exile with Charles II.[327] Like Webb, he was disappointed not to be rewarded with the Surveyorship, but, unlike Webb, he was given a major post in the Office of Works. As Paymaster he was responsible for managing the financial side of the overhaul of the royal palaces after 1660. It may be that his appearance in the queen's Privy Purse expenses reflects a financial role there also, particularly as in 1669 he was receiving £30 a year as Comptroller of her works.[328] However, at Windsor Castle where May was Comptroller, he was architect too, proving that the two positions could go hand in hand. Considering the documentary evidence which shows him being paid as one of her works staff, it would be hard to dismiss May as being the queen's architect in 1660.

Henrietta Maria's new works

In 1660 Denmark House must have looked incredibly old-fashioned to the king's mother. Despite work done on the queen's rooms in the 1620s and 1630s, the majority of the interiors were largely still those of Anne of Denmark's time. Taste had moved on enormously since 1638-9 and in the intervening 20 years Henrietta Maria had been in France, experiencing first hand the latest fashions in architecture and interior decoration. Moreover, by 1660 the type of rooms required by a queen and their uses had changed significantly. So the architect's brief must have been two-fold. First, to provide a modern suite of rooms that could be used by the queen in the manner that court etiquette of the 1660s required; and second to give the building a new face, more in tune with contemporary architectural taste.

The solution was simple but ingenious. It was proposed to build a new block of rooms on the south side of the great hall in the garden. The rooms would fit neatly between the chapel on the west and the old presence chamber on the east. A new front would be presented to the south, giving a modern impression to people moving up and

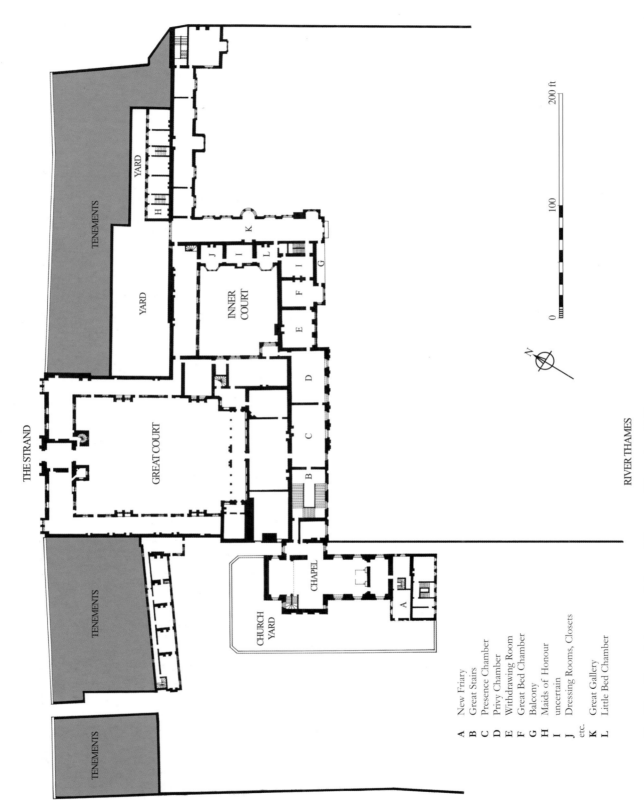

THE STRAND

TENEMENTS

YARD

YARD

TENEMENTS

H

K

INNER COURT

J I L

E F G

GREAT COURT

D

C

B

TENEMENTS

TENEMENTS

CHURCH YARD

CHAPEL

A

RIVER THAMES

N

0 100 200 ft

A New Friary
B Great Stairs
C Presence Chamber
D Privy Chamber
E Withdrawing Room
F Great Bed Chamber
G Balcony
H Maids of Honour
I uncertain
J Dressing Rooms, Closets
etc.
K Great Gallery
L Little Bed Chamber

Fig. 17. Plan of the ground floor of Somerset House in c. 1665.
(Simon Thurley; drawing Melissa Beasley)

down the river and arriving by barge at Somerset House steps (**cats 20, 21, 24, 26**). At first-floor level there were to be three great spaces, a staircase, a new presence chamber and a new privy chamber (Fig. 17). Architecturally this was difficult to handle as some of the rooms would be within the existing shell and some in the new structure. Thus while the privy chamber was fully behind the new frontispiece, the third window of the presence chamber was not. The whole staircase was in the portion to one side.

The staircase was the key to the new rooms, creating a new circulation hub for the queen's court. Pepys describes descending it and trying the 'brave echo on the stairs — which continues a voice so long as the singing three notes concords, one after another, they all three shall sound in consort together a good while most pleasantly'.[329] Little wonder it echoed, for at its tallest it rose through almost four storeys (Fig. 19). Webb managed the landings of the stairs so that, for the first time, a route was created from the state apartments to the tribune of the chapel. Now Henrietta Maria could process from her inner rooms through the outer chambers down a processional flight of stairs and into the chapel (Figs 17, 19). This was a significant change as it symbolized the much closer relationship of house and the friary, making the chapel much more akin to the royal chapels in other palaces.

The Tudor great hall now became the guard chamber, entered from the great court. From here a door in the centre of the south wall took visitors to the dowager's presence chamber. This was a much larger room than that which it replaced and was intended for a specific Court event.

The principal Court occasion in the queen's weekly calendar was the Circle. This was an event instituted by Henrietta Maria in the 1630s whereby the queen's presence chamber was thrown open to select ladies and gentlemen of the court who would gather round the queen, seated under her throne canopy, for conversation and gossip.[330] The innovation was probably French, an event that was later known as a *salon*, but which was, in the 1630s and 1640s, epitomized by the gatherings held by Madame Rambouillet in her chateau outside Paris. Henrietta Maria reinstated these Circles immediately on returning to England, making them the most important social gatherings at court. Before Charles II had a queen, these events were even more significant as his mother took on the ceremonial role of consort. After the king's

marriage to Catherine of Braganza, Henrietta Maria's Circle remained the leading Court social event, the young queen joining her mother-in-law beneath the throne canopy.

It was to provide a modern setting for the queen's Circle that the new rooms were built on the south front of Somerset House. The huge presence chamber leading from the big new guard chamber was carefully sited to facilitate the operation of the Circle, courtiers arriving in the great court and assembling in the old great hall before moving into the queen's presence. The great staircase allowed the king, queen, Duke and Duchess of York to disembark from their barges and cross the garden ascending the spectacular staircase to enter the Circle directly. In September 1662 Samuel Pepys attended a Somerset House Circle, being ushered into the presence chamber by the surgeon James Pierce. Under the canopy there was the queen mother and the queen attended by the Countess of Castlemaine and the Duke of Monmouth amongst others. Soon they were joined by the king and the Duke and Duchess of York.[331]

Does all this mean that Henrietta Maria requested a building of specifically French form? The Parisian social circles that were later to be known as *salons* required a specialized type of room; not the alcove bedchambers reserved for intimate discourse, nor the much larger *salles* which were for more public events. What developed in France was the *salle de compagnie* or *salle d'assemblée* where social circles regularly met. During the eighteenth century the social gathering known as a *salon* began to meet in a room of the same name, normally positioned in the centre of the main front in the middle of the suite of rooms. In the 1660s the marriage of room and event was still far from common, but some of Charles II's courtiers began to design houses with a large central dining room called a saloon in imitation of the great French chateaux like Vaux-le-Vicomte. The saloon was to become important in the design of English eighteenth-century large houses, in town and country.[332]

Yet in 1660 this was a long way off and Henrietta Maria's new rooms on the south front of Somerset House are not easily identifiable with this later tradition. They were, however, designed for a specific purpose and the presence chamber in particular was a much larger, grander and more central room than before. As the queen's Circle metamorphosed into an event called a Drawing Room and switched its location from the presence

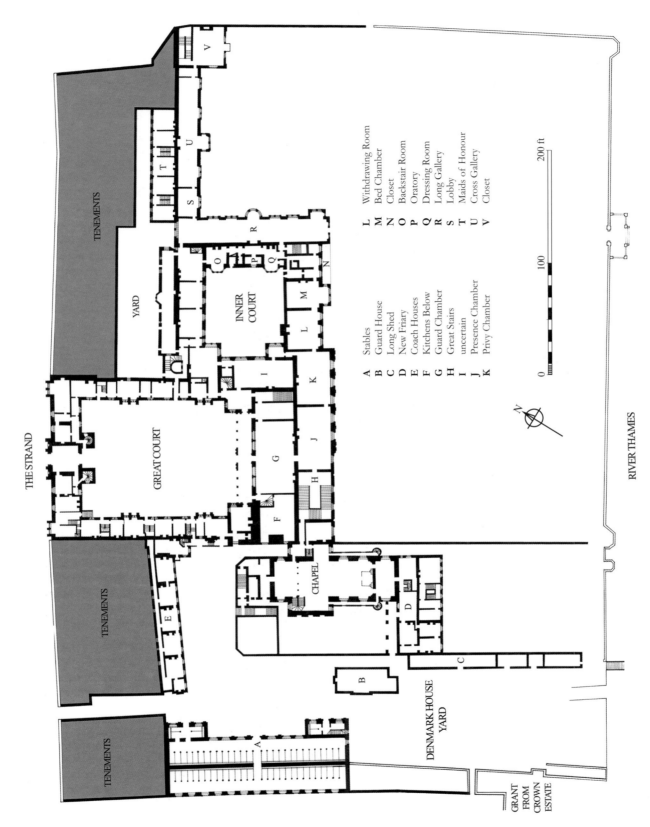

TENEMENTS

TENEMENTS

TENEMENTS

TENEMENTS

YARD

GREAT COURT

INNER
COURT

CHAPEL

DENMARK HOUSE
YARD

GRANT
FROM
CROWN
ESTATE

RIVER THAMES

A	Stables
B	Guard House
C	Long Shed
D	New Friary
E	Coach Houses
F	Kitchens Below
G	Guard Chamber
H	Great Stairs
I	uncertain
J	Presence Chamber
K	Privy Chamber
L	Withdrawing Room
M	Bed Chamber
N	Closet
O	Backstair Room
P	Oratory
Q	Dressing Room
R	Long Gallery
S	Lobby
T	Maids of Honour
U	Cross Gallery
V	Closet

N

0   100   200 ft

Fig. 18.   Plan of the ground floor of Somerset House in *c.* 1680.
(Simon Thurley; drawing Melissa Beasley)

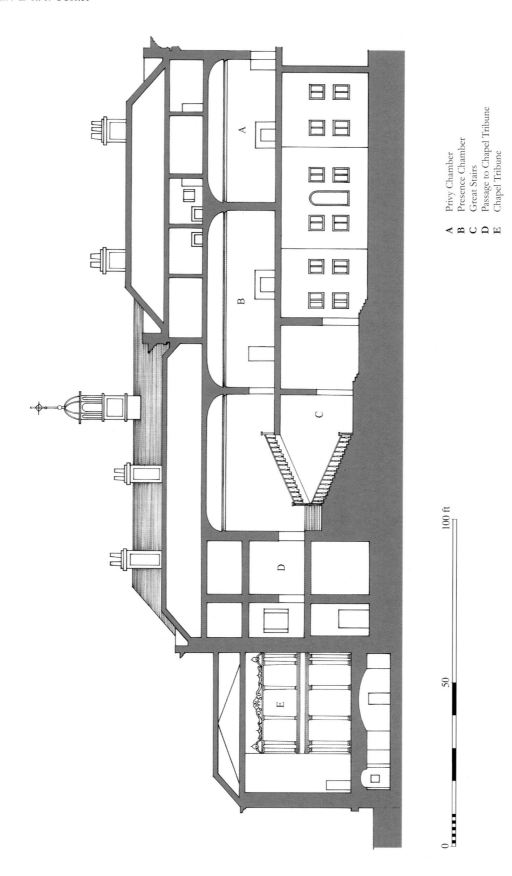

A   Privy Chamber
B   Presence Chamber
C   Great Stairs
D   Passage to Chapel Tribune
E   Chapel Tribune

100 ft

50

0

Fig. 19.   East-west elevation and cross-section of Somerset House in *c.* 1680. See fig. 18 for plan.
(Simon Thurley; drawing Melissa Beasley)

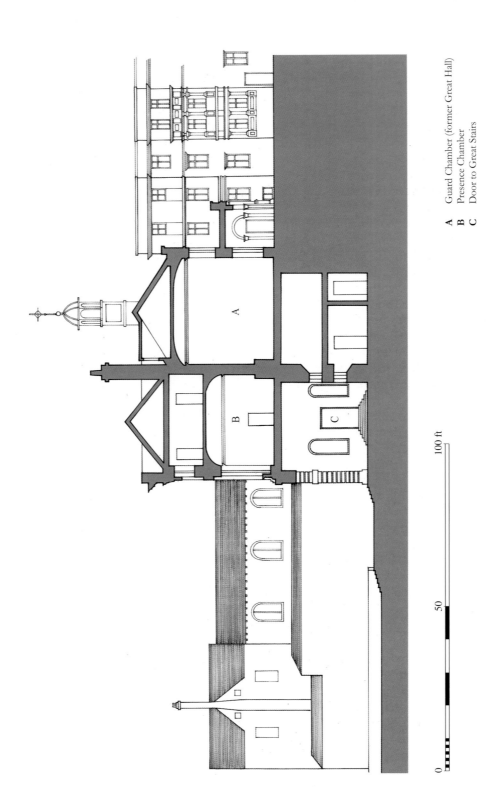

A   Guard Chamber (former Great Hall)
B   Presence Chamber
C   Door to Great Stairs

100 ft

50

0

Fig. 20.   North-south elevation and cross-section of Somerset House in c. 1680. See fig. 18 for plan.
(Simon Thurley; drawing Melissa Beasley)

chamber into the room of the same name, the fusion of event and space occurred as it had done in the *salons* of France 50 years later. The Queen of England's drawing room henceforth became one of the most important rooms socially and architecturally, culminating in the great east front drawing room at Hampton Court.[333]

The new building dominated the south front of the palace. It was a carefully composed frontispiece most likely based on an engraving of the Palazzo Magnani in Bologna, but ultimately derived from arcades illustrated by Serlio in his fourth book.[334] Its construction, as we have seen, was paid from the dowager queen's Privy Purse, for which no detailed accounts now survive. We do, however, have the draft accounts of the queen mother's Treasurer and Receiver General, Henry Jermyn Earl of St Albans, covering the period. They show that £23,501 was spent, partly through Sir John Denham and the Office of Works, and partly through direct contracts made between her officers and individual craftsmen. In none of this is any individual part of the building specified.[335] This is frustrating as it deprives us of any chance of visualizing the interiors which are otherwise unrecorded. We should not doubt that they were fitted up with great magnificence, probably with deep coved ceilings with richly moulded plaster-work, heavy panelling and cornices and architectural fireplaces with pediments. In Figure 19 I have shown what I regard to have been the likely effect and proportion.

Two entries in the draft accounts might suggest that the queen brought Frenchmen to design and execute part of the work. One Monsieur Ambrey was paid £109 for unspecified tasks. Was he a painter, a plasterer or a designer? So far he remains unidentified. More promising is the payment of £15 for 'ye ffrench joyners'. It is possible that they were responsible for laying the parquet floors illustrated in Richards's edition of Palladio's *First Book of Architecture* published in 1676 (**cat. 17**). These he included as they were a 'novelty in England' at the time.

When Henrietta Maria returned to London in August 1662, Somerset House was not quite finished so for a few weeks she resided at Greenwich. Yet by the end of the month she was using the new rooms, although work continued on perfecting them for another year or so.[336] Pepys visited in February 1664 and remarked that the chapel was complete and full of worshippers, and that the new building would be in every respect 'mighty magnificent and costly'. When he visited again in October he saw the completed rooms furnished and thought them 'stately and noble'.[337]

The queen's chapel and other improvements

The new stone front to the river was the principal domestic concern but the rehabilitation of the chapel was perhaps the queen's first priority. The dowager queen reinstated her Catholic chapel on arrival in England, indeed many of her chapel were the same personnel as before the war — Father Cyprien [de] Gamache and Abbé Montagu the foremost amongst them. They immediately resumed their ministry where they had left off and the chapel once again became a magnet for Catholics from all over London.[338]

Some preparations for this had been made before the queen returned, principally the eviction of the French Church from the queen's chapel to the Savoy Chapel next door. The Office of Works had provided a new altar and a pulpit brought from Whitehall.[339] This was not going to be enough either for the queen or for Father Cyprien, and so in the period 1660-4 the chapel was entirely refitted.[340] There are no accounts for this, but I have argued elsewhere that the new reredos (**cat. 23**) was inspired by Jesuit models from Paris.[341] It is quite clear that the design and decoration of the chapel owed a great deal to the influence of the queen's Capuchins. Father Apolinaire, who arrived in England with the queen in August 1662, 'was charged to keep the Queen's chapel always duly adorned'. He spent his time increasing the 'splendour and the majesty of the altar' with 'rare pieces of workmanship'.[342] Once again we come up against the question of the designer. We do not know who designed the reredos, but whoever did had detailed knowledge of what was happening in Paris, and so it may be that Father Apolinaire or one of the Frenchmen mentioned in the accounts had a hand in its design.

While the chapel was being refitted, the private house that had replaced the friary was vacated and itself refashioned to make it suitable for the queen's friars. Thus the new friary of 1662-4 was in fact a converted town house of the 1640s.[343]

The great rebuilding of 1662-4 also included some more mundane aspects. The 'new bricke building three storeys high for her magestie the queen-mother adjoyninge to the stone gallery next ye garden', otherwise known as the 'new bricke building at the end of the crosse gallery in the back court of Somersett house', was a major piece of work. This block of lodgings, presumably designed for the queen's household, can be easily identified on the 1706 plan (**cat. 19**) where they are called 'French Buildings' and on the 1775 plan (**cat. 33**) where they are called 'Maid of Honour's Court'. Raised up on a basement there were seven lodgings, some one room, some two and one three. They looked out over a narrow court on the north side, and presumably into the upper windows of the tenements on the Strand.

Finally the queen ordered the garden to be refashioned. In her draft accounts her gardener is identified as John Smith, but Roger Looker described himself as 'gardener to her majesty'.[344] The bowling green was dug up and laid out with grass plots and gravel walks, and new plinths were provided for statues in front of the loggia.[345]

In the spring of 1665 Henrietta Maria decided to return to France.[346] Her health was not good — a fact she blamed on the climate; the plague was beginning to strengthen in the city and she missed her daughter. Father Cyprien travelled with the queen, but the other Capuchins remained behind just as in 1642. For the next four and a half years the house was maintained partly by the Office of Works and partly by the queen. Little of note is recorded in the Works accounts, other than the painting of the chapel ceiling in 1666.[347]

Catherine of Braganza

On 10 September 1669 Henrietta Maria died and the following month Catherine was finally granted Somerset House and its contents.[348] Many expected her to move there from Whitehall as Henrietta Maria has done before the Civil War.[349] Catherine, however, never made Somerset House her residence while she was queen, much preferring to remain in her apartments at Whitehall while she was in London.[350] Yet the queen was faced with a dilemma. Since 1662, she had maintained a Catholic chapel at St James's where she had built a new friary for her Capuchins and English Benedictines. The chapel had been refitted, too, at some expense. The Somerset House chapel was, however, far superior, larger and much better suited to Catholic worship. Since she was not allowed to keep two establishments by the terms of her marriage agreement, should she move her chapel establishment to Somerset House?[351] This is in fact what Catherine resolved to do. She shut down the chapel at St James's and

moved the whole establishment to Somerset House. Certainly a primary motivation behind the move was the growing number of Catholics and the greater capacity at Somerset House, but it was also probably regarded as being a more central location than remote St James's, ideal for attracting both residents and converts from the populous Strand and Covent Garden.[352]

Work immediately started on what was called 'the new buildings at the friary'. Henrietta Maria seems to have made some minor improvements to the Commonwealth town house for her friars, but not converted it into a fully functioning Capuchin house. A comparison of Hollar's view (**cat. 10**) with William Morgan's map of 1682 (**cat. 18**) shows the new westward extension to the friary built by Catherine; Kip and Knyff's view (**cat. 20**) shows the new building to have a characteristically late seventeenth-century hipped roof with a cornice.

This accords with what is known from the Works accounts, as this new building was paid for, not out of the queen's own private income as at St James's, but from the Treasury.[353] We learn that bricks were brought from the waterside for the new friary and a timber roof was framed up. A cloister was erected with 'columns' entered through a gate with a pediment.[354] The cloister was in reality more of a pentice, allowing the friars to get from the gate to the friary under cover. This arrangement can be clearly seen on the 1706 plan on the south side of the friars' burial ground (**cat. 19** and Fig. 15).

Some details of the internal fitments are recorded: four partitions were made for the friars' beds, and in one room a 'porthole' was made presumably to create a line of sight from one of the friars' rooms to an altar. The chapel itself was re-ordered, the choir stalls moved and more seats installed. Joiners finished 'a greate chaire in ye chappell and turning ye doores of ye railes by ye high alter and making a partition in it for father Constantine and a place enclosed by it'. A bell was hung, and we learn of the friars' kitchen, laundry, house of office and pissing place. At the bottom of the garden, clearly discernible on historic plans (**cat. 19**), was a five-sided summer house for the friars to relax in.[355] These works were probably specified by the superior, Father Constantine, who died in August 1672 and was buried in the new cloister.[356]

The most important architectural commission of Charles II's reign was a new stable building for

56 horses designed by Robert Hooke (**cat. 13**). It has been suggested that Hooke won the commission through his friendship with the queen's Treasurer, John Hervey.[357] There are no accounts for the building and so details of its construction are lost; the cost was presumably born by the queen's Privy Purse. Why such a large and architecturally pretentious building was required when the queen was not habitually residing there is unclear. It seems likely that they were erected in 1669 or 1670 before it was fully clear how the queen would use the house. Nevertheless, it is also true that the house was conspicuously without stables and that other great London mansions had buildings of some pretension designed, like Hooke's, to look like a small country house.[358] Near the stable and close to the friary door was a new guard house erected in 1671 (fig. 18). This can be seen on the 1706 plan, for instance (**cat. 19**).[359]

Although the queen did not live at Somerset House, as soon as she took possession of it her household and administration took up lodgings there. Senior officers had apartments in the main house and Somerset Yard was full of the more junior officers: officers of the guard, the clerk of works, the locksmith, glazier, footmen, necessary women, priests, the queen's staff of the robes, her cooks, her doctor and surgeons. Her Master of the Horse enjoyed a large apartment in Hooke's new building over the stables.[360]

The palace was thus fully staffed and equipped, and in the queen's absence the state apartments continued to be used, on an occasional basis, for their traditional functions. After his death in January 1670 the body of the architect of the Restoration, George Monck the Duke of Albemarle, was laid out in the state rooms (**cat. 14**); two years later another military hero, the Earl of Sandwich, was laid in state in the same rooms after being killed when his flagship blew up fighting the Dutch.[361] Important foreign guests were accommodated there, too.[362] Although Catherine rarely used the state apartments, she attended services there on a regular basis, not only on holy Days of Obligation, but on Sundays and occasionally vespers and other minor services, too.[363]

Although Catherine had moved her chapel establishment to Somerset House, it was never to enjoy much stability there. In March 1675 all English-born Catholic priests were expelled from Court, depleting the queen's chapel and causing her to send to Portugal for more Capuchins to replace the Benedictines lost from Somerset

House.[364] The Portuguese chapel continued to minister to Catholics at large, not just the queen's household. Yet the core of the congregation were English courtiers. Typical, perhaps, were Sir Samuel and Lady Tuke. Tuke was a royalist officer who had converted to Catholicism, his wife Mary was a dresser in service to the queen. They had rooms at Somerset House and saw their son Charles baptized in the chapel there in July 1672. The godparents included the king, Henry Arundell, Lord Wardour (Henrietta Maria's former Master of Horse and a leading parliamentary Catholic) and the peeress, the Countess of Huntingdon. On Sir Samuel's death in 1674 he was buried in the chapel cloister.[365]

In 1675 the queen decided to spend Easter at Somerset House so she could enjoy the full observances of Holy Week. The state apartments were refurnished: new furniture was delivered, including a great cloth of state bearing Catherine's arms, a standing bed of blue damask and matching hangings; tapestries were delivered to hang in the guard chamber.[366] Huge crowds of Catholics were expected and it was decided to add galleries to the chapel to make more space. Two galleries erected 'on the east and west sides ... cont in length 37 foot long each and breadth 4 foot' with windows looking out and staircases at each end. Six doors, presumably three on each side, were made to provide access to the galleries.[367] These can be seen on Kip's view (**cat. 20**) and eighteenth-century plans (**cat. 30**).

This Easter visit was, as far as we can tell, exceptional, but she did use the house every year for her own Catholic Maundy ceremony in the guard chamber. Just as with the king in the Banqueting House in Whitehall, a section of the room was railed off for the ceremony and after the service the Maundy men dined on long tables in the Presence Chamber next door.[368]

The intensive use of the house for Catholic liturgy and ceremonial by the queen and an inner circle of courtiers did nothing to improve its image with Londoners at large; indeed, it contributed to the queen and her palace being the focus of scandal surrounding the Popish Plot of 1678. The fabricated plot centred on the murder of the king to clear the way for Catholic James to ascend the throne. The queen was allegedly complicit in this, and to cover up the evidence it was claimed that Catherine's Catholic servants had murdered the investigating magistrate, Sir Edmund Godfrey, at Somerset House with the queen's knowledge and approval. Somerset House was even searched for evidence. Despite the passing of the 1678 Test Act and the subsequent reduction of the queen's Portuguese household, the queen and Somerset House remained symbols of popery and fear, so much so that in 1680 she was publicly insulted on her way to chapel. These threats caused two troops of horse and a foot regiment to be quartered at Somerset House.[369] Rough treatment at the gates of her own house finally convinced the queen to shut up the Somerset House chapel and move her Capuchins back to St James's, which was closer to her apartments at Whitehall and removed from the violent populace further east.

The abandonment of the chapel and friary coincided with the appointment of Edward Hyde, the second Earl of Clarendon as her Treasurer and Receiver General of Revenues. The empty friary was now converted into a residence for him; he clearly used the house, as John Evelyn records dining with him there.[370]

On the death of Charles II Catherine moved, with her household, from Whitehall to Somerset House. An estimate prepared by Sir Christopher Wren in February 1685 lists £1,813 worth of repairs that were required for her arrival. Much of the work was for the queen's chapel and the friary. The chapel had been stripped of many fittings when it had moved back to St James's in 1680 and the friary had been turned into the Earl of Clarendon's house. The house was refitted for the friars, 'with conveniences suitable to their rules of living' and the chapel restored. The queen's lodgings needed little work in comparison, and Wren noted that no allowance had been made for sprucing up the three hundred or so servants' rooms in the palace.[371]

Catherine's dowager life at Somerset House was architecturally uneventful,[372] but during the reign of James II music and worship in her chapel flourished.[373] The chapel, being the most prestigious place of Catholic worship in England, was the site of the consecration of the Vicars Apostolic, the Catholic bishops who were, King James hoped, to evangelize in England.

At the crisis of James II's reign, there was an eruption of anti-Catholic violence in the capital directed against Catholic places of worship. Although after much pressure James ordered all Catholic chapels to be shut up, the order did not include the royal chapels at Somerset House, St. James's and now Whitehall. On 11 December, the night James left the capital, huge crowds attacked houses where priests were supposed to be lodging, as well as the private chapels of Catholic ambassadors. With the king gone and protection withdrawn from the royal chapels, the crowd then turned their attention to them. The provisional government only just managed to save the Catholic chapel at St James's Palace from destruction; a mob was already inside dismantling the altar and organ when troops arrived to protect it. At Somerset House the dowager queen was in fear of her life — a huge angry, violent mob had assembled outside the palace. Counter-measures by the government foiled a planned assault, and from that time three companies of guards and 20 horse were stationed there.[374]

After the coming of William III, royal protection was once again extended to the Dowager and her palace, but the relationship between William and Catherine was never very warm or understanding. Indeed, William seemed to regard her prominent occupation of Somerset House as an embarrassment. In March 1692, after a number of false starts, the necessary agreements between England and Portugal were in place and the queen packed her bags. She left Somerset House in a great cavalcade of carriages making for Dover. As they passed over London Bridge the great guns of the Tower fired a salute. Somerset House's last resident queen consort had finally left.[375]

Despite her departure the house was still Catherine's, and in it remained a skeleton staff of caretakers, maintenance officers and retainers under the Earl of Feversham, her keeper. Many of these people had rights of occupation and enjoyed large apartments at the queen's favour.[376] Various attempts were made by William to evict Feversham and the rump of the old queen's household, but it was only on the queen's death in December 1705 that the palace finally became free for a new use.

IX. DECLINE

Introduction[377]

BY the 1670s Somerset House as a royal residence was becoming increasingly out of place. Soon after the Restoration, the main concentration of aristocratic residences moved westwards. One reason is that new men now held positions of importance in Court and Government, but did not inherit the existing aristocratic mansions and so needed to build. The relaxation of controls over building on new sites meant that the fields north and west of Westminster were now available for them to do this. Sir Edward Hyde, first Earl of Clarendon, the Lord Chancellor, leased a mansion in the Strand (Worcester House) until his own mansion in Piccadilly, designed by Roger Pratt, was completed in 1665. Another important and influential politician, Henry Bennet, Earl of Arlington, Secretary of State, acquired Goring House on the west side of St James's Park, which was rebuilt in 1674 as Arlington House. John Berkeley, first Lord Berkeley of Stratton, built Berkeley House, designed by Hugh May, in Piccadilly next to Clarendon House.[378] These mansions encouraged a new fashion in building and led owners of the old-fashioned mansions in the Strand to move to more spacious surroundings. New building near St James's Palace was also providing modern town mansions, more modest in scale but in a more convenient location for Court and Parliament. Old-fashioned, decaying, hemmed in and in the wrong location, the old mansions of the Strand could make way for redevelopment with streets of brick houses, which continued to be in increasing demand for the middle classes, artisans, and retailers.

On the south side of the Strand after the Restoration, the Howard family no longer used Arundel House as their main London residence, and redevelopment of the site began in the 1670s, when Surrey, Norfolk, and Arundel Streets were laid out over the northern half of the site, with the mansion itself being demolished *c.* 1680 (**cats 24, 27**).[379] At Essex House, where the third Earl of Essex had died in 1642, the eventual owner, Lord Hertford, Duke of Somerset from 1660, and his duchess occupied the house, but rebuilding in the grounds started in the 1660s. After the duchess died in 1674, the mansion and houses fronting the Strand were sold and the site was laid out by 1679 with Essex Street and rows of new houses in Milford Lane. Worcester House continued to be used by the Herbert family until 1681, when the house was demolished and Beaufort Buildings, Herbert Street, and Fountain Court were laid out. To the east, Little Salisbury House was converted into Middle Exchange with shops by 1671; new houses were built in Salisbury Street in 1673, and Salisbury House itself was demolished in 1694 and replaced with Cecil Street.

On the north side of the Strand, the Cecil family received a licence to demolish and rebuild on the sites of Exeter House, Little Exeter House and Wimbledon House in 1671, and Exeter and Burleigh Streets were laid out, with the Exeter Change, used amongst other things for large public entertainments, being built on the site of Exeter House. East of the Cecil family's property, the White Hart, a large medieval tavern belonging to Brasenose College, Oxford, was demolished in 1673 to make a new connection, Catherine Street, between the area of Covent Garden and the Strand, opening up the area still further. To the west of the Cecil estate, Bedford House remained the home of the Russell family until the death of the first Duke of Bedford in 1700, when his heir moved to Bloomsbury. The house was demolished 1705-6 and Southampton Street was built across the site. In addition to the many smaller houses being built in and around the Strand for middle-class occupants, a new church was finally built for the parish of St Mary-le-Strand in 1714-17, on the island site in the middle of the Strand.

All this left Somerset House high and dry, a surviving relic of a past way of life, a topographical, architectural and social dinosaur trapped in a web of new streets and houses, occupied not by royalty and nobility but by a new middle class of Londoners.

Queen Anne

By 1718 Sir John Vanbrugh judged Somerset House to be in the worst condition of any royal palace. For the preceding 40 years only what was absolutely necessary had been done to keep the building from collapse — and that reluctantly.

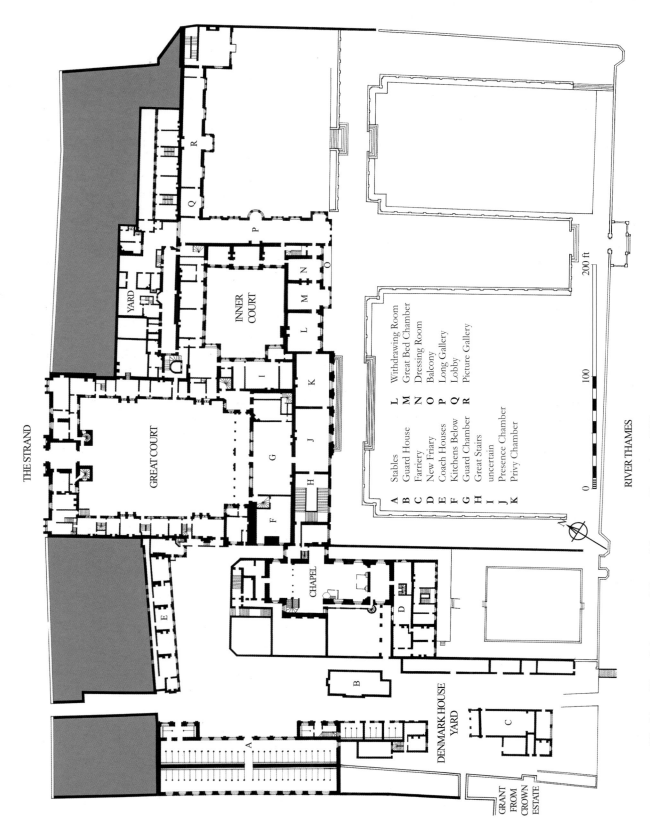

THE STRAND

GREAT COURT

YARD

INNER COURT

CHAPEL

DENMARK HOUSE YARD

GRANT FROM CROWN ESTATE

RIVER THAMES

A   Stables
B   Guard House
C   Farriery
D   New Friary
E   Coach Houses
F   Kitchens Below
G   Guard Chamber
H   Great Stairs
I   uncertain
J   Presence Chamber
K   Privy Chamber

L   Withdrawing Room
M Great Bed Chamber
N   Dressing Room
O   Balcony
P   Long Gallery
Q   Lobby
R   Picture Gallery

0   100   200 ft

Fig. 21.   Plan of the ground floor of Somerset House in *c.* 1760.
(Simon Thurley; drawing Melissa Beasley)

This book has been about the physical development of Somerset House and its impact on the Court, on politics and on London, a story that comes to an end in 1692 with the death of Catherine of Braganza. As a conclusion this short chapter will cover the old palace's last years. The intention is not to repeat what the *History of the King Works* or Needham and Webster's book on *Somerset House* have covered, but to add to that story in the context of what this book has taught us about the palace.[380]

In August 1706, soon after the house fell into the possession of Queen Anne, plans were laid for ejecting Catherine of Braganza's remaining servants and officials. Orders were given by Wren for the Clerk of Works at Somerset House to make a list of the fittings and fixtures in the apartments so that they could not be stolen by the departing occupants.[381] The inventory has recently been purchased by the Somerset House Trust and shows in detail the contents and architectural features in 1706. With the house vacated the queen's plan was to set it aside for visiting ambassadors, and to that end a survey was commissioned of the whole building (**cat. 19**). Together the 1706 survey and inventory present a unique snapshot of the house at the end of its use as a fully functional royal residence.

In February 1707 orders were given for fitting up Somerset House for the Venetian ambassadors. The cost was £20,057 18s 4d, the bulk of which was for joiners' work, especially in the kitchens, but work was fairly comprehensive and included painting, plastering, brickwork and even repairing the great clock over the guard chamber. The same year there was a large order for new furniture.[382] In all, in the years after 1707 over £8,000 was spent on restoring the house.[383] Queen Anne may have envisaged a permanently maintained ambassadorial residence; if she had, the idea soon died. The house was not kept up after this initial burst of expenditure and soon the house and gardens were being plundered for works of art to furnish other palaces.[384]

Georgian Somerset House

After the death of Queen Anne in August 1714 the throne passed to Hanoverian George I who arrived in England with his son, the future George II and his wife, the intelligent and cultured Caroline of Brandenburg-Ansbach. In 1715 Somerset House was settled on Caroline, as

Princess of Wales, with a dowry of £50,000.[385] The princess could have decided to take the house on and make it a modern residence and social hub, but this was almost certainly never contemplated. The social gravity of London had moved much further west and the centre of her life was to be at St James's and Leicester House. In fact there had been a huge social deterioration on the Strand from the 1670s and the Middle Exchange, only a few doors away from Somerset House, had been known as the Whore's Nest.[386] The tenements that had provided such an important stream of income for the queens of England were not seen as an asset by William III, and so had been granted to the Earl of Dorset in 1694. They were quickly redeveloped with shops on the ground floor and three storeys of accommodation with attics above. The effect of this on Somerset House can be best seen on Antoine Benoist's engraving (**cat. 25**). John Strype, writing in 1720, describes the 'stately Pile of new Brick Houses on both sides of *Somerset House*; which much eclipse that palace'.[387] He was right; the old Strand façade now looked very small and dilapidated next to the handsome new Georgian terraces.

Nevertheless, the Prince and Princess of Wales were happy to try any location at their disposal to create a gay and lively court, throwing that of George I into the shade, and Somerset House was used for a series of balls in 1716, apparently with some success.[388] Sporadically over the next half-century the house would briefly burst into life, with a masquerade in 1749 and the stay of the Venetian ambassador in 1763.

In 1730 Anne of Denmark's bedchamber and privy chambers on the east side of the inner court collapsed, and the south and east walls of the court needed to be rebuilt. The effects of this can be seen by comparing the 1706 plan (**cat. 19**) with the 1775 plan (**cat. 33**), also see Figure 18. The new work presumably created slightly more modern and commodious rooms for royal guests.

Most of the time Somerset House was host to a mixed collection of grace-and-favour residents given lodgings at royal whim as a reward for services or as compensation for hard times. In 1775 the last list of occupants was drawn up showing who was living there, by what right and since when.[389] Some had lodgings 'by right of office', in other words being in possession of a Somerset House sinecure, such as Mary Campbell of Mamore who was appointed keeper of the house by Queen Caroline when she and her husband got into financial difficulties.[390] Others were grace-and-favour residents living there, at the 'king's indulgence'.

In 1761 Somerset House was settled on Charlotte of Mecklenburg Strelitz, George III's queen. Her tenure did not herald an improvement in the old palace's fortunes. It was used to accommodate the Venetian ambassador in 1763 and, in the following year, it housed its last royal visitor, the Hereditary Prince of Brunswick Luneburg, who was negotiating for the hand of George III's daughter, Augusta. Neither stay could have been very comfortable in the vast, cold and decaying building. During the rest of the 1760s, while grace and favour continued, parts of the house were used as a barracks.[391] Only one part of the old palace was now serving its original function — the chapel. When she left for Portugal, Catherine of Braganza took her Catholic priests with her, leaving the chapel and friary empty. After her death Queen Anne decided to reconsecrate the chapel as an Anglican place of worship. This was done on Easter Day 1711 by John Robinson, the bishop diplomat, to whom Queen Anne had granted grace-and-favour lodgings at Somerset House.[392] The chapel became, like the Whitehall chapel, a fashionable place to get married, be christened and, up until 1775, be buried. It was in this way that the chapel, that had been the scourge of seventeenth-century London, and that had been implicated in the downfall of kings, ended its life as part of the social circuit of fashionable eighteenth-century society.

In 1771 the state apartments were granted to the newly-constituted Royal Academy of Arts, which George III had a major hand in founding. The first of their annual dinners (which continue to this day) was held that St George's Day. However, by 1771 the idea of using the site of Somerset House for a new and very ambitious project had already been mooted. The project was to unite the various offices of government in a new building on one site, a concept, at that date, without precedent in Europe.

On 6 May 1774 the Board of Works reported that the old palace was, indeed, ruinous, and four days later the king and the Prime Minister, Lord North, discussed the matter. On 17 May George III finally authorized the demolition of one of England's oldest royal palaces. It is unlikely that this was a reluctant act, as his agreement was part of a wider deal with the government. In exchange for Somerset House the king was effectively given a grant to purchase Buckingham House in St James's and convert it into a new dower house for the queen. This was confirmed in an Act of Parliament in 1775.[393] Demolition of Somerset House began the following year, but not before a number of artists had made a record of the old building (**cats 33-7**). The old palace was dismantled in sections as the new buildings rose around the ruins. This provided considerable opportunity for tourists to watch the demolition and artists to record it (**cats 38-41** show views of the house as it was demolished).

Thus, by exchanging the ruins of an ancient Tudor palace, the British monarchy gained the royal residence which, after several centuries of alteration, expansion and improvement, is now its principal seat. Meanwhile, thanks to Sir William Chambers, the architect chosen to build the new government offices, London gained, perhaps, its finest eighteenth-century architectural work: New Somerset House.

APPENDIX. FRAGMENTS OF DECORATIVE PLASTERWORK EXCAVATED AT SOMERSET HOUSE

by CLAIRE GAPPER

Introduction

Since no decorative plasterwork has survived *in situ* in any of the royal palaces of the Tudor and early Stuart monarchs, it has been exciting to see fragments of some of those early schemes emerge during recent excavations at Somerset House.[394] Significant finds of decorative plasterwork were made at two separate locations on the site, entirely different in character. The previous history of the site meant that it was not possible to date these fragments or establish their original location on the basis of the archaeological investigation alone. Documentary evidence exists to supplement stylistic analysis, but the clerks of the royal works were neither exhaustive nor consistent in their descriptions of decorative schemes. With these provisos in mind, these building accounts supply an additional means of dating the plaster fragments.

Group 1

During Chambers's rebuilding of Somerset House great quantities of rubble were used to infill the site of the existing great staircase in the south range of the great court. Amongst the shattered fragments emerged some recognizable pieces of decorative plaster — a grotesque mask, part of a 'jelly mould' boss, an artichoke and a pear (all on display at Somerset House) (Figs 22-25).

It is clear to the naked eye that these pieces were produced from moulds, but the mask and boss were made using a different lime plaster mix from the artichoke and pear, indicating that they are not of the same date. No hair is visible in the lime plaster, but, while crushed brick was used as aggregate for the mask and boss, quartz sand bulked out the plaster of the artichoke and pear, resulting in a colour differentiation between the two mixes.

The backing coat of the mask had been applied to laths, with two iron armatures providing additional support. Remains of an iron ring are held in the mouth of the mask (perhaps to hold a chandelier), whose lips are painted red. Plentiful traces of gilding survive around the exaggerated eyebrows of the face and on the boss, which also retains blue paint between the foliate decoration of its outer circle. The mask measures 220 mm high and 180 mm wide.

The artichoke and pear are most likely to belong to a post-Restoration scheme, after Henrietta Maria's return to Somerset House. The accounts provide no confirmation of this stylistic analysis as they are incomplete and perfunctory in their descriptions.

Group 2

A second group of fragments was excavated at the eastern end of Anne of Denmark's cross gallery (Figs 26-28). Among these were several pieces of lime plaster which still bore their original gilded decoration. The mouldings are of an architectural nature, suggesting not only wall or ceiling ribs, but also moulded cornices and framing elements that would have been run *in situ*. The gold leaf decoration is also architectural in its vocabulary, including water-leaf, guilloche, overlapping coin ornament and dentils. The lime plaster mix is very similar to that of the mask and boss, with no hair and an aggregate of crushed brick. It is therefore likely that all these fragments are close in date.

Dating

The most plausible date for a ceiling incorporating the grotesque mask and boss would be the period of major rebuilding undertaken by Queen Anne between 1609 and 1613. There would have been plenty of old bricks available to be crushed into aggregate for the lime plaster as Anne of Denmark replaced much of Somerset's earlier brick-built structure.

During this period no fewer than eleven 'frett Ceilings' were provided by James Leigh, the royal Master Plasterer, ranging in cost from 3s 4d to 4s 6d per yard, with materials mainly supplied by the royal works. In 1609-10 he created ceilings for the privy gallery (3s 8d per yard), the bedchamber and the attiring chamber.[395] The following year saw the addition of decorative ceilings in the library at the

Fig. 22.   A grotesque mask in lime plaster showing traces of gilding and red paint.
© Museum of London.

end of the cross gallery, the return gallery, the withdrawing chamber, the cabinet chamber, the privy chamber, the presence chamber and the lobby.[396] In 1611-12 the cabinet chamber also received 'a Frett with a freeze of one yarde depe', expensively priced at 5s 6d per yard, which suggests that it was probably hand-modelled. Finally, the 'great room' (at the eastern end of the cross gallery) was lavishly plastered with a decorative ceiling (for which Leigh also supplied 25 pendants at 12d each), a frieze and two 'greate window toppes' at the top rate of 4s 6d per yard.[397]

Although the plasterwork of the privy gallery was not the most expensive of the designs commissioned by Queen Anne, it was the only one to receive any additional colouring; all the others appear to have been left white. Whereas the clerks making up the accounts usually restricted themselves to references to 'frett worke' ceilings, giving no hint of the actual appearance of the plasterwork, the entry for John de Critz's embellishment of the ceiling in 1615-16 provides more clues. The sergeant painter applied gilding to 72 'maske heades', 72 roses, 36 square and 24 round pendants and 749 bosses, which were additionally 'layd rounde about with a blewe Coulor'. The 110 marigolds, which were the same size as the roses, were painted, but this cost just as much as the gilding. There is no specific mention of the gilding of any architectural elements, but he was also paid 'for paynting and guylding both the endes of the gallery betweene the waynscott and the roofe'.[398] Altogether, the ceiling must have made a dazzling contribution to the sumptuous appearance of the privy gallery.

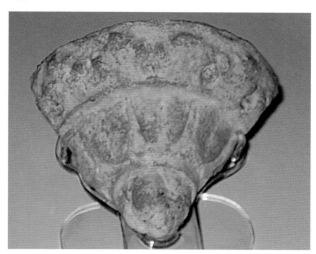

Fig. 23.   A ceiling boss in lime plaster with traces of gilding and blue paint.

© Claire Gapper, by permission of the Museum of London.

Figs 24 and 25.   Fragment of an artichoke and a pear in lime plaster.
© Claire Gapper, by permission of the Museum of London.

The accounts give the size of the mask heads as 9½ inches 'ouer the pece' (241 mm). The excavated mask measures 220 mm in height, and allowing for losses to the head during the demolition process this seems very close indeed.

Decorative plaster ceilings were the height of fashion in interiors of the early seventeenth century, combining enriched ribs, motifs from moulds, pendants and bosses in typically rich Jacobean style. Similar grotesque masks from moulds can be found on other London ceilings of this period,[399] derived from sets of engravings such as those by Cornelis Floris, whose *Maskers* was published in Antwerp in 1555. Once Inigo Jones's style of ceiling design became the dominant mode in royal palaces from 1620 onwards, bosses such as

Fig. 26.   Lime plaster fragments of architectural mouldings with applied gilded guilloche decoration.
© Andy Chopping, Museum of London Archaeology.

Fig. 27.   Lime plaster fragment with applied gilded dentils.

© Claire Gapper, by permission of Museum of London Archaeology.

Fig. 28.   Lime plaster fragment with applied gilded water-leaf ornament.

© Claire Gapper, by permission of Museum of London Archaeology.

that excavated at Somerset House would have served no purpose. Moreover, the survival of Queen Anne's privy gallery is attested by the repair of the painting and gilding of the ceiling of the 'Royal Gallery' in 1725-6 and it was still in place in 1776 when, during a final visit to the old palace before demolition, Joseph Moser remarked on 'the stuccoed ceiling, from which still depended part of the chains, etc, to which had hung chandeliers' in the gallery.[400] Taking all this circumstantial evidence into account, it seems reasonable to assign the mask and boss to Anne of Denmark's privy gallery.

The fragments of plaster with gilded architectural ornament were made with a lime plaster very similar to the mask and boss and may belong to the same extended building campaign. On the other hand, they could belong to one of the rooms decorated for Henrietta Maria in the late 1620s when a similar mix of lime plaster was probably still being used by the royal works (although James Leigh was no longer royal Master Plasterer). In 1628-9 the queen's new Cabinet Room (at the east end of the cross gallery, very close to the site of the excavated finds) was decorated by Matthew Goodrich, involving much painting and gilding including the cornice and architrave and their 'severall members'.[401]

Could the fragments have survived from Somerset's building? Mention has been made of Somerset's employment of Giles Gering in 1548. Five separate bills had been submitted by Gering between April and September of that year, totalling £246 13s 4d, but no details of his work are given.[402] Gering was described in 1545 as 'overseer of certain of our [Henry VIII's] white workes' and as 'the moldemaker at Nonesuch', which suggests that he was heavily involved in the stucco decoration of the exterior of that palace. It is possible that he was employed in a similar role by Somerset. A drawing of 1775 by James Hunter (**cat. 31**) shows relief decoration on the frontispiece that might have been in lime plaster rather than carved stone — most notably, the Nike in the spandrels of the ground floor and reclining figures of Zeus and Poseidon in the panels beneath the outer windows of the second floor.[403] There are also three empty niches that might once have contained figures in plaster. But the Strand was not the only site where the Protector was building, and Gering could have been employed elsewhere.[404] This tantalizing reference must, therefore, remain entirely inconclusive.

There is no reason, moreover, to assume that Gering or Nicholas Bellin of Modena ever produced decorative plaster ceilings for either Henry VIII or Somerset. The fashion for such interior decorative features was not established until the second half of the sixteenth century and the one reference to a ceiling of Somerset's period referred to the painting and trimming of the withdrawing chamber roof, which appears to have been of timber, in the manner of many Henrician palace ceilings.[405]

NOTES

ABBREVIATIONS

BL   The British Library

Cal. Pat. Rolls   *Calendar of the Patent Rolls*

Cal. S.P. Dom.   *Calendar of State Papers, Domestic Series*

Cal. S.P. Ven.   *Calendar of State Papers and Manuscripts Relating to English Affairs in the Archives and Collections of Venice and in other Libraries of Northern Italy*

Commons Journal   *The Journal of the House of Commons*

HMC   Historical Manuscripts Commission

HKW   Howard Colvin, ed., *The History of the King's Works*, 6 vols (London: HMSO, 1963-82)

L.&P.   *Letters and Papers, Foreign and Domestic of the Reign of Henry VIII*, 21 vols, J. S. Brewer, R. H. Brodie and J. Gairdner, eds, (London: Longman & Co., 1862-1932)

NLW   National Library of Wales

Oxford DNB   *Oxford Dictionary of National Biography*, Colin Matthew, Brian Harrison and Lawrence Goldman, eds (Oxford: Oxford University Press, 2004)

TNA   The National Archives

[1] Leeds Barroll, *Anna of Denmark, Queen of England. A Cultural Biography* (Philadelphia, 2001), p. 39.

[2] A. F. Pollard, *England Under Protector Somerset; an Essay* (London, 1900), pp. 314-23. Pollard's view is essentially followed by W. K. Jordan in *Edward VI: The Threshold of Power. The Dominance of the Duke of Northumberland* (Harvard, 1970), pp. 105-10; the opposing view is put forward most powerfully by M. L. Bush in *The Government Policy of Protector Somerset* (London, 1975), pp. 160-1.

[3] See the debate between M. L. Bush, G. W. Bernard and Ethan H. Shagan in *English Historical Review* (February 2000), pp. 103-33.

[4] Diarmaid MacCulloch, *The Boy King: Edward VI and the Protestant Reformation* (New York, 2001), pp. 41-51.

[5] Nikolaus Pevsner, 'Old Somerset Place', *Architectural Review* CXVI (1954), p. 167. Sir John Summerson does not even address the role of the patron of Somerset Place in his *Architecture in Britain 1530-1830* first published in 1953.

[6] Maurice Howard, *The Early Tudor Country House. Architecture and Politics 1490-1550* (London, 1987), pp. 188-94; Malcolm Airs, *The Tudor and Jacobean Country House: a Building History* (Gloucester, 1995), pp. 31-2, 89.

[7] The background to this can most conveniently be found in *HKW* IV (ii), pp. 367-401.

[8] *HKW* IV (ii), p. 379.

[9] 'Parish of Hackney part 1: Brooke House', *Survey of London* XXVIII (1970), p. 73.

[10] L. R. Shelby, *John Rogers. Tudor Military Engineer* (Oxford, 1967), pp. 5, 49, 67, 99, 113-14, 115-16, 117, 119, 126.

[11] John Harvey, *English Medieval Architects, A Biographical Dictionary down to 1550* (Gloucester, 1984), pp. 175-7; Marcus Merriman, 'Sir Richard Lee', *Oxford DNB*.

[12] For Italians in France, see *HKW* IV (ii), pp. 386-7.

[13] For a convenient summary of who was working where, see Marcus Merriman, 'Italian Military Engineers in Britain in the 1540s', in Sarah Tyacke, ed., *English Map Making, 1500-1650: Historical Essays* (London, 1983), pp. 57-67.

[14] *HKW* IV (ii), p. 380.

[15] TNA SP1/216, f. 74 (L&P XXI (i), no. 507).

[16] TNA SP1/211, f. 42 (L&P XXI (i), no. 1159).

[17] L&P XXI (i), no. 1133.

[18] M. L. Bush, op. cit. (2), pp. 23-4.

[19] W. K. Jordan, *The Chronicle and Political Papers of King Edward VI* (New York, Cornell, 1966), pp. 35, 104, 138-9.

[20] HMC, *MSS of the Marquess of Bath* IV (Seymour Papers 1532-1686), p. 338. The total given in the HMC volume is incorrect — the subheadings actually total £27,385 17s 9¾d.

[21] Malcolm Airs, op. cit. (6), p. 99.

[22] For Wolsey's office which is the closest direct parallel to Seymour's, see S. Thurley, 'Cardinal Wolsey's Domestic Building Works', in S. J. Gunn and P. G. Lindley, eds, *Cardinal Wolsey, Church, State and Art* (Cambridge, 1991), pp. 76-81.

[23] HMC, *Salisbury* I, p. 96.

[24] HMC, *MSS of the Marquess of Bath* IV, p. 112.

[25] HMC, *MSS of the Marquess of Bath* IV, p. 338.

[26] TNA E351/408.

[27] BL, Egerton MS 2815.

[28] Malcolm Airs, op. cit. (6), pp. 94-5.

[29] Barrett L. Beer, 'Edward Seymour', *Oxford DNB*.

[30] Maurice Howard, op. cit. (6), p. 36.

[31] HMC, *MSS of the Marquess of Bath* IV, pp. 325, 331.

[32] The letters relating to the new house are printed in J. E. Jackson, 'Wulfhall and the Seymours', *The Wiltshire Archaeological and Natural History Magazine* XV (1875), pp. 178-86.

[33] A recent review of the evidence can be found in Graham Bathe, 'The Duke of Somerset's Grand Mansion at The Brails, Great Bedwyn: A Review of the Evidence', *Wiltshire Archaeological and Natural History Magazine* 99 (2006), pp. 236-45.

[34] Simon Thurley, *Hampton Court a Social and Architectural History* (Yale, 2003), pp. 70-1.

[35] *HKW* IV (ii), p. 272.

[36] *Cal. Pat. Rolls* 1547-8, p. 130.

[37] An account book in the National Archives covers the manufacture of items here and at Mortlake, TNA E351/3199.

[38] Crucially there appears to be a gallery and closet between the privy and withdrawing chambers. This is a very specific plan form associated with Henry VIII's palaces (S. Thurley, *The Royal Palaces of Tudor England* (Yale, 1993), pp. 125-7).

Most often this appears between the privy and presence chambers, but late in his reign Henry may have been using the withdrawing chamber as a privy chamber and thus the gallery and closet are in the right place. This suggests that perhaps Henry VIII completed a suite of lodgings there.

[39] BL Egerton, MS 2815.

[40] W. K. Jordan, *The Chronicle and Political Papers of King Edward VI* (Cornell, 1966), p. 40.

[41] *HKW* IV (ii), pp. 272-3; VCH, *Middlesex* XIII (forthcoming, 2009), pp. 103-4.

[42] TNA E351/3231, E351/3218, E351/3227. See also G. R. Batho, 'Syon House: The First Two Hundred Years, 1431-1632', *Transactions of the London and Middlesex Archaeological Society* n.s. 19 (1958), pp. 1-17; G. R. Batho, 'Henry, Ninth Earl of Northumberland and Syon House, Middlesex', *Transactions of the Ancient Monuments Society* n.s. IV (1956), pp. 95-104. Also see Bridget Cherry and Nikolaus Pevsner in *The Buildings of England: London 3: North West* (1991), pp. 443-4.

[43] His Grace the Duke of Northumberland, Syon MSS B.XIII, 2c. See G. R. Batho, 'Henry Ninth Earl of Northumberland', p. 96 n. 4; West Sussex Record Office PHA 1630, pp. 6-7.

[44] J. Stow, *The Survey of London* (London, 1618), pp. 829-30.

[45] VCH has posted detailed histories of the properties in the Strand on its website, www.victoriacountyhistory. ac.uk/Middlesex, under Work in Progress, and is publishing them in Volume XIII, part 1, *City of Westminster: Landownership and Religious History* (forthcoming, Summer 2009). This section on the background to Somerset Place is based on that work.

[46] Also see Christopher Phillpotts, 'The Houses of Henry VIII's Courtiers in London', in David Gaimster and Roberta Gilchrist, eds, *The Archaeology of Reformation 1480-1580* (Society for Post-Medieval Archaeology, 2003), pp. 299-309.

[47] Discussed in 'A Place in Town: Palaces, Mansions, and Suburban Houses in Medieval and Early Modern Westminster', paper given by Patricia Croot to a Local and Regional seminar at IHR in 2000.

[48] TNA, CP 40/134, rot. 203.

[49] *Cal. Pat. Rolls* 1301-7, p. 367.

[50] TNA, C 143/149, no. 13; *Cal. Pat. Rolls* 1321-4, p. 12.

[51] TNA, E 149/14, no. 9.

[52] See below, towards the end of this section.

[53] *Reg. Godfrey Giffard*, II. 149.

[54] Worcester County Record Office, 821/BA 3814, ff. 103v-104v; *Cal. Pat. Rolls* 1307-13, p. 148; TNA, C 143/74, no. 7; CP 25/1/149/39, no. 24.

[55] HMC, *Cal. MSS D.&C. Wells* II (1914), 198.

[56] F. A. Inderwick, ed., *The Inner Temple: History and Records, 1505-1603* (London, 1896), p. 460.

[57] H. H. L. Bellot, *Inner and Middle Temple* (London, 1902), p. 239.

[58] TNA, DL 42/2, f. 217, no. 11; C 143/72, no. 3; *Cal. Pat. Rolls* 1307-13, p. 286.

[59] For detailed history of lawyers' inns in Westminster, see www.victoriacountyhistory.ac.uk/Middlesex, under Work in Progress.

[60] TNA, E 326/11959; E 315/48, no. 285.

[61] Mary D. Lobel, ed., 'The City of London from Prehistoric Times to c.1520', *The British Atlas of Historic Towns* 3 (Oxford 1989).

[62] TNA, C 54/333, m. 7d.

[63] *L.&P.* XII (1), p. 233.

[64] *L.&P.* XII (1), pp. 357, 363, 526; XIII (1), p. 76.

[65] TNA, E 315/34, no. 101; *L.&P.* XIV (1), p. 404.

[66] TNA, E 318/19/968; BL, Add. Ch. 40224; *Cal. Pat. Rolls* 1547-8, pp. 114, 258, 260.

[67] TNA, E 326/12005.

[68] *Cal. Pat. Rolls* 1549-51, pp. 430-2.

[69] TNA, E 326/11959.

[70] TNA, E 326/12061.

[71] TNA, E 328/164; E 328/173.

[72] *Cal. Pat. Rolls* 1558-60, p. 346.

[73] *Cal. Pat. Rolls* 1572-5, p. 252 (no. 1329).

[74] TNA, DL 25/3604; *Cal. Pat. Rolls* 1572-5, p. 252 (no. 1329).

[75] TNA, E 328/164.

[76] C. J. Kitching, ed., *London and Middlesex Chantry Certificates 1548*, London Record Society 16 (1980). Returns to the chantry commissioners probably made March to May: ibid., p. xii.

[77] *Home Counties Magazine* I, p. 117, 1899.

[78] *Cal. Pat. Rolls* 1566-9, p. 93.

[79] Stephen Alford, *Kingship and Politics in the Reign of Edward VI* (Cambridge, 2002), pp. 74-81.

[80] Derek Keene, Arthur Burns and Andrew Saint, eds, *St. Paul's. The Cathedral Church of London 604-2004* (Yale, 2004), pp. 33-44.

[81] Samuel Pegge, *Curialia or an Historical Account of Some Branches of the Royal Household, Part I A Succinct History of Somerset House* (London, 1806) notes this on p. 7**.

[82] Howard Colvin and Susan Foister, eds, *The Panorama of London circa 1544* (London Topographical Society 151 in association with the Ashmolean, Oxford, 1996), p. 11, drawing III.

[83] Some, but not all, of his account is based on Stow.

[84] Barrett L. Beer, ed., *The Life and Raigne of King Edward the Sixth by John Hayward* (Kent, Ohio and London, 1993), pp. 100-1.

[85] Simon Thurley, *Whitehall Palace. An Architectural History of the Royal Apartments 1240-1698* (Yale, 1999), pp. 13-64; Gervase Rosser and Simon Thurley, 'Whitehall Palace and King Street Westminster: The Urban Cost of Princely Magnificence', *London Topographical Record* XXVI (1990), pp. 57-77.

[86] Maurice Howard, op. cit. (6), pp. 136-64.

[87] His attempt to pull down St Margaret's Church Westminster met with violence from the local population and was abandoned. See Gervase Rosser, *Medieval Westminster 1200-1540* (Oxford, 1989), pp. 275-6.

[88] Details of the mechanics of compiling the list are in TNA E351/3326 and the list is TNA E351/408.

[89] A point proved by entries in the list of debts at the duke's death in TNA E351/408.

[90] The best white glass came from Normandy. L. F. Salzmann, *Building in England Down to 1540* (Oxford, 1952), p. 183.

[91] TNA E351/408; *HKW* III (i), pp. 61-3.

[92] TNA E351/408; *HKW* III (i) p. 71.

[93] BL Egerton, MS 2815; *HKW* III (i), p. 408.

[94] M. Whinney, *Sculpture in Britain 1530-1830* (Harmondsworth, 1964), pp. 16-17.

[95] TNA E351/408; *HKW* III (i), p. 411.

[96] Josephine C. Turquet, 'The Inner Court of Nonsuch Palace' (unpublished PhD thesis, London, 1983).

[97] Rob Poulton with major contributions by Alan Cook and Simon Thurley, *Excavations at Oatlands Palace 1968-73 and 1983-4* (Guildford, 2009); Simon Thurley, 'Nonsuch: A Palace Fit for a Prince?', *Country Life*, 11 August 2005, pp. 42-5.

[98] In 1544 the same person, Joyce Wastall, was paid 40s by Seymour. HMC, *MSS of the Marquess of Bath* IV, p. 123.

[99] C. L. Kingsford, ed., *A Survey of London by John Stow* (reprinted from the text of 1603, Oxford, 1908), II, p. 45.

[100] TNA E351/3204, f. 14v; E351/3219, f.13; E351/3224, f. 11; E351/3228, f. 11; E351/3220, f. 6; E351/3229, ff. 9v, 10.

[101] *Cal. S.P. Dom.* Edward VI, I (1547-53), nos 503, 506, 528, 567, 569.

[102] On this also see John Norman King, 'Protector Somerset, Patron of the English Renaissance', *The Papers of the Bibliographical Society of America* 70 (1976), p. 307.

[103] Mary Dewar, *Sir Thomas Smith, A Tudor Intellectual in Office* (London, 1964), pp. 26-35.

[104] Simon Bradley and Nikolaus Pevsner, *The Buildings of England: London 6: Westminster*, (Yale, 2003), p. 318.

[105] Simon Thurley, op. cit. (34), pp. 22-6.

[106] At the time of writing (2007) these are still being cleaned and assessed, but I had the chance to examine them in some detail at the Museum of London's store at Mortimer Wheeler House.

[107] Barney Sloane and Gordon Malcolm, *Excavations at the Priory of the Order of the Hospital of St. John of Jerusalem, Clerkenwell, London* (MoLAS monograph 20, Museum of London, 2004), pp. 174-8.

[108] Susan James, 'Edward Seymour, Duke of Somerset? Re-examining a Tudor Portrait', *The British Art Journal* II (2) (Winter 2000/1), pp. 14-21; Karen Hearn, ed., *Dynasties. Painting in Tudor and Jacobean England* (Tate, 1995), pp. 50-2.

[109] Unpublished report available from the Greater London Historic Environment Record, English Heritage: Somerset House, City of Westminster Regeneration of the Great Court. Assessment Report on Phase III of Archaeological Watching Brief. The Somerset House Trust, May 2005.

[110] Sydney Anglo, *Spectacle Pageantry and Early Tudor Policy* (Oxford, 1969), p. 215; Simon Thurley, *Whitehall Palace. An Architectural History of the Royal Apartments, 1240-1698* (Yale, 1999), Simon Thurley, op. cit. (85), pp. 60-1; Jacques Androuet Du Cerceau, *Exempla arcuum, partim ab ipso inventa, partim ex veterum sumpta monumenta* (Orléans, 1549).

[111] Mark Girouard, *Robert Smythson and the Elizabethan Country House* (Yale, 1983), pp. 41, 308 n. 8.

[112] Mark Girouard, 'The Development of Longleat House between 1546 and 1572', *Archaeological Journal* CXVI (1959), p. 209.

[113] TNA E351/3237.

[114] 'The Strand (The Parish of St. Martin-in-the-Fields, part III)', *Survey of London* XVIII, 1937, pp. 86-8; David Starkey, *Elizabeth* (London, 2000), pp. 94-6.

[115] David Starkey, op. cit. (114), pp. 109-10; *Survey of London*

XVIII, pp. 94-6. Note that the *Survey* confuses Edward and Thomas Seymour in note †. Bill for the limitation of the Duke of Somerset's lands, *Cal. S.P. Dom.* Edward VI, I (1547-53), no. 590, p. 224.

[116] During Edward's reign £90 17s 7½d had been spent on securing the house and unused materials for the king's use. TNA E351/3326.

[117] J. G. Nichols, 'The Diary of Henry Machyn', *Camden Society* 42 (1842), p. 37; David Starkey, *Elizabeth*, pp. 112-24, David Starkey, op. cit. (114).

[118] The following details come from a petition written by John Revell in 1568 referring to works he had undertaken in 1553. It is in TNA E351/3330.

[119] *Cal. S.P. Ven.*, 1556-7, p. 836 (no. 743); J. G. Nichols, op. cit. (117), p. 120.

[120] David Starkey, op. cit. (114), p. 256.

[121] John Norden's remarks 'Queene Elizabeth hath within the precincts of this Cittie three faire and pleasant palaces: namely Whitehall ... St. jeames ... and Somerset house builded by the Duke of Somerset about the yeere of Christ 1549', *Speculum Britanniae* (London, 1593), p. 46.

[122] TNA E351/3326.

[123] John Norden, 'Notes on London and Westminster', from his *Description of Middlesex* (1592) (BM, Harl. MS 570), p. 94.

[124] TNA E351/3218; E351/3224.

[125] HMC, MSS of the Marquess of Bath (Seymour Papers 1532-1686, London, 1968), p. 159.

[126] TNA E351/3205; E351/3208.

[127] TNA E351/3206.

[128] John Nichols, *The Progresses and Public Processions of Queen Elizabeth*, 3 vols (London, 1823), I, p. 83; TNA E351/3213. Also see Samuel Pegge, op. cit. (81), pp. 60-1.

[129] TNA E351/3205. A longer list of those who were lodged at Somerset House can be found in Samuel Pegge, op. cit. (81), pp. 59-61; R. Needham and A. Webster, *Somerset House* (London, 1905), pp. 58-64; E. K. Chambers, *The Elizabethan Stage*, 4 vols (Oxford, 1923), I, p. 10.

[130] 1558, 1562, 1571, 1573, 1582, 1583, 1585, 1587, 1588, 1589, 1590, 1593, 1594, 1599.

[131] TNA E351/3221.

[132] HMC, MSS of the Marquess of Bath, IV, p. 159. The construction of the covered pulpit appears in TNA E351/3219.

[133] Peter E. McCullough, *Sermons at Court. Politics and Religion in Elizabethan and Jacobean Preaching* (Cambridge, 1998), p. 47.

[134] Victor von Klarwill, *The Fugger Newsletters* (London, 1926), p. 184.

[135] Derek Keene, op. cit. (80), pp. 171-3.

[136] Ann Saunders, ed., *The Royal Exchange* (London Topographical Society 152, 1997), pp. 44-5.

[137] John Nichols, op. cit. (128), II, p. 537.

[138] TNA E351/3204; E351/3219; E351/3224; E351/3228; E351/3220; E351/3229.

[139] In 1570-1, to provide greater capacity, a new kitchen and a number of kitchen offices were erected, including a boiling house, larder, rush house and chaundry. E351/3205, f. 3.

[140] TNA E351/3235.

[141] TNA E351/3241.

[142] For the great hall, see TNA E351/3219, and the Savoy, see TNA E351/3222. Elizabethan accounts mention a chapel near the great stair in TNA E351/3216.

[143] W. B. Rye, ed., *England as seen by Foreigners, in the days of Elizabeth and James the First* (London, 1865), p. 117; HMC, *Salisbury* XVI, p. 212; XVII, pp. 441, 520.

[144] TNA E351/3205; E351/3216; E351/3217; E351/3237.

[145] HMC, *Salisbury* XV, p. 348, printed in E. Lodge, *Illustrations of British History, Biography and Manners, etc.* (London, 1791), pp. 206-7. Also see Lodge, pp. 210-12 for a full list of the jointure.

[146] W. B. Rye, op. cit. (143), p. 204.

[147] *Cal. S.P. Ven.*, 10, p. 143.

[148] TNA SC6/jasI/1650.

[149] TNA E317/Middx/81.

[150] TNA E317/Middx/85.

[151] TNA E317/Middx/81.

[152] A useful comparison can be made by looking at John Schofield, *The London Surveys of Ralph Treswell* (London Topographical Society 135, 1987), pp. 11-28.

[153] This and next four paragraphs are based on accounts of the individual estates in VCH, 'City of Westminster', *Middlesex* XIII (forthcoming 2009).

[154] Maureen M. Meikle, 'A Meddlesome Princess: Anne of Denmark and Scottish Court Politics, 1589-1603', in Julian Goodare and Michael Lynch, eds, *The Reign of James VI* (East Linton, 2000), pp. 126-7; Leeds Barroll, 'The Court of the First Stuart Queen', in Linda Levy Peck, ed., *The Mental World of the Jacobean Court* (Cambridge, 1991), pp. 194-8.

[155] Aonghus MacKechnie, 'James VI's Architects and their Architecture', in Julian Goodare and Michael Lynch, eds, *The Reign of James I* (East Linton, 2000), pp. 161-5.

[156] See the summary of evidence in Aonghus Mackechnie, 'The Royal Palace of Dunfermline' in Richard Fawcett, ed., *Royal Dunfermline* (Society of Antiquaries of Scotland, 2005), pp. 119-26; J. G. Dunbar, *Scottish Royal Palaces. The Architecture of the Royal Residences during the late Medieval and Early Renaissance Periods* (East Linton, 1999), pp. 87-94; Deborah Howard, *The Architectural History of Scotland* (Edinburgh, 1995), pp. 26-30; Charles McKean, *The Scottish Chateau. The Country Houses of Renaissance Scotland* (Stroud, 2001), pp. 190-1.

[157] A view shared by Charles McKean, *ibid.*, p. 190.

[158] E. Lodge, op. cit. (145), III, p. 1.

[159] Leeds Barroll, op. cit. (154), p. 199.

[160] TNA SP14/67, p. 79.

[161] *HKW* III (i), pp. 105-20.

[162] Mara R. Wade, *Triumphus Nuptialis Danicus. German Court culture and Denmark. The 'Great Wedding' of 1634* (Wiesbaden, 1996), pp. 47-56.

[163] The inventory is published in M. T. W. Payne, 'An Inventory of Queen Anne of Denmark's "Ornaments, furniture, householde stuffe, and other parcels" at Denmark House, 1619', *Journal of the History of Collections* 13 (1) (2001).

[164] *HKW* IV (ii), pp. 254-61.

[165] Roy Strong, *The Renaissance Garden in England* (London, 1984), pp. 87-93.

[166] HMC, *Salisbury* XVI, pp. 182-3; HMC, *Salisbury* XXIV (Addenda 1605-68), pp. 216-17; TNA SC6 1650 Jas 12-15.

[167] TNA E317 Middlesex 82.

[168] E. Lodge, op. cit. (145), p. 213; *Cal. S.P. Dom.*, 1603-10, p. 141; HMC, *Salisbury* XVI, pp. 182-3.

[169] Marja Smolenaars, 'John Gerard', *Oxford DNB*; TNA SP40/2, f. 67r.

[170] *Cal. S.P. Dom.*, 1611-18, p. 17.

[171] *Cal. S.P. Dom.*, 1603-10, p. 490; Marja Smolenaars, 'John Gerard', *Oxford DNB*.

[172] HMC, *Salisbury* XXI, pp. 130-1.

[173] Maureen M. Meikle, 'Holde her at the Oeconomike rule of the House: Anne of Denmark and Scottish Court Finances, 1589-1603', in Elizabeth Ewan and Maureen M. Meikle, eds, *Women in Scotland c.1100-c.1750* (East Linton, 1999), p. 107.

[174] John S. Brewer, ed., *Dr. Godfrey Goodman, The Court of King James the First*, 2 vols (London, 1839), II, p. 37.

[175] For this, see the essays in Pauline Croft, ed., *Patronage, Culture and Power. The Early Cecils* (Studies in British Art 8, Yale, 2002).

[176] For details, see E351/3244–3250 and SP14/62. My interpretation differs from that in *HKW* in a number of important respects.

[177] TNA E351/3243, p. 20; E351/3244, p. 10.

[178] See M. T. W. Payne, op. cit. (163); the inventory lists the rooms as 'great gallery, little attiring chamber close to the gallery, little bedchamber, diet chamber, coffer chamber, great bedchamber'. The following accounts help confirm the inventory: TNA E351/2339, f. 12v; E351/3244, ff. 8, 11v; E351/3246, f. 12v; E351/3252, f. 8.

[179] The outer court was paved with stone. TNA SP14/38, p. 123.

[180] John Pitcher, ed., *Samuel Daniel, Hymen's Triumph* (Oxford, Malone Society reprints, 1994); E. K. Chambers, op. cit. (129), p. 277.

[181] See James Knowles, 'To Enlight the darksome Night, Pale Cinthia Doth Arise: Anne of Denmark, Elizabeth I and the Images of Royalty', in Clare McManus, ed., *Women and Culture at the Courts of the Stuart Queens* (Basingstoke, 2003), pp. 30-3.

[182] TNA SP14/90, Chamberlain to Carleton, 8 March 1616/17, 'The king dined that day [4 March] with the queen at Somerset house, which was then new christned and must hence forward be called Denmark house'. *Cal. S.P. Dom.*, 1611-18, pp. 422, 514. Also see E. K. Chambers, op. cit. (129) I, p. 12.

[183] John Nichols, *The Progresses, Processions and Magnificent Festivities of King James the First*, 4 vols (London, 1828), III, pp. 4, 14, 80-1, 253.

[184] *Ibid.*, III, p. 474.

[185] I am most grateful to Mark Girouard for discussing this issue with me. The most important recent work on Burghley has been Jillian Husselby, 'Architecture at Burghley House: The Patronage of William Cecil 1553-1598', 3 vols (unpublished PhD Thesis, Warwick, 1996). This covers the courtyard in detail but assumes that the open work was copied from Somerset House (II, p. 207).

[186] Lawrence Stone, 'Inigo Jones and the New Exchange', *Archaeological Journal* 114 (1957), pp. 106-21.

[187] Giles Worsley, *Inigo Jones and the European Classicist*

Tradition (Yale, 2007), pp. 10-11; John Harris and A. A. Tait, *Catalogue of the Drawings by Inigo Jones, John Webb and Isaac de Caus at Worcester College Oxford* (Oxford, 1979), pp. 13-14; John Harris and Gordon Higgott, *Inigo Jones, Complete Architectural Drawings* (London, 1989), pp. 36-7.

[188] TNA E351/3226.

[189] TNA E351/3241.

[190] See, for instance, Paula Henderson, 'The Loggia in Tudor and Early Stuart England: The Adaption and Function of Classical Form', in Lucy Gent, ed., *Albion's Classicism: The Visual Arts in Britain, 1550-1660* (Studies in British Art, 2, Yale, 1995), p. 113.

[191] Dr. Johnson, in his dictionary, defines *terrace* as '1. A small mount of earth covered in grass. 2. A balcony; an open gallery'. Both meanings are found in the Office of Works accounts from the late 1530s. Also see Fynes Moryson, *An Itinerary*, 4 vols (London, 1617), I, p. 145, where he translates 'cloyster' as 'terrace'.

[192] Bruce Allsopp, ed., *Inigo Jones on Palladio, being the notes by Inigo Jones in the Copy of I Quattro Libri dell'architettura de Andrea Palladio, 1601, in the Library of Worcester College Oxford*, 2 vols (Newcastle upon Tyne, 1970), f. 52.

[193] Malcolm Airs, 'Pomp and Glory: The Influence of Theobalds', in Pauline Croft, ed., op. cit. (175).

[194] TNA E351/3252.

[195] TNA E351/3247.

[196] TNA E351/3246

[197] TNA E351/3250.

[198] For the presence chamber, see TNA E351/3244, ff. 8, 10v; for the privy chamber, see TNA 351/3244, ff. 8, 10, 11r; for the withdrawing chamber, see TNA E351/3243, f. 20; E351/3244, f. 8.

[199] TNA E351/3239, 'making a degree for plate to stand on the table in the presence and attending to sett upp tables and taking them downe every meale', and more importantly in 1617, E351/3252. Anne of Denmark's practice in this room is referred to in Henrietta Maria's household regulations. BL, MS Stowe 561, f. 13v.

[200] Sir John Finet, *Finetti Philoxensis: Som Choice Observations of Sir John Finett, Knight, and Master of Ceremonies to the two Last Kings, Touching the Reception, and Precedence, and the Treatment and Audience, the Punctillios and Contests of Forren Ambassadors in England* (London, 1656), p. 40.

[201] BL, MS Stowe 561, f. 15r.

[202] M. T. W. Payne, op. cit. (163), pp. 37-8.

[203] HMC, *Portland*, p. 31; *Cal. S.P. Dom.*, 1611-18, p. 222.

[204] *Cal. S.P. Ven.*, 1615-17, pp. 96-7.

[205] Sir John Finet, op. cit. (200), p. 199.

[206] TNA E351/3244, E351/3247.

[207] TNA E351/3244, E351/3246.

[208] TNA E351/3224.

[209] Simon Thurley, op. cit. (85), p. 67 (fig. 75), p. 76.

[210] E. Lodge, op. cit. (145), pp. 227-8.

[211] BL, MS Stowe 561, ff. 12r–17v.

[212] BL, MS Stowe 561, f. 15r.

[213] Roger Lockyer, *Buckingham. The Life and Political Career of George Villiers, First Duke of Buckingham, 1592-1628*, pp. 19-20; John Rushworth, *Historical Collections Abridg'd and Improved*, 4 vols (London, 1702), pp. 292-3; John S. Brewer, op. cit. (174), I, p. 224.

[214] *Cal. S.P. Ven.*, 1603-7, p. 513.

[215] I owe these suggestions to Dr Helen Payne whose PhD thesis, 'Aristocratic Women and the Jacobean Court' (University of London, 2001) covers the ladies at the court of Queen Anne. I am very grateful to Dr Payne for her views and advice on this point.

[216] *Ibid.*, pp. 248-9.

[217] S. R. Gardiner, *History of England from the Accession of James I to the Outbreak of the Civil War* II (Elbron Classics, 2000), p. 255; '... those who were admitted to her privacy in Denmark House knew well that, as often as she thought she could escape observation, the Queen of England was in the habit of repairing to a garret, for the purpose of hearing mass from the lips of a Catholic priest, who was smuggled in for the purpose'.

[218] M. T. W. Payne, op. cit. (163), p. 37.

[219] In 1626 Henrietta Maria used this room and the gallery next to it as her chapel, reinforcing the likelihood that this was a chapel under Anne. For this, see below.

[220] M. T. W. Payne, op. cit. (163), p. 35.

[221] Rob Poulton, op. cit. (97).

[222] The visits were in 1606 and 1614.

[223] Joakin A. Skovgaard, *A King's Architecture. Christian IV and his Buildings* (London, 1973), pp. 57-8.

[224] TNA E351/3244.

[225] TNA E351/3246.

[226] Roy Strong, *The Artist and the Garden* (Yale, 2000), pp. 36-7; Roy Strong, op. cit. (165), pp. 87-93; Geoffrey Fisher and John Newman, 'A Fountain Design by Inigo Jones', *The Burlington Magazine* 127 (August 1985), pp. 530-3; *HKW* IV (ii), pp. 268-70.

[227] Jennifer Woodward, *The Theatre of Death. The Ritual Management of Royal Funerals in Renaissance England, 1570-1625* (Woodbridge, 1997), pp. 166-74.

[228] *Ibid.*, pp. 186-7.

[229] M. T. W. Payne, op. cit. (163), pp. 23-44.

[230] *Ibid.*, p. 27; N. E. McClure, ed., 'The Letters of John Chamberlain', *Memoirs of the American Philosophical Society*, 2 vols (1939), II, pp. 237-8, 254; *Cal. S.P. Dom.*, 1619-23, pp. 48-9, 129; TNA E351/3254, E351/3255.

[231] *Cal. S.P. Dom.*, 1619-23, pp. 204, 372; TNA E351/3255; Sir John Finet, op. cit. (200), pp. 68, 96.

[232] *Cal. S.P. Dom.*, 1619-23, pp. 516, 576, 582, 583; N. E. McClure, op. cit. (230) II, p. 494.

[233] The historiography of the debate about the influence of Henrietta Maria has been summarized by Michelle Anna White in *Henrietta Maria and the English Civil Wars* (Ashgate, 2006), pp. 1-6, and in Karen Britland, *Drama at the Courts of Queen Henrietta Maria* (Cambridge, 2006), pp. 1-14.

[234] Also see Caroline Hibbard, 'Henrietta Maria in the 1630s: Perspectives on the Role of Consort Queens in *Ancien Régime* Courts', in Ian Atherton and Julie Sanders, eds, *The 1630s. Interdisciplinary Essays on Culture and Politics in the Caroline Era* (Manchester, 2006), pp. 94-102.

[235] For the marriage of Jane Drummond, James I was 'invited to lie' at Somerset House, and accepted. See N. E. McClure, op. cit. (230) I, p. 504. Mostly the queen was at Somerset House by herself, N. E. McClure, ed., II, pp. 34, 47, 149, 159. James would sometimes come just for dinner, N. E. McClure, ed., II, p. 60.

[236] T. Rymer, *Foedera* VIII (i) (1743), pp. 211-12 (*Cal. S.P. Dom.*, 1625-6, p. 561).

[237] Society of Antiquaries MS 137. See also Pamela J. Willetts, *Catalogue of the Manuscripts in the Society of Antiquaries of London* (London, 2000), p. 63.

[238] For Henrietta Maria's role in transmitting French taste, see Caroline Hibbard, op. cit. (234), pp. 92-4; Peter Thornton, *Seventeenth Century Interior Decoration in England France and Holland* (Yale, 1983), p. 46; Caroline Hibbard, 'Translating Royalty: Henrietta Maria and the Transition from Princess to Queen', *The Court Historian* 5 (1) (May 2000), p. 25; R. Malcolm Smuts, *Court Culture and the Royalist Tradition in Early Stuart England* (Philadelphia, 1999), p. 186.

[239] An inventory of the trousseau is in BL, King's MSS 136, ff. 412-61.

[240] Ibid, f. 441.

[241] M. C. Hippeau, *Mémoires Inédits du comte Leveneur de Tillières* (Paris, 1862), pp. 89, 91. Dover had been given a make-over at the cost of £2,600, overseen by Buckingham himself as admiral of the Cinque Ports; *Cal. S.P. Ven.*, 1625-6, no. 125; M. Toynbee, 'The Wedding Journey of King Charles I', *Archaeologia Cantiana* LXIX (1955), pp. 82-3.

[242] M. Louis Delavand, Roger Gaucheron and Émile Dermenghem, *Mémoires de Cardinal de Richelieu* 5 (Paris, Société de l'Histoire de France, 1907) 31, pp. 142-3; M. C. Hippeau, op. cit. (241), p. 92. The bed was in reality even older; it is listed in the inventories as being Henry VIII's: Society of Antiquaries MS 137, f. 26v.

[243] BL, King's MSS 136, f. 433.

[244] Society of Antiquaries of London, MS 137, f. 27.

[245] *Cal. S.P. Ven.*, 1629-32, no. 439.

[246] W. L. Spiers, 'The Note Book and Account Book of Nicholas Stone', *Walpole Society* VII (1918-19), pp. 86, 88.

[247] E351/3266, f. 9v; LR5/65 (Grynder's bill January, February, March 1632).

[248] For further examples of gifts of furniture, see HMC 11th Report Appendix part I, 'MSS of Henry Duncan Skrine Esq' (1887), p. 141.

[249] N. L. W. Wynnstay, MS178.

[250] Charles Carlton, *Charles I. The Personal Monarch* (2nd edition, London, 1995), p. 186.

[251] Oliver Millar, ed., 'The Inventories and Valuations of the King's Goods 1649-1651', *Walpole Society* XLIII (1970-2), p. 338.

[252] Simon Thurley, op. cit. (34), p. 119.

[253] BL, King's MSS 136, ff. 412-14, 439-41, 448v-449v; see also a section on chapel linen, ff. 451v-452.

[254] HMC, 11th Report, Appendix part I, MSS of Henry Duncan Skrine, p. 85; HMC, Salvetti Correspondence 11th Report, Appendix part 1, pp. 25, 57, 77; TNA E351/3258; E351/3259; E351/3260; AO1/2425/57.

[255] The French ambassador Marshal Bassompierre quoted in R. Needham and A. Webster, op. cit. (129), p. 104.

[256] *HKW* III (i), pp. 195-6.

[257] T. Birch, ed., *The Court and Times of Charles I*, 2 vols (London, 1849), pp. 306-8.

[258] H. Ellis, *Original Letters*, ser. 2, III (London, 1827), p. 271.

[259] *HKW* IV, pp. 264-6; John Summerson, with a foreword by Sir Howard Colvin, *Inigo Jones* (Yale, 2000), pp. 67-71; J. Harris and G. Higgott, op. cit. (187), pp. 193-206; John Harris, *Catalogue of the R.I.B.A. Drawings Collection: Jones &*

Webb (London, 1972), p. 15, nos 36-9*:* I. Ware, *Designs of Inigo Jones* (London, 1743), fig. 30; Gordon Higgott, 'Inigo Jones's Theory of Design', *Architectural History* 35 (1992), pp. 69-70; Edward, Earl of Clarendon, *The History of the Rebellion and Civil Wars in England*, 6 vols (Oxford, 1888), II, p. 326.

[260] Simon Thurley, 'The Stuart Kings, Oliver Cromwell and the Chapel Royal 1618-1685', *Architectural History* 45 (2002), pp. 241-2.

[261] J. Harris and G. Higgott, op. cit. (187), pp. 206-9; Giles Worsley, op. cit. (187), p. 39.

[262] J. Harris and G. Higgott, op. cit. (187), pp. 198-9.

[263] Simon Thurley, op. cit. (260), pp. 258-62.

[264] See, for instance, the friary built at St James's Palace (*HKW* V, p. 246).

[265] TNA E351/3404.

[266] TNA E351/3267.

[267] For instance, see de la Serre, *l'Histoire de l'Entrée de la Reyne Mere du Roy très Chrétien dans la Grande Bretagne* (London, 1639), p. 54.

[268] J. Harris and G. Higgott, op. cit. (187), p. 198; John Harris, 'The Link Between a Roman Second-Century Sculptor, Van Dyck, Inigo Jones and Queen Henrietta Maria', *Burlington Magazine* 115 (August 1973), pp. 526-30.

[269] See Charles Avery, 'The Collector Earl and his Modern Marbles. Thomas Howard and François Dieussart', *Apollo* CLXIII (June 2006), pp. 46-53.

[270] T. Birch, op. cit. (257), pp. 311-14; Erica Veevers, *Images of Love and Religion. Henrietta Maria and Court Entertainments* (Cambridge, 1989), pp. 165-71.

[271] Indeed, often the chapel was referred to as 'the Queen's Chapel in Somerset-House-yard', emphasizing its separation from the house; William Knowler, ed., *Thomas Wentworth, Earl of Strafford, Letters and Dispatches* I (Dublin, 1711), p. 505.

[272] T. Birch, op. cit. (257), p. 315.

[273] On this subject, see Caroline Hibbard, 'Somerset House Chapel and the Topography of London Catholicism', in George Gorst and Malcolm Smutts, eds, *The Politics of Court Space in Europe and the Mediterranean, ca 1500-1750* (forthcoming, 2009).

[274] K. J. Lindley, 'The Lay Catholics of England in the Reign of Charles I', *Journal of Ecclesiastical History* XXII (3) (1971), pp. 199-200, 204.

[275] Kevin Sharpe, *The Personal Rule of Charles I* (Yale, 1992), pp. 304-7; T. Birch, op. cit. (257), p. 315; Edward, Earl of Clarendon, op. cit. (259), I, p. 194; Michelle Anna White, *Henrietta Maria and the English Civil Wars*, pp. 34-46.

[276] *Cal. S.P. Dom.*, 1638-9, p. 65.

[277] *Cal. S.P. Dom.*, 1639-40, p. 174.

[278] TNA E351/3270; E351/3271.

[279] TNA E351/3270. TNA E351/3271 mentions the ground-floor room under the queen's closet.

[280] NLW Wynnstay MS 183.

[281] TNA E351/3271; AO1/2427/69.

[282] NLW Wynnstay MS 182.

[283] Oliver Millar, op. cit. (251), pp. 119-20; Simon Jervis, '"Shadows, not substantial things". Furniture in the Commonwealth Inventories', in Arthur MacGregor, ed., *The Late King's Goods*, (Oxford, 1989), pp. 294-5.

[284] TNA E351/3271, LR5/66 (Ralph Grynder's bill for lady quarter 1638).

[285] NLW Wynnstay MS 183.

[286] John Harris and A. A. Tait, op. cit. (187), pp. 18-19; op. cit. (259), p. 16; Giles Worsley, *Inigo Jones* (Yale, 1997), pp. 84-6.

[287] See, for instance, David Lindley, *The Court Masque* (Manchester, 1984); Barbara Ravelhofer, *The Early Stuart Masque. Dance, Costume, and Music* (Oxford, 2006); Erica Veevers, op. cit. (270); Karen Britland, *Drama at the Court of Queen Henrietta Maria* (Cambridge, 2006); Clare McManus, ed., *Women and Culture at the Courts of the Stuart Queens* (Basingstoke, 2003).

[288] John Orrell, *The Theatres of Inigo Jones and John Webb* (Cambridge, 1985), pp. 80-1.

[289] *Ibid.*, pp. 78-89.

[290] The great hall in 1626, TNA AO1/2424/56; E351/3271; the presence chamber in 1632-3, TNA AO1/2427/63; E351/3267 (1633-4).

[291] John Orrell, op. cit. (288), pp. 113-27.

[292] *HKW* IV, pp. 262-3, 268-70. Also see Geoffrey Fisher and John Newman, 'A Fountain Design by Inigo Jones', *Burlington Magazine* 127 (August 1985), pp. 530-3.

[293] *Cal. S.P. Dom.*, Commonwealth 1655-6, p. 228.

[294] For a discussion of the chapel in this period in some detail, see Simon Thurley, op. cit. (260); pp. 238-74; Simon Thurley, 'The Politics of Court Space in Early Stuart London', in George Gorst and Malcolm Smutts, op. cit. (273).

[295] Proceedings of the House of Commons in BL, Add. MS 31,116 ff. 32v, 38v; The Memoirs of Father Cyprien de Gamache, translated and printed in T. Birch, op. cit. (257), II, pp. 352, 429; Albert J. Loomie, 'The Destruction of Rubens's "Crucifixion" in the Queen's Chapel, Somerset House', *Burlington Magazine* 140 (October 1998), pp. 680-2; Julie Spraggon, *Puritan Iconoclasm During the English Civil War* (Woodbridge, 2003), pp. 71-5; *The Kingdomes Weekly Intelligencer*, 28 March–4 April 1643; *Certaine Informations*, 27 March–3 April 1643.

[296] *Commons Journal* V (1646-8), p. 440; PRO AO1/2431/79.

[297] *Cal. S.P. Dom.*, 1649-50, III, p. 401.

[298] T. Birch, op. cit. (257), II, p. 429.

[299] Clarendon says that her lodgings were pillaged and stuff stolen and embezzled. Edward, Earl of Clarendon, op. cit. (259) III, p. 11 probably refers to an incident in September 1643 when the state rooms were broken into and some items were stolen; *The Journals of the House of Lords* VI, p. 215a.

[300] A summary of this is found in Oliver Millar, op. cit. (251), pp. xi-xvii.

[301] A. G. H. Bachrach and R. G. Collmer, eds and trans., *Lodweijk Huygens: The English Journal 1651-1652* (Leiden, 1982), p. 61.

[302] Jonathan Brown, *Kings and Connoisseurs. Collecting Art in Seventeenth-century Europe* (Yale, 1995), pp. 69-75.

[303] *Ibid.*, pp. 76-83; Jonathan Brown and John Elliott, eds, *The Sale of the Century. Artistic Relations Between Spain and Great Britain, 1604-1655* (Yale, 2002), pp. 60-8.

[304] *Commons Journal* IV (1644-6), p. 477; *Cal. S.P. Dom.*, Commonwealth 1649-50, p. 299.

[305] *Cal. S.P. Dom.*, Commonwealth 1649-50, pp. 228, 303.

[306] *Cal. S.P. Dom.*, Commonwealth 1649-50, p. 262; 1650,

[307] pp. 117, 526; 1651, p. 187.

[307] *Cal. S.P. Dom.*, Commonwealth 1649-50, pp. 228, 303; A. G. H. Bachrach and R. G. Collmer, op. cit. (301), p. 60.

[308] *Cal S.P. Dom.*, Commonwealth 1655, p. 127; 1658-9, p. 57. For specific embassies, see, for instance, TNA AO1/2353/71; BL, Add. MS 5751, f. 25.

[309] Roy Sherwood, *Oliver Cromwell. King in all but Name 1653-1658* (Gloucester, 1997), pp. 143-54; Laura Lunger Knoppers, *Constructing Cromwell. Ceremony, Portrait and Print 1645-1661* (Cambridge, 2000), pp. 139-45.

[310] *Journal of the House of Commons* VII, pp. 656a, 663a, 689a, 708a; Ruth Spalding, ed., 'The Diary of Bulstrode Whitelocke 1605-1675', *Records of Social and Economic History* n.s. XIII (Oxford, 1990), pp. 515, 533.

[311] TNA SP46/128, f. 196; C. H. Frith, ed., *The Memoirs of Edmund Ludlow*, 2 vols (Oxford, 1894), II, p. 102.

[312] *Cal. S.P. Dom.*, Commonwealth 1658-9, p. 340.

[313] *Cal. S.P. Dom.*, Commonwealth 1659-60, p. 115; Edward, Earl of Clarendon, op. cit. (259) VI, p. 167; Ruth Spalding, op. cit. (310), p. 565.

[314] *Journal of the House of Commons* VIII, p. 73.

[315] *Cal. S.P. Dom.*, 1661-2, p. 184.

[316] TNA Work 5/1.

[317] TNA LC5/137, pp. 4, 56; HMC *5th Report Sutherland MSS*, p. 156; Robert Latham and William Matthews, eds, *The Diary of Samuel Pepys* I (London 1970), p. 249.

[318] TNA LC5/137, pp. 225-6.

[319] *HKW* V, p. 5; Stephen Porter, 'William Crofts', *Oxford DNB*.

[320] *Cal. S.P. Dom.*, 1656-7, p. 58; City Archives of Bruges Oud Archief nr 101 Politieke Oorkonden 1st reeks no. 621, f. 5. This reference was supplied to me by Dr Anna Keay.

[321] John Webb, the Tennis Court Master, died in 1660 and had been appointed to his post under James I. He would have been a very old man in 1656 and it is hard to see why he would have travelled to Bruges to see the king. The two junior members are very unlikely to have been listed as 'Mr' John Webb as they were the lowliest members of the household.

[322] *Cal. S.P. Ven.*, 1659-61, p. 148.

[323] Simon Thurley, 'A Country Seat Fit for a King: Charles II, Greenwich and Winchester', in Eveline Cruikshanks, ed., *The Stuart Courts* (Gloucester, 2000), pp. 215, 236 n. 7; Simon Thurley, op. cit. (85), p. 99.

[324] John Harris, op. cit. (259), p. 15. This drawing has been dated to the 1660s by Gordon Higgott, to whom I am grateful for discussing the role of Webb.

[325] TNA SP29/251, p. 120. Printed in John Bold, *John Webb. Architectural Theory and Practice in the Seventeenth Century* (Oxford, 1990), p. 182.

[326] Both appear in the summary for 1662, TNA LR5/67.

[327] H. M. Colvin, *Biographical Dictionary of Architects* (Yale, 2008).

[328] *Cal. S.P. Dom.*, 1671, pp. 561-2.

[329] Robert Latham and William Matthews, op. cit. (317) VI, p. 18.

[330] Anna Keay, 'The Ceremonies of Charles II Court', (unpublished PhD thesis, London, 2004), pp. 116-26.

[331] R. Latham, op. cit. (317), III, pp. 190-1. For other accounts, see ibid., v, pp. 300-1; E. S. De Beer, ed., *The Diary of John Evelyn* III (1955), p. 334; *The Memoirs of Ann Lady Fanshawe* (London, 1907), pp. 121-2.

[332] These issues are summarized in Mark Girouard, *Life in the French Country House* (London, 2000), pp. 129-40; Mark Girouard, *Social Life in the English Country House* (Yale, 1978), pp. 126-38.

[333] Simon Thurley, op. cit. (34), pp. 213-17; Anna Keay, *The Magnificent Monarch* (London, 2008), pp. 126-32.

[334] *HKW* V, p. 256.

[335] PRO LR5/67 (formerly LR6/190, 191); the main headings are printed in *HKW* V, p. 255.

[336] *Cal. S.P. Ven.*, 1661-4, p. 171; HMC, Ormonde III, p. 23; E. S. De Beer, op. cit. (331), p. 334.

[337] R. Latham and W. Matthews, op. cit. (317), V, pp. 63, 300-1.

[338] *Cal. S.P. Dom.*, 1661-2, p. 451.

[339] T. Birch, op. cit. (257), p. 429; *Cal. S.P. Dom.*, Charles II, XVI 1660-1, p. 277; PRO, Work 5/1, ff. 364, 372. As some of the original fittings were taken to store during the Commonwealth, it is just possible that the pulpit was the original one being returned.

[340] Op. cit. (260), pp. 238-74.

[341] *Saint-Paul — Saint-Louis. Les Jésuites á Paris* (Musée Carnavalet, 12 March to 2 June 1985).

[342] T. Birch, op. cit. (257), II, pp. 458-9.

[343] T. Birch, op. cit. (257), II, p. 429.

[344] TNA LR65/67; Sandra Raphael, 'Roger Looker', *Oxford DNB*.

[345] TNA Work 5/6, f. 482.

[346] R. Latham, op. cit. (317), VI, p. 142.

[347] TNA Work 5/9, f. 421.

[348] *Cal. S.P. Dom.*, 1668-9, pp. 511, 597.

[349] See, for instance, a newsletter of 9 May 1671, BL, Add. MS 36916, f. 222.

[350] See, for instance, *Cal. S.P. Ven.*, 1671-2, no. 66 (p. 76).

[351] HMC, twelfth report VII, Fleming papers, p. 67.

[352] *Cal. S.P. Ven.*, 1671-2, no. 66 (p. 76).

[353] The following details are from TNA Work 5/15–19.

[354] TNA Work 5/17, ff. 245, 250.

[355] TNA Work 5/9, f. 222.

[356] TNA work 5/19, f. 232.

[357] *HKW* V, p. 258 n. 4.

[358] Giles Worsley, *The British Stable* (Yale, 2004), pp. 89-91.

[359] TNA Work 5/18, f. 432.

[360] TNA Work 5/29, f. 287; Work 5/32, f. 212; Work 5/32, f. 166; Work 5/33, ff. 180, 188.

[361] TNA T1/103 104, p. 350.

[362] HMC, twelfth report VII, Fleming papers, pp. 70-1.

[363] For instance, *Cal. S.P. Dom.*, 1671, pp. 294, 395; TNA LC5/2, pp. 48-57.

[364] Edward Corp, 'Catherine of Braganza and Cultural Politics', in Clarissa Campbell Orr, ed., *Queenship in Britain 1660-1837* (Manchester, 2002), p. 59.

[365] C. H. Firth, rev. A. J. Hopper, 'Sir Samuel Tuke', *Oxford DNB*.

[366] TNA LC5/141, pp. 136, 138, 311.

[367] TNA Work 5/23, f. 297.

[368] For example, TNA Work 5/23, f. 294, or Work 5/32, f. 200.

[369] *Cal. S.P. Dom.*, 1679-80, p. 364.

[370] TNA Work 5/33, ff. 154, 177; Work 5/35, f. 170; E. S. De Beer, ed., op. cit. (331) IV, p. 259.

[371] TNA Work 3/1, p. 6.

[372] Some of the minor works to the chapel and palace are covered in *HKW* V, p. 257.

[373] Peter Leech, 'Musicians in the Catholic Chapel of Catherine of Braganza, 1662–92', *Early Music* (November 2001), pp. 584-5.

[374] Robert Beddard, *A Kingdom Without a King. The Journal of the Provisional Government in the Revolution of 1688* (Oxford, 1988), pp. 44, 81, 107-8; Tim Harris, 'London Crowds and the Revolution of 1688', in Eveline Cruikshanks, ed., *By Force or Default? The Revolution of 1688-89* (Edinburgh, 1989), pp. 51-2.

[375] R. Needham and A. Webster, op. cit. (129), p. 167.

[376] See the list of inhabitants in BL, Add. MS 20,726, ff. 39-41.

[377] This introductory section is written by Patricia Croot.

[378] Accounts of Clarendon, Goring, and Berkeley estates in VCH, *Middlesex* XIII (forthcoming 2009).

[379] This paragraph and the next is based on accounts of individual estates in VCH, *Middlesex* XIII (forthcoming 2009).

[380] *HKW* V, pp. 258-263; R. Needham and A. Webster, op. cit. (129), pp. 168-89.

[381] TNA Work 6/14, p. 140.

[382] TNA Work 6/3, p. 15; AO1/2447/141; LC5/154, pp. 238-9.

[383] TNA T1/154 51, 21 November 1712.

[384] TNA Work 6/3, p. 19.

[385] TNA T1/192 62, p. 200, 13 October 1715.

[386] Lawrence Stone, 'Inigo Jones and the New Exchange', *Archaeological Journal* 114 (1957), p. 120; Elizabeth McKellar, *The Birth of Modern London* (Manchester, 1999), p. 23.

[387] John Strype, ed., *Stow's Survey of London* (London, 1720), p. 112.

[388] J. M. Beattie, *The English Court in the Reign of George I* (Cambridge, 1967), p. 262; R. Needham, op. cit. (129), pp. 173-6.

[389] TNA T1/518/13A-38A.

[390] Ruth M. Larsen, 'Mary Campbell', *Oxford DNB*.

[391] R Needham and A. Webster, op. cit. (129), pp. 181-3.

[392] J. B. Hattendorf, 'John Robinson', *Oxford DNB*.

[393] David Watkin, *The Architect King. George III and the Culture of the Enlightenment* (London, 2004), pp. 113-23; John Harris and Michael Snodin, eds, *Sir William Chambers, Architect to William III* (Yale, 1997), pp. 111-24; *HKW* V, pp. 261-3, 363-80.

[394] Duncan Wood and Julian Munby, 'The Historical Development of Somerset House: An Archaeological Investigation', *Transactions of the London and Middlesex Archaeological Society* 54 (2003), pp. 79-110.

[395] TNA E351/3244, Taskwork: James Lee.

[396] TNA E351/3245, Taskwork: James Lee.

[397] TNA E351/3246, Taskwork: James Lee.

[398] TNA E351/3250, Taskwork: John De Critz.

[399] Examples include Canonbury House (1599), 'Old Palace', Bromley-by-Bow (*c.* 1606), Tottenham Priory (1620).

[400] Cited in *HKW* V, pp. 259-60 and 262.

[401] TNA E351/3262, Taskwork: Matthew Goodrich.

[402] BL, Egerton MS 2815.

[403] TNA Work 30/263.

[404] The cofferer's account lists Syon, Reading, Odiham, Wolfhall and Banbury as building sites in addition to Somerset Place.

[405] See *HKW* IV, pp. 253-4.

CATALOGUE

This catalogue publishes for the first time all the principal topographical sources for Old Somerset House. It focuses on the primary evidence and does not reproduce derivative views or prints of watercolours or drawings where the originals survive. Nor does it include the drawings by Inigo Jones for the remodelling of Somerset House for the Stuart queens as these have been comprehensively illustrated and discussed in John Harris and Gordon Higgott, *The Complete Architectural Drawings of Inigo Jones*. It is arranged chronologically and contains a commentary that complements, rather than duplicates, the main text.

Catalogue 1

Anthonis van den Wyngaerde, *Panorama of London from the River* (*c*. 1544)

Ashmolean Museum, Sutherland 51 drawings I, III

Pen and ink on paper; 9⁴/₁₀in. × 16¹/₂in. (24cm × 42cm)

Wyngaerde was one of the most important topographical artists working in Europe in the sixteenth century. Born in the Low Countries, he was working in London on his panorama by 1543-4. As there were no maps of London at this date his ambitious view lacks dimensional accuracy. Yet Wyngaerde's drawing shows the future site of Somerset Place still occupied by the inns of the bishops of Chester and Llandaff. Definitively untangling the buildings shown is now probably impossible, but in 1544-5 the future Duke of Somerset was certainly living on the site in at least some of the structures shown.

BIBLIOGRAPHY

Howard Colvin and Susan Foister, and Ann Saunders, ed., *The Panorama of London circa 1544* (London Topographical Society 151, in association with the Ashmolean, Oxford, 1996), p. 11, drawing III.

Catalogue 2

a) Unknown, *The Woodcut Map of London* (1561-70)

28¹/₂in. × 72¹/₂in. (72.4cm × 184.2cm)

b) G. Braun and F. Hogenberg, *London* (from *Civitates Orbis Terrarum*, 1572)

12¹/₂in. × 18⁷/₈in. (31.8cm × 47.9cm). Detail illustrated in this catalogue at 290% of original size.

Both the woodcut map and Braun and Hogenberg's plate of London from their 1572 atlas *Civitates Orbis Terrarum* derive from the lost 'copperplate' map of London of 1553-9. Unfortunately the section of the copperplate map showing Somerset Place has not, so far, been found. This means that Braun and Hogenberg and the woodcut map, usually known as 'Agas', are the earliest interpretations of the original depiction of Elizabethan Somerset Place.

The two maps essentially show the same view, but the woodcut map is clearer and seems more precise in many of the details. The map shows, for the first time, the topography of the newly-built mansion. The division between the three principal medieval properties on the site is still evident. Worcester Inn, on the left, with its gatehouse, was later to become Somerset House Yard. The principal mansion and garden are mainly on the site of Chester Inn and the church. To the right, still largely undeveloped, is the site of Strand Inn bounded by Strand Lane.

The view shows piles of rubble, or perhaps building stone, in Strand Inn, capturing the site in transition. We know that Somerset Place was not completed by 1553-9 but the map is not clear enough to be definitive about the stage which the mansion had reached. What is, however, clear is that the house was perceived as being a castellated building, including, it appears, the Strand front.

BIBLIOGRAPHY

Stephen Powys Marks, *The Map of Mid-sixteenth Century London; an Investigation into the Relationship between a Copper-engraved Map and its Derivatives* (London Topographical Society 110, 1964).

Ann Saunders and John Schofield, ed., with contributions by Peter Barber, Stephen Powys Marks and John Schofield, *Tudor London: A Map and a View* (London Topographical Society 159, 2001).

Ida Darlington and James Howgego, *Printed Maps of London circa 1553-1850* (London, 1964), no. 2, pp. 51-2.

Cat 1.

Cat 2a.

Cat 2b.

Catalogue 3

John Norden, map of Westminster, *Speculum Britanniae* (1593)

6in. × 8in. (15.2cm × 20.3cm)

John Norden was a cartographer specializing in county histories. His map of Middlesex from his atlas *Speculum Britanniae* shows Westminster and the palaces along the Strand in an engraving by Pieter van den Keere. The view was reprinted at least twice, including the extraordinary 'double view' in the Royal Library Stockholm, but the details are very similar.

Somerset Place is shown from a higher angle than in the woodcut map, allowing us to see inside the great court and get a feeling of the inner court to its right (east). The threefold division of the medieval landholdings is still apparent and there still seems to be a pile of rubble or building material on the site of the former Strand Inn. The architecture of the south front accords closely with what we know from later views which gives credence to the suggestion that the Strand front was originally crenellated.

BIBLIOGRAPHY

A View of London in 1660, by John Norden (London Topographical Society 94, 1961).

Norden's Maps of London and Westminster, engraved by Pieter van den Keere, 1593 (London Topographical Society 7, 1889).

James Howgego, *Printed Maps of London circa 1553-1850* (2nd edition, 1978), no. 5, p. 46.

Henry B. Wheatley, *Notes upon Norden and his Map of London, 1593* (New Shakespeare Society series VI, 1876), pp. lxxxix-cvi.

Catalogue 4

Unknown, *The Somerset House conference of 1604*

National Portrait Gallery 665

Oil on canvas; 81in. × 105½in. (205.7cm × 268cm)

In May 1604 representatives of Spain, the Spanish Netherlands and England met together in London to hammer out a peace treaty ending the long period of Elizabethan hostility and war. James I made Somerset House available for the envoys and

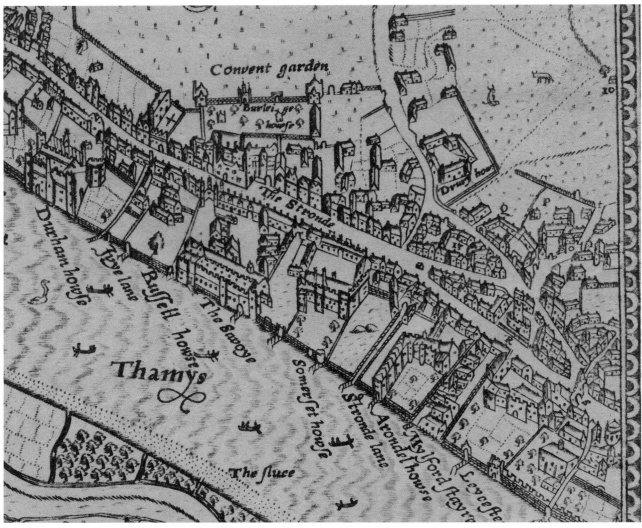

Cat 3.

for the conference that was to negotiate terms. The conference met in eighteen sessions in the Somerset House council chamber concluding their business in mid-July and signing a treaty at Whitehall on 19 August. The conference was an occasion of huge international importance and was celebrated in both England and Spain with the utmost magnificence. Gifts were exchanged between the various delegates and this painting was made as a record of the occasion.

Two versions survive, one in the National Portrait Gallery which seems to be the primary version, and the other in the National Maritime Museum, Greenwich, which appears to be a slightly later copy executed, perhaps, in Spain. Although it is unclear who painted either picture (the NMM version seems more Spanish in style) the likelihood is that the NPG version was painted

in England as a record of the event and returned to Spain with the delegation.

The outer court at Denmark House mainly contained lodgings, but it also contained the queen's council chamber depicted in this painting. The queen's council was responsible for the administration of her jointure, and queens at least since the time of Henry VIII had had similar councils. Anne of Denmark's was specifically modelled on the council which she had in Scotland and was headed, in 1603, by Robert Cecil who appears prominently in the painting.

In 1605 King James I was anxious to regularize the business of government while he was on his peripatetic hunting trips outside the Home Counties. He decided to do this by ordering the council to meet once a week at the queen's court, in other words often at Denmark House (G. P. V.

Cat 4.

Akrigg, ed., *Letters of King James VI & I* (Berkeley, CA, 1984, p. 247). The Privy Council records for this period are lost and so it is unclear how often, in reality, the council met at Somerset House, but this requirement may help to explain the prominence and size of the room.

In the painting the Spanish negotiators are seated in front of a tapestry which may show a scene from the story of David; the moment when he sends Uriah the Hittite to a certain death. The tapestry has a date of 1560, suggesting that it may be from life, such a specific reference is otherwise hard to understand. On the opposite side of the table are the English delegation with Sir Robert Cecil in the bottom right-hand corner. Various symbolic items are included, such as the rose growing on the back right side of the painting, but the table carpet and chairs are entirely consistent with the sort of furniture at court at the turn of the century.

An inscription identifies all the sitters and their portraits are lifelike and recognizable, once again suggesting that the group portrait shows a real view. Architecturally speaking, this seems to be the case. The large four-light casement window is one of those looking out into the great court. The view through the window into the outer court is particularly important. In 1604 the west side of the courtyard was incomplete and the view through the window shows it before Anne of Denmark added great bay windows matching the Strand frontage. The wall seems to be of stone and the roof of tiles with dormer windows. The view thus captures the inner court before it was modernized by Anne of Denmark and shows that the Duke of Somerset's courtyard was plain and simple.

BIBLIOGRAPHY

Roy Strong, *Tudor and Jacobean Portraits*, 2 vols (London: National Portrait Gallery, 1969), I, pp. 351-3.

Karen Hearn, *Talking Peace 1604. The Somerset House Conference Paintings* (Gilbert Collection, London, 20 May–25 July 2004).

N. R. R. Fisher 'The Queenes Courte in her Councell Chamber at Westminster', *English Historical Review* (1993), pp. 313-17.

Elizabeth Ewan and Maureen M. Meikle, eds, *Women in Scotland c.1100-c.1750* (East Linton, 1999), pp. 105-10.

E. Lodge, *Illustrations of British History, Biography and Manners, etc.* (London, 1791), pp. 208-14.

Catalogue 5

Unknown, *First floor plan of the Strand range of Somerset Place* (*c.* 1608-11)

Hatfield Maps, Hatfield House, Hertfordshire CPM II 56

Pen and ink on paper; 11in. × 16in. (28cm × 40.6cm)

The Earl of Salisbury was appointed Keeper of Somerset Place in 1603 (*Cal. S.P. Dom.*, 1603-10, p. 441). In 1605-6 the first-floor gallery overlooking the Strand and the great room in the centre were subdivided to make lodgings for him (TNA E351/3241). This plan shows the effect of the alterations, and is the earliest surviving plan of part of the house. As Cecil had a magnificent house a matter of yards away (see p. 33), these lodgings were presumably used as administrative space for the supervision of the queen's financial affairs and her building works.

It is worth noting that the gatehouse contained at first-floor level a single large room with windows looking out over the Strand and into the outer court. This could presumably be accessed via the spiral stairs from the ground floor and thus be used as a prospect room or grandstand for watching public events.

BIBLIOGRAPHY

HMC, *Salisbury*, XXIII, p. 102.

R. A. Skelton and J. Summerson, *A Description of Maps and Architectural Drawings made by W. Cecil [...]* (Roxburgh Club, 1971), pp. 77, 83.

Catalogue 6

Robert Smythson, *Ground plan of Somerset Place and gardens* (*c.* 1611)

RIBA Drawings Collection I/13

Pen and ink on paper with incised lines by metal stylus; 11in. × 10½in. (27.9cm × 26.7cm)

Inscriptions read '*The Platforme: of Somersett garden/the Queenes house*' and '*The Newe adition at/Somersett house*'.

In 1611 when he came to London, the mason turned architect Robert Smythson was in his late seventies but with an undimmed curiosity about architecture. The fashionable world must have been closely watching the most important London project of the day, the reconstruction of Somerset Place, and Smythson would have been keen to see this work at first hand. He seems to have had access

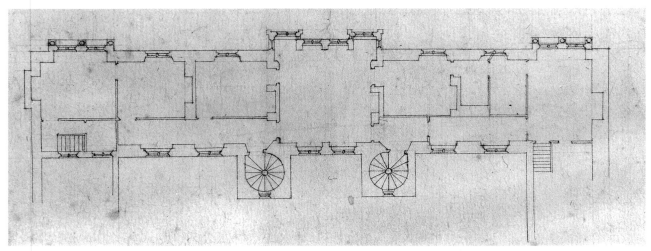

Cat 5.

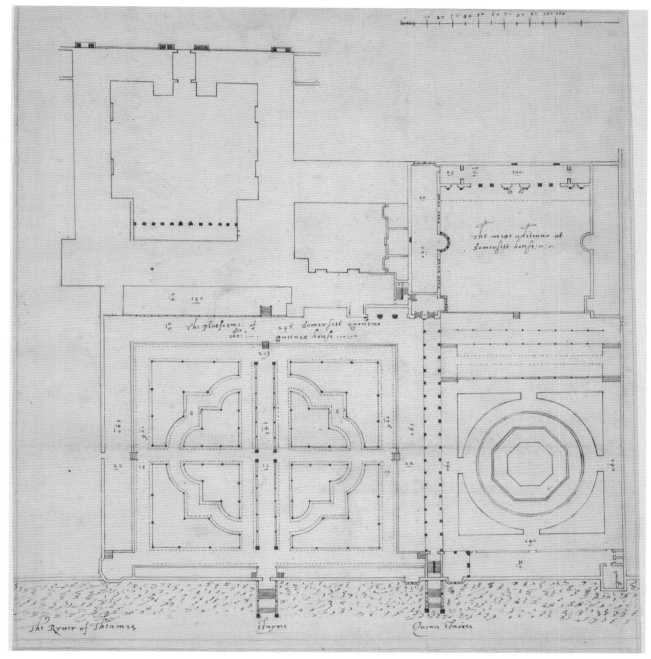

Cat 6.

to the Office of Works as his plan is a copy of one or more master plans that must have been in the office at the time. The drawing suggests detailed knowledge of both royal intentions and the progress of work. By 1611 the purchase of additional land had just been agreed and the plan shows, for instance, a gallery on the site of Sergeant Goodrowse's house, although this was never built.

The plan makes a careful distinction between what already existed and what was intended. It is,

in fact, incomplete and some parts have incised lines ready for inking that were never inked up. Figure 8 is based on this, showing the room divisions indicated by underscoring. Smythson recorded the rooms around the inner court but not the details of the outer court. This may have been because the details were not finalized in 1611 — the outer court was just under construction.

In a wider context, the plan of the gardens is particularly important, giving a significant amount of detail. The octagonal feature on the right is the rock grotto known as Parnassus designed by Isaac de Caus.

BIBLIOGRAPHY

Mark Girouard, 'The Smythson Collection of the Royal Institute of British Architects', *Architectural History* 5 (1962), p. 33.

Mark Girouard, 'Robert Smythson', *Oxford Dictionary of National Biography*.

Roy Strong, *The Renaissance Garden in England* ((London, 1984), pp. 86-93.

Geoffrey Fisher and John Newman, 'A Fountain Design by Inigo Jones', *The Burlington Magazine* 127 (August 1985), pp. 530-3.

Catalogue 7

John Thorpe, *Elevation of the Strand front and ground plan of the first courtyard of Somerset Place c.1610-11*

John Thorpe's copy of a presentation plan prepared for Simon and Edward Basil to present to Anne of Denmark in 1610-11

Sir John Soane's Museum, vol. 101, pp. 87–88.

Pen and ink with pencil under drawing and pencil additions on paper; 16^{7}⁄$_{10}$in. × 11in. (42.5cm × 27.6cm)

Left-hand cresting on the elevation has been patched

Inscriptions read: (outer court) '*All ye sides round abouts are leadyd / & ballistes after ye order of ye front: / & cort mayne ground & a story of offices under/ round about also*'; '*This court 120 fo longe and it should be 90 fo wide*'; '*Thes wyndoes are such * as those in ye front*'. (East wing) '*Thes Lodgings are but 2 stories hie above ye ground*'. (West wing) '*And all ye offices are under both sides round about wth kychens & sellers*'. (Top left) '*This way is ye great Chamber, Prsence, etc. / & gallery returning wch make an other square cort*' and *A square cort hear...o fo*'. (The hall) '*54 fo*'; '*this should be 30fo: wide*'; '*square bay windoe / 4 lightes forw / :of W 7fo*'. (On terrace) '*here are wyndowesabove * this terrace and leaddyd round*'; '*seats*'; '*Terrace above this walke 10 fo*'.

This drawing, seminal for the interpretation of Somerset Place, has too often been uncritically accepted as being first a record of what Protector Somerset built and second a drawing produced speculatively by John Thorpe in 1603. There is good reason to believe that neither is the case.

In 1966 Sir John Summerson dated this drawing to *c.* 1603 as he believed that was the date at which

Thorpe would have been most likely to put forward a proposal for the alteration and completion of Somerset Place or make a copy of someone else's scheme. As has been argued above, in 1603 there was no stated intention that the house was to be rebuilt. It was not until five years into James's reign that plans were formulated for the reconstruction of Somerset Place. This contrasts strongly with the plan Thorpe made of Eltham Palace in 1603 where James hurriedly spent nearly £4,000 on alterations. Thus it is most unlikely that anyone would have made plans for work at Somerset Place before late 1608.

Moreover, when work started on redesigning the house as a residence for the queen, it was not the outer court that was the priority. It was in the queen's privy lodgings that work started in the spring of 1609. Work on the completion and modernization of the outer court only began in 1611-12 and presumably detailed plans for this were in hand from late 1610. Thus the most likely date for the Thorpe drawing is 1610-11, not 1603.

In the first decade of the century Thorpe had been busy on a variety of commissions; some royal, others for aristocrats and the upper gentry. From 1607 he had again been increasingly working for the Crown, and in 1610 an office, under the surveyor Ralph Treswell, was created for the continuous survey of royal properties and Thorpe was to be one of Treswell's two assistants. His duties and works, as one of 'His Majesties surveyors', are poorly recorded, but Thorpe was at the centre of royal property administration at the crucial point in the redesign of the outer court at Somerset Place.

On 16 March 1610 an estimate was prepared of 'the charges of such worcks as are intended to be don on the first court at Somersett House', signalling the existence of a scheme for the outer courtyard. The section dealing with masonry makes it clear that the proposal was to make significant alterations to the Strand elevation. First, the walls were to be heightened and given a balustrade: 'the north side towards the streete to be raised higher with ashlar cornish, railes and ballesters'. Then the 'square windowes towards the streete to be raised higher with ashlar and other open worcks, pedestals, architrave, freize and cornice'. The frontispiece seems to have been proposed to be altered, too: 'the fore front to be clensed and the railes and ballesters amended' (TNA SP14/62, no. 33).

These additions can be identified on Thorpe's elevation. The cresting over the 'square windows'

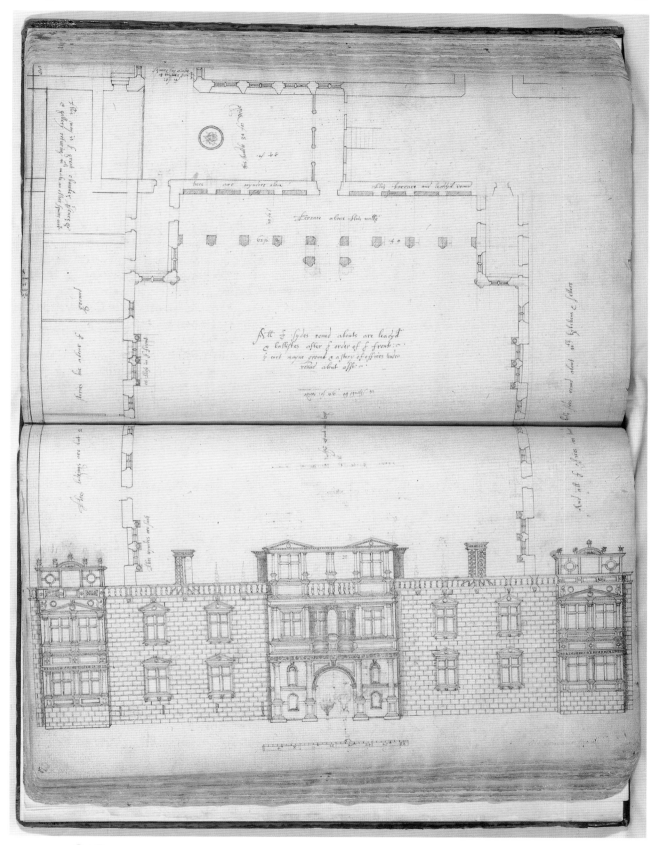

Cat 7.

and balustrades with Jacobean finials and corbels are prominent and, according to the estimate, additions to the original. The plan section of Thorpe's drawing accords with the proposals in the estimate, too, showing the 'square returns' with windows, the proposal for erecting 'square windows' and completing the west range.

The question is, of course, whether the proposed 1610 scheme was Thorpe's or whether his drawing was a copy of someone else's scheme. Thorpe was not in the Office of Works, and Simon Basil, the Surveyor of the Works, would have had responsibility for the design. The only record that exists mentioning a drawing is in the account for 1610-11 and records a fee of 40s being paid to Edward Basil, the clerk of works at Somerset Place and brother of Simon. There is no record of Edward or his more senior brother being draughtsmen, and the plan prepared 'against her majesties coming hither' was a presentation plan. In other words, one designed to convey to the queen what the end result would look like. Could Basil have employed Thorpe to draw up his proposals and ideas? In which case, is Thorpe's drawing a copy of a presentation plan for Queen Anne of Denmark? This would certainly explain its unusual form combining the elevation and plan and only covering the area to be worked upon in 1611-12.

Was the work shown on the presentation plan actually undertaken? Although it is not possible to isolate the charge for this work in the enrolled account, a separate list of task work for July 1611 contains a mason's bill for just over £500 for works including the 'railes and ballisters' for the front (TNA SP14/65, no. 61). More importantly, later elevations of the façade confirm that most of the design was, in fact, executed. But most telling, perhaps, is the date 1612 and the initials 'IR' and 'AR' on the rainwater heads shown on James Hunter's drawing of 1775 (**cat. 31**).

Four reliable elevational records of the Strand façade, including a measured drawing (**cats 25, 29, 31, 36**) agree on its appearance in 1750-77. All differ from Thorpe's view. Some of the differences can be easily explained. The balustrade and the frets over the bay windows were certainly added in 1611-12 as they can be seen from the rear in Kip's engraving of 1702 (**cat. 20**). They were probably removed soon after. Thorpe and the eighteenth-century views agree on the details of the windows at either end of the elevation in all their essentials, but the upper part of the central feature differs significantly. Thorpe shows two

windows surmounted by pediments with an open loggia between them. The loggia has a balustrade at the front, converting it into a covered balcony looking over the street. We have no plan at this level, but Kip's engraving suggests that it was the façade to a single great second-floor room. But was it ever built as shown, and if so was it part of Somerset's house or erected by Anne of Denmark?

The 'amending' of the balusters and rails on the 'fore front' certainly seems to indicate that in 1610-11 the intention was to alter the frontispiece. The creation of a loggia would have been not dissimilar to that which Jones designed for the Queen's House only six years later, only cruder. It is known that Somerset House was used as a viewing gallery for important state and civic processions. In May 1615, for instance, King James watched a procession of newly-created knights of the garter from a vantage point at Somerset House (*Cal. S.P. Dom.*, 1611-18, p. 287). Was this from the upper loggia? Eighteenth-century views show the loggia with two transom and mullion windows on a blank pedestal flanked by two pedestals with carved semi-recumbent figures (**cat. 31**). This arrangement did not preclude the feature being used as a grandstand as **cat. 25** shows. The loggia, however, was either an unexecuted proposal or it was altered at a later date.

The middle tier of the central feature as shown by Thorpe is corroborated by the later views. All show two projecting windows flanked by pilasters with a projecting niche on the same plane in the middle set between two recessed windows. The niche is empty in Thorpe's elevation; was it intended to take a statue of King Edward as at Nonsuch, or a figure of Somerset himself? The lower part is shown in all views as having a heavy Tuscan order and a round-headed archway. The eighteenth-century views show winged victories in the spandrels, which Thorpe omits (together with the other sculpted panels shown in later views). Thorpe shows a pair of lower niches with string-courses; these are not there by the eighteenth century. The upper niches are at the level shown by Thorpe and so it is possible that the lower ones were built and later removed, possibly as they attracted the attention of passers-by as seats or receptacles for rubbish.

In conclusion, this important drawing shows neither Protector Somerset's House nor the house as altered for Anne of Denmark. It is for this reason that it has been so misread.

BIBLIOGRAPHY

John Summerson, ed., 'The Book of Architecture of John Thorpe in Sir John Soane's Museum', *Walpole Society* XL (1966), cat. T87-88, pp. 69-70, pl. 41.

Nikolaus Pevsner, 'Old Somerset House', *The Architectural Review* CXVI (1954), pp. 163-7.

H. M. Colvin, *A Biographical Dictionary of British Architects 1600-1840* (3rd edition, 1995), p. 979.

Malcolm Airs, 'John Thorpe', *Oxford Dictionary of National Biography*.

J. Schofield, ed., *The London Surveys of Ralph Treswell* (London Topographical Society 135, 1987), p. 10.

Catalogue 8

Marcus Gheeraerts, *Portrait of Queen Anne of Denmark with the gardens of Denmark House in the background* (*c.* 1611-14)

Woburn Abbey

Oil on canvas; 87in. × 51 in. (221cm × 131cm)

It is not certain that the garden shown in the background of this portrait is that of Denmark House, but the portrait is one of a group of Jacobean royal portraits where James and Anne expressed the sophistication of their artistic patronage by appearing against the background of a newly-commissioned building or structure. James I's portrait by Paul van Somer shows the newly erected Whitehall Banqueting House in the background and the south front of Oatlands appears in the background of van Somer's equestrian portrait of Anne of Denmark (Oliver Millar, *The Tudor, Stuart and Early Georgian Pictures in the Collection of Her Majesty the Queen*, 2 vols (London, 1963), I, no. 105). That Anne should be painted in front of the garden in *c.* 1611-14 is significant and the only garden it could realistically be is that at Denmark House. The layout of hedged compartments and turf beds in geometric patterns is very similar to the design in Smythson's plan. If this is right, the vantage point is probably the gallery between the privy chamber and great gallery. The arched top of the loggia can be clearly seen on views of the house from the south.

BIBLIOGRAPHY

Roy Strong, *The Renaissance Garden in England* (London, 1984), pp. 87-8.

Roy Strong, *The Artist and the Garden* (Yale, 2000), pp. 36-7.

Karen Hearn, ed., *Dynasties. Painting in Jacobean England 1530-1630* (Tate Gallery, London, 1995), pp. 192-3.

Catalogue 9

Cornelius Bol, *Somerset House from the River Thames* (*c.* 1640-50)

Dulwich Picture Gallery DPG360

Oil on canvas; 25in. × 42⅕in. (63.5cm × 108.7cm)

In the late 1630s John Evelyn commissioned Cornelius Bol to paint views of Arundel House, the Tower of London and Denmark House. Bol was a painter from Antwerp who was active in London in the late 1630s and 1640s. The paintings he executed, still in the Evelyn Collection, were shown at the Royal Academy in 1960. The Dulwich Picture Gallery version of the Denmark House view is one of a number of copies, but signed by Bol.

The painting is an extremely important source for understanding Denmark House at the end of the early Stuart period. It provides the only known view of the side elevation of the chapel and the private house that occupied the site of the friary buildings. It also shows clearly the difference between the brick tower at the south end of the great gallery and the rendered south front painted to look like stone. It also shows details of the garden and water gate.

BIBLIOGRAPHY

Richard Beresford, *Dulwich Picture Gallery: Complete Illustrated Catalogue* (London, 1998), pp. 42-3.

The Age of Charles II (ex. cat., RA, 1960), pp. 67-8.

M. D. Whinney and O. Millar, *English Art, 1625-1714* (1957), pp. 262-3.

George Vertue, *Notebooks,* 6 vols, Walpole Society 1930-1955, IV, p. 53.

Christies, Important British Paintings, London, Wednesday 6 June 2007, lot 63.

Catalogue 10

Wenceslaus Hollar, *Bird's-eye plan of the west central district of London* (*c.* 1660)

British Museum, Q 6.136

Cat 8.

Cat 9.

Etching; [whole etched area] 13³/₁₀in.× 17⁴/₅in. (33.8cm × 45.1cm), [plate] 13⁹/₁₀in. × 18in. (35.3cm × 45.7cm)

Wenceslaus Hollar was born in Prague to a Protestant family and moved to Cologne where he established himself as a printmaker. In 1636 the Earl of Arundel, travelling through Cologne, spotted Hollar and brought him back to London where he joined Arundel's household and married one of Lady Arundel's ladies-in-waiting. Arundel did not deliver the patronage that Hollar expected, and from about 1639 he began to produce commercial prints.

At the Restoration Hollar proposed a hugely ambitious project, the production of a huge wall map 10ft long and 5ft deep, covering the whole of London in perspective. Subscribers were sought for this project at £3 each. Hollar's great project was overtaken by the fire that destroyed the city he sought to depict. Subsequent royal patronage yielded no financial reward and the project ground to a halt. This section is the only surviving of what would have been perhaps as many as 24 sheets.

The print is usually dated to *c.* 1660-6, but the drawings from which it was made must have been made before the end of 1660 as the early Stuart south front of the house which is clearly shown on his print was already being demolished by then.

This is a particularly important view capturing Denmark House's appearance during the Civil

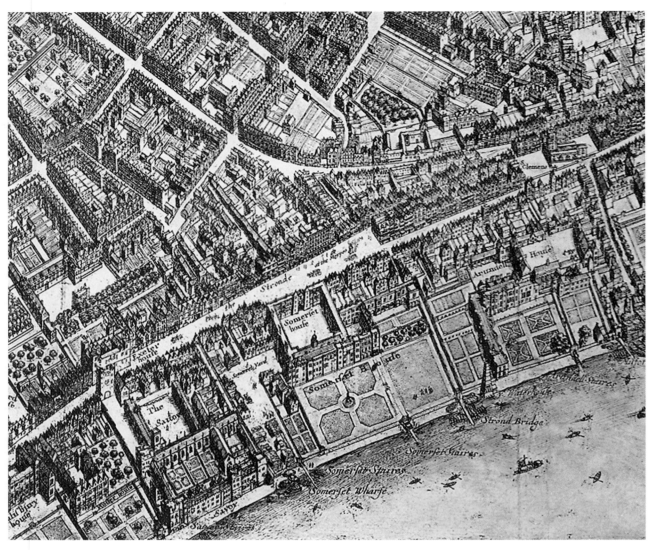

Cat 10.

War before Henrietta Maria's renewed building works of 1660. In essence, it shows in bird's-eye the early Stuart palace. Particularly important are the glimpses of the interiors of the inner and great court and the chance to understand the relationship between the Strand tenements and the royal palace. The plot sizes of the tenements are shown although these cannot be accurately related to the more or less contemporary parliamentary survey discussed in Chapter 5.

Somerset Yard is shown with the chapel in use as the French church and the west side before the new stable block was built for Catherine of Braganza. To the south of the chapel is the private house built in the 1640s on the site of the demol-

ished friary. The gardens are shown shorn of statuary by Oliver Cromwell.

BIBLIOGRAPHY

Hollar's West-Central London, c. 1658, a bird's-eye view (engraved by Walker and Cockerell), (London Topographical Society 12, 1902).

W. R. Lethaby and Rhys Jenkins, 'Hollar's Map', *London Topographical Record* II (1903), pp. 109-11.

Arthur M. Hind, *Wenceslaus Hollar and his Views of London and Windsor in the Seventeenth Century* (London, 1922), no. 6, pp. 33-4, pl. 14.

Richard Pennington, *A Descriptive Catalogue of the etched work of Wenceslaus Hollar 1607-1677* (1982), p. 169.

Catalogue 11

Wenceslaus Hollar, attrib. to, *Somerset House from the river c.1658*

Pen and ink on paper; 2in. × 6in. (5.3cm × 15.2cm)

Pepys Library Magdalene College, Cambridge, 2972, 237f.

This drawing, which is unsigned but generally accepted as being by Hollar, may be a preliminary study for his bird's-eye engraving (**cat. 9**). It neatly shows the castellated form of the house from the river front: even the waterfront wall has crenellations. The structure on the far right side, east of Strand Lane, is the water house of Arundel House.

BIBLIOGRAPHY

7 drawings photographed from the original drawing in the Pepysian Library by permission of the Master and Fellows of Magdalene College, Cambridge (London Topographical Society 50, 1922).

Robert Latham, gen. ed., *Catalogue of the Pepys Library at Magdalene College Cambridge* III, Prints and drawings; part I: General (1981), p. 21.

Catalogue 12

The Portraiture of his Royal Highness Oliver late Protector in his life and death

Printed for Edward Thomas 1659

7⅜in. × 5½in. (20.0cm × 14.0cm)

Oliver Cromwell's funeral effigy is shown standing beneath a throne canopy in the presence chamber of Somerset House. While not an image taken from life, this extraordinary print shows both the monarchical nature of Cromwell's power and the place that Somerset House occupied in the life cycle of a seventeenth-century English monarch.

BIBLIOGRAPHY

Laura Lunger Knopper, *Constructing Cromwell — Ceremony, Portrait and Print* (Cambridge, 2000), pp. 140-2.

Catalogue 13

Robert Hooke, *Plan and elevation for a stable for 70 Horses to be built at Somerset House* (*c.* 1669-70)

BL Add. MS 5238, f. 89

34³⁄₁₀in. × 44³⁄₁₀in. (87.1cm × 113.3cm)

Robert Hooke was one of Wren's most talented and prolific architectural contemporaries. He was a capable, but not inspired, draughtsman and a good architect. A number of his drawings survive, including this one, of Catherine of Braganza's new stables at Somerset House. Comparing Hooke's design with the stables shown in Kip's engraving (**cat. 20**) and the plan of 1706 (**cat. 13**), it can be seen that the building was constructed as shown, possibly making this drawing a presentation drawing for approval.

BIBLIOGRAPHY

Wren Society V (1928), pl. XXXII.

History of the King's Works V, p. 258.

H. M. Colvin, *A Biographical Dictionary of British Architects 1600-1840* (3rd edition, Yale, 1995), pp. 506-8.

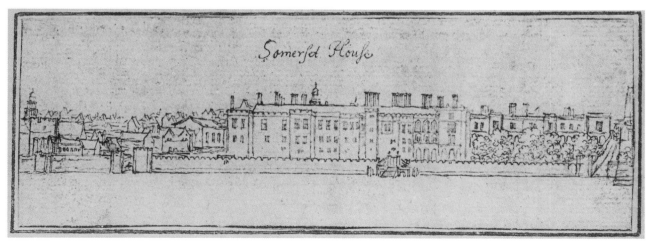

Cat 11.

Cat 12.

Catalogue 14

'A Prospect of the Chamber and Bed of State in which the Effigies of the Duke of Albemarle lay in State' from the Order and Ceremonies used for the Solemn internment of ... George Duke of Albemarle... collected by Francis Sandford 1671

British Museum Prints and Drawings 1849, 0315.40

Engraving by Robert White after Francis Barlow; 9⁷/₁₀in. × 13in. (24.7cm × 33cm)

This print is the first of a series of twenty showing the funeral procession of the Duke of Albemarle. On his death in January 1670 George Monck was honoured by Charles II with a lying-in-state at Somerset House and a state funeral and a monument (*Cal. S.P. Dom.* Charles II, 1670, pp. 16, 182). His lying-in-state reflects a tradition that grew up during the Commonwealth, that of allowing the lying-in-state of figures of state as well as members of the royal family.

The room is hung in black and lit by silver one-branch sconces and a large central chandelier. The duke's arms are hung round the room at frieze level, while his effigy lies on a state bed of typical design for the 1660s. Any architectural details are hidden by the heavy mourning cloths.

BIBLIOGRAPHY

Anthony Griffiths, *The Print in Stuart Britain* (1998), cat. 136.

MS account of the funeral and lying-in-state, BL Add. MS 10177, f. 237.

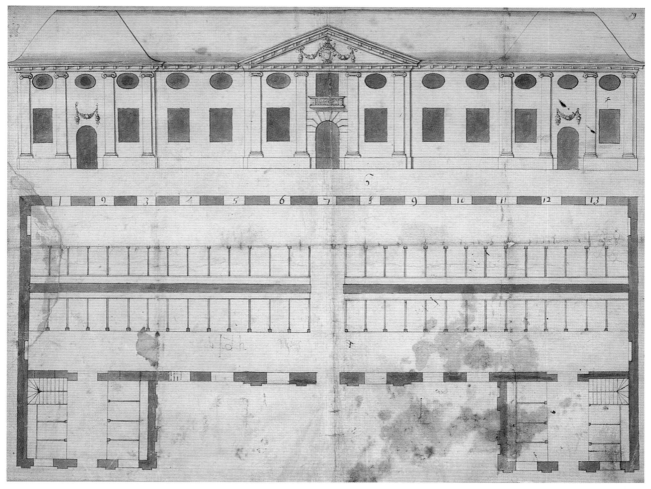

Cat 13.

Catalogue 15

William Lodge, *Old Somerset House from the South Bank of the Thames* (c. 1675)

British Museum Prints and Drawings 1866, 1114.676

Pen and ink; 11½in. × 5½in. (29.2cm × 14cm)

William Lodge, the etcher and landscape draughtsman, came from a prosperous family, and after practising law at the Inns of Court inherited £300 a year and devoted himself to drawing and etching. Many of his drawings were topographical and he enjoyed making views of towns.

Lodge's view of Somerset House captures the house not long after Henrietta Maria's work of the 1660s, viewed from the other side of the river. Unusually it shows the whole length of the building in elevation and the buildings on the site of the Savoy to the west. Notable is an accurate elevation of the house at the south end of the chapel later converted into a friary. A small sketch in the top right-hand corner captures the details of Henrietta Maria's new frontage.

BIBLIOGRAPHY

Antony Griffiths, 'Lodge, William (1649–1689)', *Oxford Dictionary of National Biography*.

Edward Croft Murray and Paul Hulton, *Catalogue of British Drawings in the British Museum. I: XVI-XVII Centuries* (London, 1960), pp. 426-8 and pl. 225.

Catalogue 16

John Ogilby and William Morgan, *Large and Accurate map of the City of London* (1676)

60in. × 97½in. (152.4cm × 247.7cm)

Ogilby and Morgan's map of 1676 was the first true map of London with all the features laid out in plan and to scale. Indeed, its accuracy and detail was not to be matched until the publication of the

Cat 14.

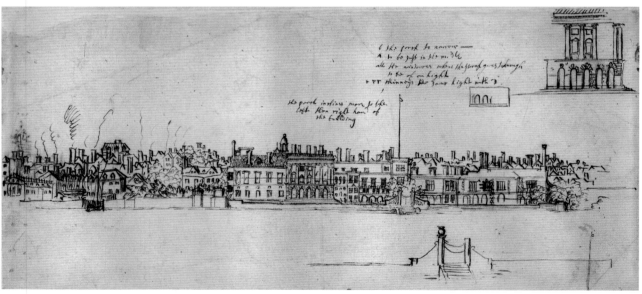

Cat 15.

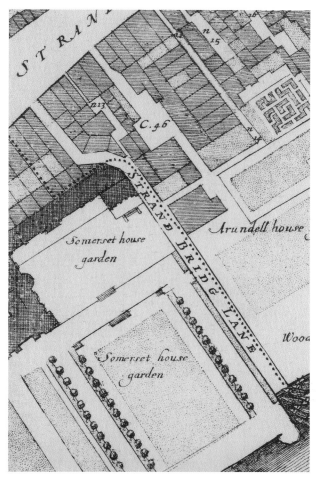

Cat 16.

Cat 17.

first edition of the Ordnance Survey. Twenty sheets covered the city and sheet 16 at the map's westernmost edge shows the Strand, Fleet Street and most of Somerset House at a scale of 1in. to 100ft. Sadly, the map ends without covering the whole of Somerset House, making it an interesting, accurate, but very partial source.

BIBLIOGRAPHY

James Howgego, *Printed Maps of London circa 1553-1850* (2nd edition, 1978), no. 28, pp. 58-9.

Charles Welch, ed., *A Large and accurate Map of the city of London [...] 1677. (London survey'd, or, An explanation of the Large Map of London [...]* (LAMAS, 1895).

Ralph Hyde, ed., *London &c. Actually Survey'd [...] by William Morgan* (Harry Margary and Guildhall Library, 1977).

Catalogue 17

Godfrey Richards, trans., *Le Muet's edition of Palladio's First Book of Architecture*

5¼in. × 3⁴⁄₁₀in. (13.3cm × 8.6cm)

This plate from Godfrey Richard's shows 'floors of small squares of carpentry work' at Somerset House installed for Henrietta Maria in 1662.

BIBLIOGRAPHY

Godfrey Richards, trans., 'Le Muet's edition of Palladio', *First Book of Architecture* (3rd edition, 1676), pp. 132-3, pl. 36.

Cat 18.

Catalogue 18

William Morgan, *Survey of London and Westminster* (1682)

Twelve sheets, each 44¼in. × 93in. (112.4cm × 236.2cm)

Ogilby and Morgan's map of 1676 showed only a part of Stuart London, just including at its western edge Somerset House. William Morgan set out to create a map covering the whole of London (including Westminster) with popular appeal, rich in elevations and perspectives, as well as containing the ground plan of the City. A number of ancient and modern buildings, including the relatively recently completed south front of Somerset House, were included. An engraved panorama designed to run as a frieze either at the top or the bottom of the map shows every building in detail. The view of Somerset House is unfortunately on the junction of two sheets. Nevertheless, it represents Henrietta Maria's remodelled façade accurately.

The plan, which also shows stylized elevations of Somerset House, is the first to plot the new stables and accurately show the relation of the tenements and rents to the palace buildings.

BIBLIOGRAPHY

James Howgego, *Printed Maps of London circa 1553-1850* (2nd edition, 1978), no. 33, pp. 15-16, 62-4.

William Morgan, *Survey of London 1682* (Harry Margary, Lympne Castle, in association with the Guildhall Library, with an introduction by Ralph Hyde).

Catalogue 19

William Dickinson, *Plans of two floors of Somerset House* (engraved by Barak Longmate) (1806)

Plan 1, 23.2cm × 31.4cm

Plan 2, 18.7cm × 23.5cm

These two plans are the earliest to show the whole palace in detail and seem to be very accurate, despite being engraved copies of an original drawing. For instance, the stables as engraved agree in detail with Robert Hooke's original plan of them (**cat. 13**).

In 1706 Queen Anne decided to reserve Somerset House for the accommodation of ambassadors, and in preparation the Office of Works was instructed to undertake a comprehensive survey of it. This was to comprise a new accurate plan and a list of inhabitants. Francis Bickerton, later an assistant of Henry Flitcroft, was paid £20 for 'plotting down in a map the whole Pallace of Denmark House', and this was then redrawn to a smaller scale by one of the best draughtsmen in the office, William Dickinson. The plan was set in a frame, and the list of inhabitants copied out in neat. Both were then presented to the queen (TNA E351/3311 m4).

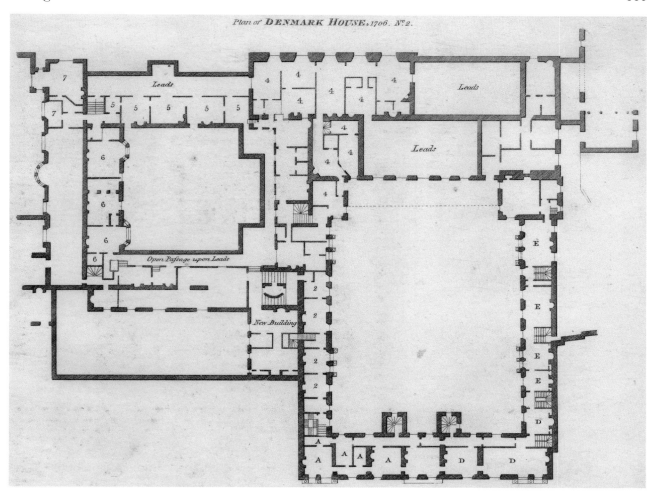

Plan of DENMARK HOUSE, 1706. Nº 2.

Cat 19a.

The original plan (or a copy of it and the list) were acquired, in due course, by the antiquary Richard Gough. Gough was a gentleman of private means who devoted himself to antiquarian study, travelling the country amassing information on history, topography and architecture. How he came into possession of the plans is unclear, but it is possible that when the Society of Antiquaries, of which he was a director, moved to Somerset House in 1780 he obtained a copy from the Office of Works.

Gough was a close friend of another member of the Society, Samuel Pegge. Pegge was the son of a distinguished antiquary of the same name who had wide-ranging interests and was closely associated with the circle of antiquaries who included Francis Grose and John Nichols. Through the patronage of the Duke of Devonshire, Pegge the younger was appointed groom of the privy chamber to George III in 1762. In this position he

acquired a deep curiosity and fascination with the royal court and household. He set out to amass a huge amount of primary information on his chosen subject and published it in two major works. The first was *Curialia, or, An historical account of Some Branches of the Royal Household*, which was published in five parts between 1782 and 1806. The last two parts were edited by John Nichols. His second work, *Curialia Miscellanea, or, Anecdotes of old times, regal, noble, gentilitian, and miscellaneous, including authentic anecdotes of the royal household*, was also edited by Nichols and published in 1818.

Parts IV and V of *Curialia* contained 'A succinct history of Somerset House from the commencement of its erection in 1549', written (all but the last two pages) by Pegge before his death and published by Nichols in 1806. Pegge was very interested in Somerset House and was the first person to write its history. His account utilizes primary materials as well as printed sources. He

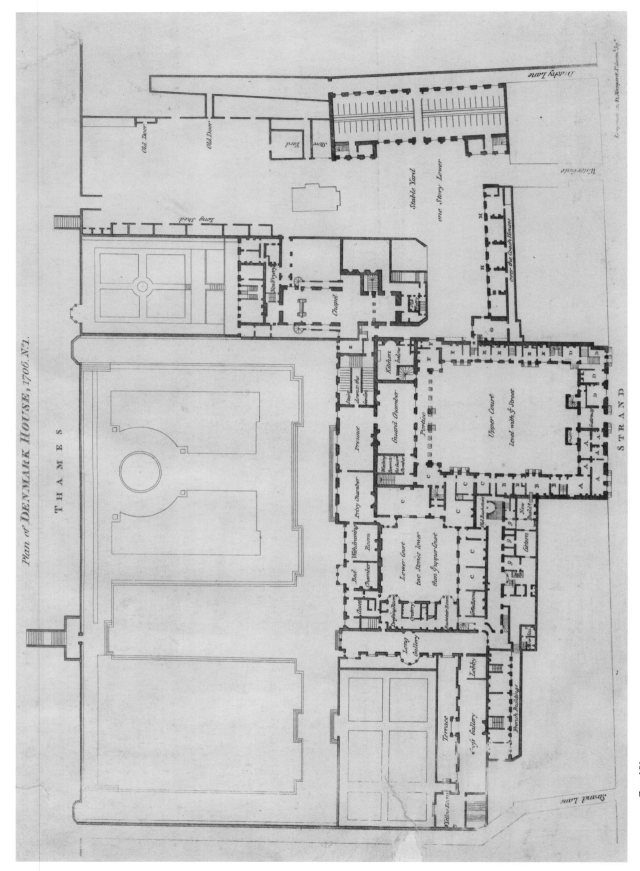

Plan of *DENMARK HOUSE*, 1706. N.º 1.

THAMES

Cat 19b.

almost certainly knew of Smythson's plan which was at the time in the hands of the Revd D'Ewes Coke of Broke-hill, Pinxton, Derbyshire. Pegge mentions his collection in his *Bibliotheca Topographica Britannica* (1793).

Nichols got Gough to agree to append to this essay his plans and the list of accommodation at Somerset House (*Curialia*, pp. ii-iii). The plans were engraved by Barak Longmate the younger (1768-1836), who moved in the antiquarian circle of Nichols and Pegge and had already engraved plans for the *Gentleman's Magazine*.

The list of accommodation which is printed in full by Pegge is very detailed and records the inhabitants of almost every room in the house in 1706. The principal groups of lodgings are identified by either a letter or a number on the plans as follows:

A: Rooms occupied by the Countess of Fingall
B: The former rooms of the Master of the Robes occupied by Mr Rowland
C: The Earl of Feversham

D: Countess of Arlington
E: Sir Richard Bealing
F: Madam Melows, the Earl of Feversham's niece
G: Clerk of Works
H: 'Works House'
K: Father Christopher

2: Madam Roper
4: Vice-Chamberlain's Porter
5: 'the Portugal Lady's lodgings'
6: Mr Stephens
7: Lady Joanna Thornhill
9: Mr Sayers

The picture painted by the list of accommodation is of a building containing a large and varied grace-and-favour community living in close proximity. The history of grace-and-favour has not yet been written, but recent work on Whitehall (Simon Thurley, *The Whitehall Palace Plan of 1670* (London Topographical Society 153, 1998), pp. 16-26) and Hampton Court (Simon Thurley, *Hampton Court a Social and Architectural History* (Yale, 2003), pp. 327-32) have sketched out the bare bones of how

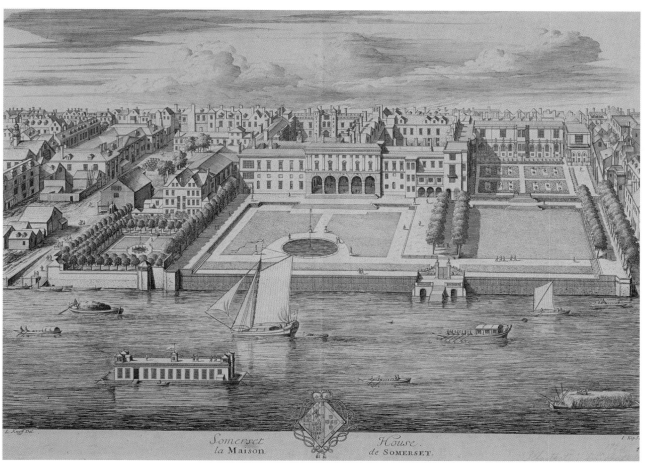

Somerset House
la Maison　　*de* SOMERSET.

Cat 20.

lodgings were allocated and to whom. The Somerset House list and accompanying plans portray what King William IV was later to describe as 'a quality poor house', a community of economically distressed gentry and nobility living in faded grandeur. The effect of this community on the Strand is not chronicled, but the presence of this large group of *nouveax pauvres* would have been striking.

The plans show that a few improvements and alterations were made in the latter part of Catherine of Braganza's time, particularly a room and staircase in the north-west corner of the inner court. This staircase must have been architecturally pretentious and caused the removal of the queen's council chamber to a new location on the south front.

BIBLIOGRAPHY

Samuel Pegge, *Curialia or an Historical Account of Some Branches of the Royal Household &c.* part IV (London, 1806).

'Obituary of Barak Longmate', *Gentleman's Magazine* V, 25 February 1836.

Thompson Cooper, rev. K. D. Reynolds, 'Samuel Pegge', R. H. Sweet, 'Richard Gough', *Oxford Dictionary of National Biography*.

Catalogue 20

Leonard Knyff and Jan Kip, *Britannia Illustrata or Views of Several of the Queen's Palaces also of the Principal Seats of the Nobility and Gentry of Great Britain* (1707)

16.5cm × 24.3cm

The Dutch landscape painter Leonard Knyff and his lesser-known brother Jacob were pioneers of the bird's-eye view in England. In the late 1690s Leonard conceived an idea for a great book of bird's-eye views depicting the country houses of England. His concept was perhaps modelled on Jacques Androuet du Cerceau's *Plus Excellent Bastiments de France* of 1568, the equivalent of which had never been made in England. Subscribers were sought for this in mid-1701. Sixty of Knyff's drawings were engraved by Jan Kip and the book was published in 1707 as *Britannia Illustrata* and sold by the publisher and bookseller David Mortier.

The first six plates of the book were of royal palaces and the seventh of Lambeth Palace. The buildings were shown in order of precedence, with St James's Palace and Park being the first two and Somerset House the third. It was followed by the Tower of London, Hampton Court and Windsor Castle.

It is not clear how Knyff achieved such clear and accurate drawings, but he must have made hundreds of preliminary drawings and sketches of the inside of courtyards and the flanks of walls. His visualization of Somerset House is very accurate and many details can be corroborated form other sources. His prospects are quite unlike those produced by the Amsterdam engraver Johannes de Ram in about 1690, who issued a view of Somerset House in *c*. 1690. De Ram's engraving, which was widely reproduced (for instance, in Coronelli's *Viaggi* of 1697 and Beeverell's *Delices de la Grand Bretagne* of 1707) was inaccurate, distorted and even fanciful.

Kip created the defining view of Somerset House and his image was widely copied and reproduced. It was used in Overton's *Prospects* (*c*. 1720-30), in the 1720 edition of Stow's *Survey of London* and in many later books.

BIBLIOGRAPHY

John Harris and Gervaise Jackson-Stops, ed., *Britannia Illustrata* (Bungay: The National Trust, 1984).

Bernard Adams, *London Illustrated 1604-1851. A Survey and Index of Topographical Books and their Plates* (London, 1983).

Catalogue 21

Colen Campbell, Elevation of the Great Gallery in Somerset House to the River, *Vitruvius Britannicus* I (1715), pl. 16

24.9cm × 37.8cm

Colen Campbell (1676-1729) took the survey of English architecture one stage further than Knyff and Kip had done. Their *Britannia Illustrata* contained perspective views of great seats; it omitted much that was new and presented buildings in a topographical rather than technical elevational mode. Campbell's three volumes, eventually to depict 103 buildings, presented detailed scaled plans and elevations for the first time. His choice of buildings was strongly affected by missionary zeal, for *Vitruvius Britannicus* was as much a prospectus of what he wanted English

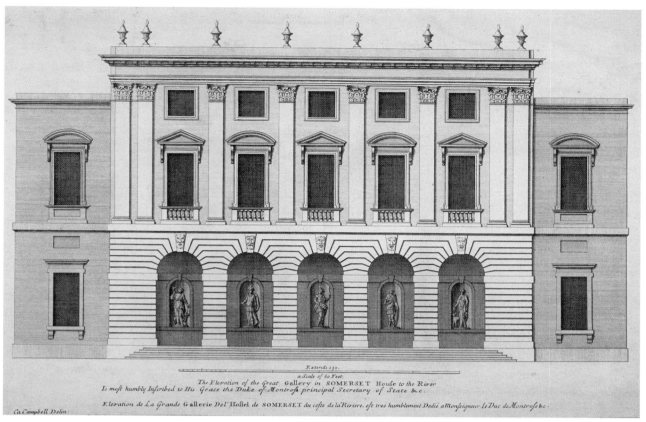

Cat 21.

Cat 22.

architecture to be as a record of what it was. The focus of the work was a celebration of the work of Andrea Palladio and Inigo Jones, whom he believed provided a model for modern architect to follow.

This explains the inclusion of the south façade of Somerset House which was, according to Campbell, taken from a design by Inigo Jones but erected by 'another hand', by which he meant John Webb. This book argues that this is a misattribution and that the front was designed entirely from scratch after the Restoration and that it was probably by Hugh May.

By 1715 Somerset House was in decay and out of fashion, so it is a measure of the respect accorded to this frontispiece that it made it into volume I of *Vitruvius Britannicus*. However, the elevation is more important for its symbolic value than its accuracy, which is doubtful; a more accurate rendition of the façade is **cat. 34**.

BIBLIOGRAPHY

Paul Breman and Denise Addis, with an introduction by John Harris, *Guide to Vitruvius Britannicus. Annotated and Analytic Index to the Plates* (New York, 1972).

Catalogue 22

Henry Flitcroft, *Measured drawing of the Ceiling of the Somerset House Chapel made for Lord Burlington* (c. 1735)

Royal Institute of British Architects Drawings Collection

Pen and wash; 13⁴/₅in. × 20¹/₂in. (35cm × 52cm)

Henry Flitcroft, who ended his career as a leading architect and doyen of the royal Office of Works, started out as a brilliant and clinical draughtsman working for Lord Burlington. Some of his duties were realizing on paper the earl's own designs, but perhaps more important was recording the work of Inigo Jones and John Webb. Many of these drawings were published in William Kent's *The Designs of Inigo Jones* in 1727.

The drawing of the Somerset House Chapel ceiling never made it to publication, and forms a pair with a section of Inigo Jones's chapel at St James's (**cat. 23**, also in the RIBA Drawings Collection). The drawing gives to scale all the plan and sectional information required to reproduce all or part of the ceiling if required. It shows a flat-beamed structure with rich embellishment on the deep beams like that at the Banqueting House. The central rectangle contained a painting until the Civil War. The portion of ceiling over one presbytery was treated with a Roman coffered ceiling. The section shows that the screen to the upper tribune (**cat. 23b**) was very thin. The drawing does not show the transept ceilings suggesting that they were at a lower level.

BIBLIOGRAPHY

John Harris, *Catalogue of the Drawings Collection of the Royal Institute of British Architects. Inigo Jones and John Webb* (London, 1972), p. 15, **cat. 39** and Fig. 35.

John Harris and Gordon Higgott, *The Complete Architectural Drawings of Inigo Jones* (London, 1989), p. 198.

Catalogue 23

Isaac Ware, *Survey drawings prepared for engraving showing the frontal of the tribune and the reredos in Somerset House Chapel* (c. 1735)

Sir John Soane's Museum

8¹/₂in. × 9³/₄in. (21.6cm × 24.8cm)

Isaac Ware was a long-standing employee of the Office of Works with his own private practice. Like so many architects of his age he was brought up in the circle of Lord Burlington, and in 1727 subscribed to William Kent's *Designs of Inigo Jones*. Six years later, with a private commission under his belt, Ware published his own collection of drawings entitled *Designs of Inigo Jones and Others*, which included designs by Lord Burlington and William Kent.

The two drawings of Somerset House chapel were engraved by P. Fourdrinier for Ware's *Designs* as plates 29 and 30. It is possible that the original surveys from which Ware's drawings were prepared were, in fact, made by Henry Flitcroft at the same time as he recorded the ceiling for Lord Burlington (**cat. 22**).

It is likely that Ware knew that the reredos was not by Jones as he gives the screen to Jones but does not make an attribution for the altar piece. The drawings, together with Flitcroft's record of the ceiling, paint a picture of the queen's chapel interior in the late 1660s after Henrietta Maria had left for France. By 1735 the chapel had been Anglican for some years, but the principal architectural features seem to have survived.

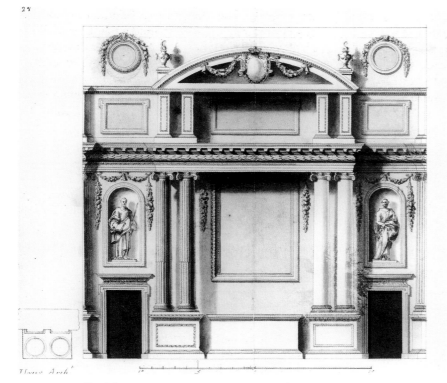

Cat 23a.

Cat 23b.

Cat 24.

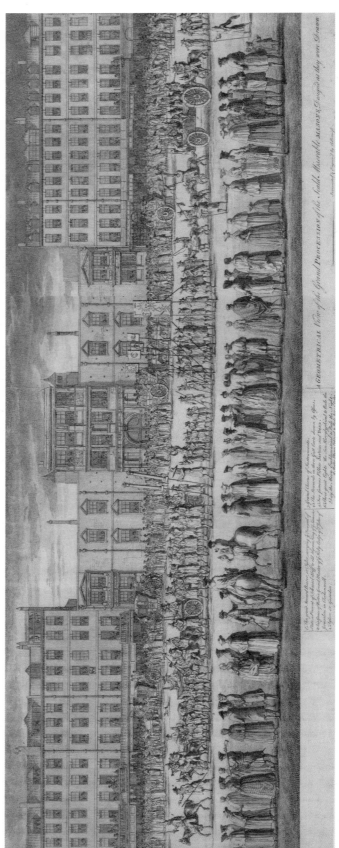

Cat 25.

BIBLIOGRAPHY

John Harris and Gordon Higgott, *The Complete Architectural Drawings of Inigo Jones* (London, 1989), pp. 198, 200.

H. M. Colvin, *A Biographical Dictionary of British Architects 1600-1840* (3rd edition, Yale, 1995), pp. 1020-1.

Simon Thurley, 'The Stuart Kings, Oliver Cromwell and the Chapel Royal 1618-1685', *Architectural History* 45 (2002), pp. 247, 258-61.

Catalogue 24

Unknown, *View of Somerset House from the Thames* (*c.* 1734)

British Museum Prints and Drawings, Crace Portfolio VI, sheet 13, no. 206

Pen and ink with watercolour; 24in. × 3¼in. (61cm × 8.2cm)

This handsome view of Somerset House from the river is by an unknown, but proficient, hand. Like **cat. 25** (which shows the Strand elevation), **cat. 24** shows the old palace in its elevational context in the period of its decline. It shows, from left to right, the Somerset House stables and Somerset House Yard. The buildings at the south end of the chapel are immediately to the left of the main building. The cross gallery is partly obscured by trees but to the right of it, across Strand Lane, are the houses developed on the site of Arundel House after its demolition in about 1680. Surrey Street, Norfolk Street and Arundel Street formed a grid of new development shown in plan form by Roque's Map of 1746 (**cat. 27**).

This view, like **cat. 25**, makes the point that in the 1730s Somerset House was looking very old-fashioned against its more modern and domestic-scaled neighbours.

Catalogue 25

Unknown, *A geometrical View of a Procession of the Scald Miserable Masons passing Somerset House on 27 April 1742*

Engraved by Antoine Benoist and published by F. Vivares, 1771

Guildhall Library P7489056

22.9cm × 60.6cm

Benoist was a French draughtsman and engraver who came to London in about 1735 and, despite occasional trips to Paris, made his home in London where he died in 1770. His engraving of the Scald Miserables Procession is one of his most remarkable works. The image, 24in. (61cm) long, shows a parade of mock Freemasons on the Strand on 27 April 1742, the procession passing in front of Somerset House. The whole of the south side of the Strand is shown in geometrical elevation, including the shops and houses built by the Earl of Dorset in around 1700.

In the early eighteenth century freemasonry in London underwent a period of public hostility. The annual procession of masons to the Grand Lodge in full regalia was ridiculed in a series of spoof processions in 1741, 1742, 1744 and 1745. These mass events led to the permanent abandonment of Masonic processions in 1747 (Robert F. Gould, *A History of Freemasonry* (New York, 1994), p. 44). The record of Somerset House is incidental but important. It is the only complete depiction of the Strand elevation of the house in context and should be compared with Thomas Bowles's print (**cat. 29**).

A smaller and earlier version of this view was published by Thomas Hurst, Edward Chance & Co. in 1742. The artist and engraver of this are anonymous. A copy can be found in the Guildhall Library (P7488950).

BIBLIOGRAPHY

Timothy Clayton and Anita McConnell, 'Anthony Benoist', *Oxford Dictionary of National Biography*.

Catalogue 26

Giovanni Antonio Canal (Canaletto), *Old Somerset House from the River Thames* (*c.* 1746-50)

Yale Centre for British Art, Paul Mellon Collection, acc. no. B1977.14.6111

Pen and brown ink with grey wash; 16½in. × 28½in. (41.6cm × 72.7cm)

Giovanni Antonio Canal, better known as Canaletto, arrived in London in 1746 seeking to continue his highly profitable business of view-painting in England from where many of his clients had always come. Canaletto's first English paintings were views of and from the Thames, and for his first two years he barely left the capital. In

Cat 26.

1748 he began to paint views of country houses, but returned to London in 1749-50 to paint some of his greatest London views, including the two majestic panoramas of London from the terrace of Somerset House. These views were instantly popular and the one looking east was published as a print in 1750. There are a number of versions of these paintings, the largest of which are in the Royal Collection. The primary version of the painting is now agreed to be the one in a private collection. A very similar version was sold at Christie's, New York, 2 June 1988, having been widely exhibited as the prototype (for instance at Somerset House in 1977 (cat. *London and the Thames*), and Birmingham (Michael Liversidge and Jane Farrington, ed., *Canaletto and England* (ex. cat. Birmingham Museums and Art Gallery, 1993), p. 93).

Canaletto was later to paint a much tighter view of Somerset House from the river for which a drawing survives in the Paul Mellon Collection. It is this drawing which is reproduced here as Canaletto's most accurate and clear rendering of Somerset House. This is no preliminary sketch; it is a carefully finished drawing presumably intended to show the effect of a painting to a prospective client. Yet a careful comparison between the drawing and the better-known painting reveals that for the finished painting Canaletto

tidied up the view, making the house and garden look less dilapidated, pruning the trees, removing weeds from the waterfront and adding smart visitors to the gardens. This drawing is thus a valuable record of the south front of the old palace in decay.

BIBLIOGRAPHY

Charles Beddington et al., *Canaletto in England: A Venetian Artist Abroad,* (Dulwich Picture Gallery, Yale, 2006), pp. 70-5.

W. G. Constable (revised J. G. Links), *Canaletto*, 2 vols (Oxford, 1976, 3rd edition 1989), I, pl. 138; II, nos 428a, b; 429; 430; 743.

Catalogue 27

John Rocque, *London and Westminster* or even *An exact Survey of the Cities of London and Westminster, the Borough of Southwark, with the Country near ten Miles round.* (London, 1746).

In 1746 the first new map of London since William Morgan's 1682 venture was published. It was produced by John Rocque, a Huguenot surveyor who lived in Soho. His 'exact Survey of London' was commissioned and partly financed by John Pine, royal engraver and friend of William Hogarth. It was started in about 1737 and took

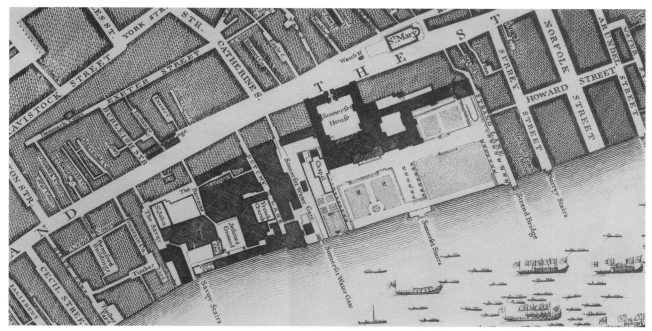

Cat 27.

Cat 28.

nine years to measure. The finished map was 13ft (3.96m) wide and 6½ ft (1.98m) deep, rather unwieldy but undoubtedly impressive — the map went through at least eight editions by 1769.

Rocque recorded Somerset House in its last phase of its history, now surrounded by more modern development and fronting the regularized and paved Strand. It is the first map to show St Mary-le-Strand consecrated in 1724 and built out of the proceeds of the 1711 Act of Parliament for the construction of fifty new churches. The church replaced its distant predecessor demolished in 1548 for the construction of Somerset Place.

The chapel is still shown as a separate entity in its own garden in Somerset House Yard. The public landing stage, Somerset Water Gate, is prominently marked.

BIBLIOGRAPHY

Ida Darlington and James Howgego, *Printed Maps of London 1553-1850* (London, 1964), no. 94, pp. 94-5.

Paul Laxton, 'John Rocque', *Oxford Dictionary of National Biography*.

Ralph Hyde, 'Portraying London Mid-Century — John Rocque and the Brothers Buck' in Sheila O'Connell, ed., *London 1753* (London, 2003), pp. 28-34.

Cat 29.

Catalogue 28

Paul Sandby, *View from the Gardens of Somerset House looking East* (*c.* 1750)

British Museum G.13.31

Watercolour with grey wash and pen and ink over graphite 1ft 8¹/₅in. × 6ft 2¹/₂in. (51.4cm × 189.3cm)

Thomas Sandby and his younger brother Paul were born in Nottingham, and Thomas came to London at the age of 19 where he joined the Ordinance Office at the Tower of London as a draughtsman. He was soon joined there by his brother. Both were to go on to work for the Board of Ordinance in Scotland and, while Thomas rose to be official draughtsman to the Duke of Cumberland, Paul was to enjoy posthumous fame as the father of English watercolour.

It is difficult to tell the work of the two brothers apart, particularly as they often collaborated on large pictures. However, it is generally agreed that it was Paul Sandby who painted a series of views of London from the gardens of Somerset House. His intention was not primarily to show the old palace but to capture the sweep of the Thames panorama. In doing this he was probably following the example of Canaletto (**cat. 26**), but perhaps more immediately influenced by an engraving by J.

Maurer published in 1742. It has been pointed out that Sandby's view includes most of the features shown by Maurer.

Sandby's painting is particularly important as it shows the differences between the parts of the south front built in brick and stone demonstrating that the earlier parts of the house on the riverfront had, at their lower levels, been built of stone. Windows inserted can be clearly seen punched into the earlier wall.

Another view by Sandby, not included here (British Museum G.13.30) shows the view looking west, with a glimpse of the lower parts of Somerset House amongst the trees. A third in the Royal Collection shows a more focused view of the south front of Somerset House (Michael Liversidge and Jane Farrington, ed., *Canaletto and England* (ex. cat. Birmingham Museums and Art Gallery, 1993), p. 132).

Bibliography

Sheila O'Connell, ed., *London 1753* (London, 2003), pp. 125-6 and col. pl. 5.

L. Stainton, *British Landscape Watercolours* (London, 1985), no. 21a.

Luke Hermann, *Paul and Thomas Sandby* (London, 1986).

Catalogue 29

Thomas Bowles III, A View of Somerset House with St. Mary's Church in the Strand published by Robert Sayer 1753

Guildhall Library P7489033. Also BM P&D 1880, 1113.2891

Print; 10³/₁₀in. × 15⁴/₅in. (26.2cm × 40.2cm)

Thomas Bowles (d. 1767), a print- and map-maker and seller, made a number of views of London scenes in the mid-eighteenth century, operating from his family's print shop in St Paul's Churchyard. In 1753 two views of Somerset House were published, one of the river front and gardens by the Swiss topographical draughtsman John Maurer (copy in Guildhall P7488950), the other an anonymous view looking east down the Strand towards St Mary-le-Strand (copy in Guildhall P7489027). The print shown here is a version drawn and engraved by Bowles and published by Robert Sayer, showing the Strand façade of Somerset House from an oblique angle looking east. It gives unique information about the upper level of the great room and loggia, over the frontispiece.

BIBLIOGRAPHY

Timothy Claton, 'The Bowles Family', *Oxford Dictionary of National Biography*.

Susanna Fisher, 'Robert Sayer', *Oxford Dictionary of National Biography*.

Catalogue 30

Unknown, *Plan of the state apartments at Somerset House (c. 1762)*

Royal Collection RL 31278

Pen and ink with coloured wash; 28in. × 13¼in. (71.1cm × 33.65cm)

The Royal Library has an album of six drawings of the first-floor plans of the state apartments of royal palaces: St James's, Kensington, Hampton Court, Windsor Castle, Somerset House and the Queen's House (Buckingham House). They are all in the same confident and competent hand and bound in red morocco.

At some later date several of the plans have been annotated in pencil. The plan for St James's is heavily marked, showing a potential rebuilding of the south front. The gallery at Windsor also has pencil annotations suggesting a rebuilding. Less prominent pencil markings can be found on the Hampton Court drawing.

The Somerset House plan has faint pencil lines on 'E' the bedchamber and 'D' the dining room, suggesting the removal of a bay window and a change in fireplace position. The Long Gallery has pencil lines suggesting division into four rooms.

The plan which is key to dating and understanding this album is that of the Queen's House. The Queen's House was acquired by George III in 1762 for £28,000. Technically it was purchased as a dower house for the queen, in effect to replace the historic function of the decaying Somerset House. The plan in the Royal Collection album shows the first floor of the central pavilion of Buckingham House with the room designations as they were in 1762. Alterations soon took place and the plan as captured in the album soon became a record of the original state of the main central rooms.

The plans in the album were thus drawn in *c.* 1762 and were probably an aid to making decisions about future use and possible alteration for the new king. The pencil annotations were perhaps part of the process of deciding on the use and layout of rooms. This plan pre-dates the definitive survey of Somerset House undertaken by Kenton Couse in 1775, and the minor differences between the plans illustrate the changes made early in George III's reign in the state apartments. The Royal Library plan has the bedchamber between the drawing room and dressing room, Kenton Couse has the dressing room in the middle. However, as neither George II nor Queen Charlotte never used the rooms, this change is unlikely to have any functional significance.

Catalogue 31

James Hunter, *Elevation of the Strand façade of Somerset House and a sectional plan of its front wall* (1775)

TNA Work 30/263 (contained in Work 30/259)

Pen and wash on paper; 36½in. × 24½in. (92.7cm × 62.2cm)

This drawing is one of a pair made immediately before the demolition of Old Somerset House. They are in the same hand and are a set as can be seen by the addition of a plan at the bottom of

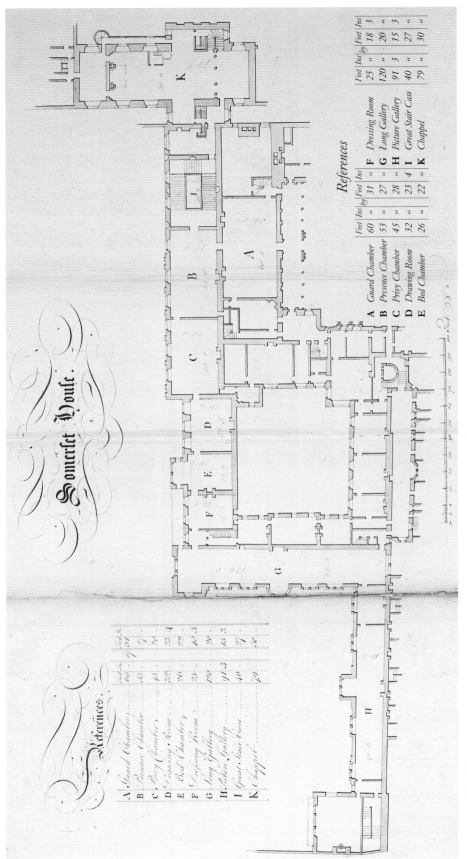

References

		Feet Ins	by	Feet Ins					Feet Ins	by	Feet Ins
A	Guard Chamber	60	"	31	"	F	Dressing Room	25	"	18	3
B	Presence Chamber	53	"	27	"	G	Long Gallery	120	"	20	"
C	Prity Chamber	45	"	28	"	H	Picture Gallery	91	3	15	3
D	Drawing Room	32	"	23	4	I	Great Stair Case	40	"	27	"
E	Bed Chamber	26	"	22	"	K	Chappel	79	"	30	"

Cat 30.

Cat 31.

Cat 32.

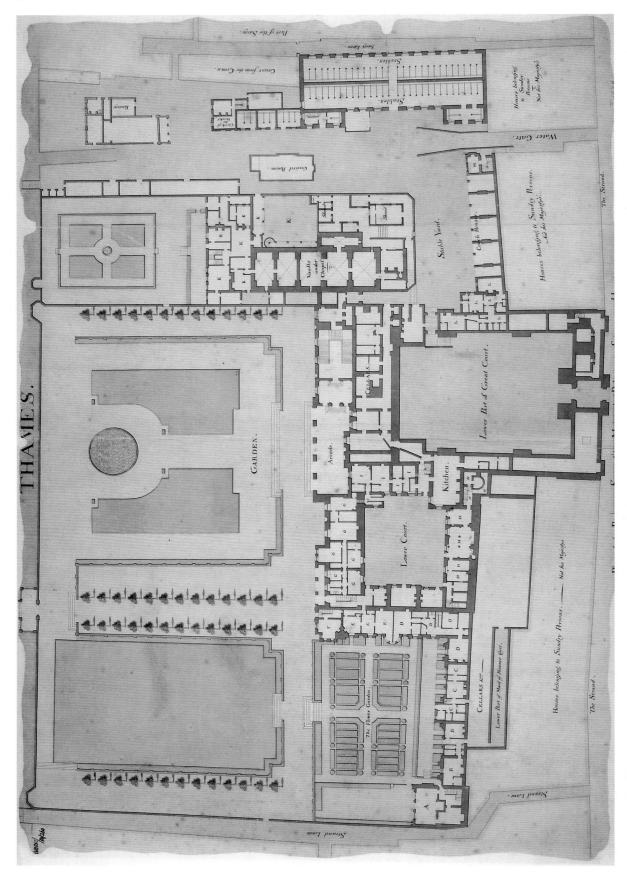

THAMES.

GARDEN.

The Flower Garden.

Lower Court.

Lower Part of Great Court.

Stable Yard.

Guard Room.

Arcade.

Kitchen.

CELLARS.

CELLARS &c.

Vaults under Chapel.

Strand Lane.

Strand Lane.

The Strand.

The Strand.

Water Gate.

Stables.

Stables.

Savoy Lane.

Part of the Savoy.

Grant from the Crown.

Clerk of the Works.

Nursery.

Lower Part of Maid of Honour Court.

Houses belonging to Sundry Persons. — Not his Majesty's.

Houses belonging to Sundry Persons. Not his Majesty's.

Houses belonging to Sundry Persons. Not his Majesty's.

Coach House.

Cat 33a.

each. **Cat. 32** is signed and dated by James Hunter, who can most likely be identified with the man of the same name who was an apprentice to James Arrow, Inspector of Repairs to the Admiralty from 1774. Arrow was also a joiner and played a large part in the construction of New Somerset House between 1776 and 1795 (*HKW* v, p. 446). Hunter was admitted to the Royal Academy Schools at Somerset House in 1773, aged 17, and was a successful draughtsman and artist, winning the silver medal in 1775.

These two drawings ended up in the collection of the Office of Works together with Kenton Couse's careful survey (**cat. 35**), and this suggests that they were part of the office's record of the building on the eve on its demolition. Whether the Office of Works commissioned the young draughtsman to execute these fine drawings, whether he offered them speculatively or whether his patron James Arrow obtained the commission for him is not known. At any rate, both Hunter and Arrow had a personal interest in Somerset House.

The drawing is the most important record of the Strand elevation of Somerset House as it is to scale and represents what was actually there in 1775. As such it can be compared to John Thorpe's plan and elevation (**cat. 7**). There are substantial survivals of both Protector Somerset's work and of Anne of Denmark's alterations, including dated and initialled lead hopper heads. This drawing give a detailed impression of the sculptural work on the façade, little of which is shown by Thorpe and, of course, since the early eighteenth century the parapet has been cut down and the frontispiece given a shallow attic.

BIBLIOGRAPHY

H. M. Colvin, *A Biographical Dictionary of British Architects 1600-1840* (3rd edition, Yale, 1995), pp. 79, 521.

Catalogue 32

James Hunter, *Measured details of the chimney stacks on the Stand range of Somerset House with a plan of the loggia on the south side of the great court* 1775. On the reverse is a sketch for the elevation of the centre-piece on the Strand front

TNA Work 30/264

Pen and wash on paper; 37in. × 24½in. (94cm × 62.2cm)

Signed 'James Hunter, 1775'

It is perhaps not surprising that the Tudor chimneys on the Strand front should command the interest of James Hunter and end up in the archive of the Office of Works. They are superb examples of Tudor workmanship and may well date to the Duke of Somerset's period. Rather than the chevrons and barley-twists of earlier Tudor stacks at, for instance, Hampton Court, these adopt an up-to-the-minute decorative vocabulary directly from Serlio. The shaft on the left is taken directly from a design in Serlio's fourth book (Ch. 12, f. 69).

The plan of the 'Arcade in the Great Court' is less decorative, but still records what was in its day an innovative part of the building.

BIBLIOGRAPHY

H. M. Colvin, *A Biographical Dictionary of British Architects 1600-1840* (3rd edition, Yale, 1995), p. 521.

Catalogue 33

Kenton Couse, *Plans of the basement storey, principal floor and upper storey of his Majesties Palace at Somerset House* 1775

TNA Work 30/260-2

Work 30/262 is signed by Couse and Work 30/261 has a K in the corner. The plans are undated

Pen and wash on paper; each measuring 35in. × 23in. (88.9cm × 58.42cm)

On 6 May 1774 the Board of the Office of Works submitted to the Treasury a report which stated that, on the basis of a survey that they had commissioned, Somerset House was in such as poor state of repair that it would be uneconomical to put it into order, especially as any royal use had long since ceased. Eleven days later George III agreed that the building be completely demolished. Work on demolition did not start until 1776 and in the meantime Kenton Couse was ordered to make a new measured plan of the building.

Couse had been apprenticed to Henry Flitcroft, Clerk of Works at Whitehall, Westminster and St James's, and in 1746 gained his own junior position in the Office of Works. He was a conscientious administrator and a competent architect who was also a fine draughtsman. In 1775 he was appointed

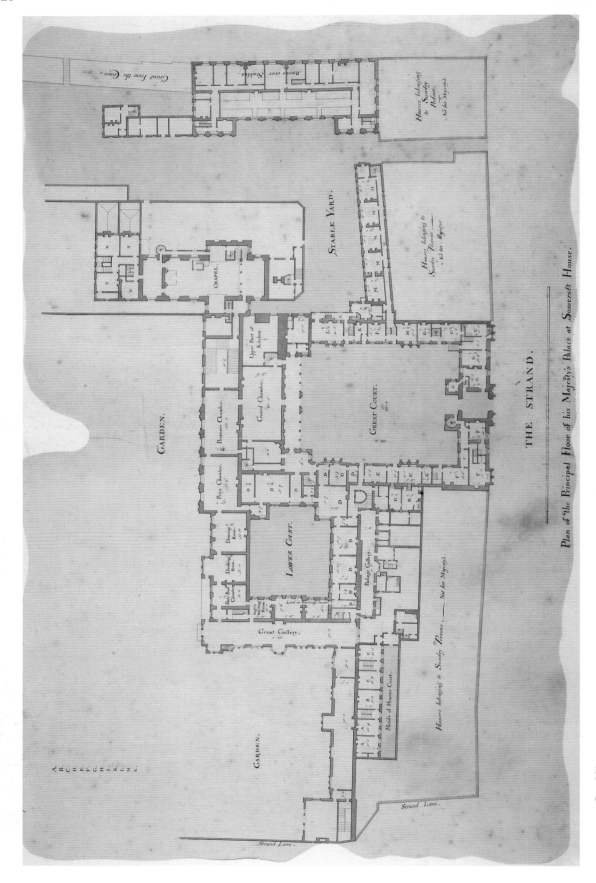

Cat 33b.

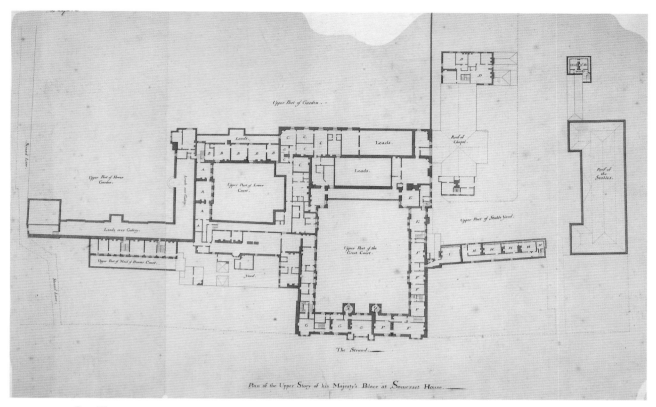

Cat 33c.

Secretary to the Board of Works, Clerk Itinerant and Draftsman and Clerk of the Works at the Queen's Palace. This latter role was primarily directed at Buckingham House but included responsibility for Somerset House, which was still officially part of the queen's 'palace'. These duties were taken up on 10 October 1775, only months before the demolition was to start and fifteen months after the Board of Works presented their survey to the Treasury. Couse's authorship of the plans demonstrates that the plans must have been drawn in 1775.

Why such a high-quality plan should be made of a building on the eve of its demolition is open to question. One reason may have been to record the lodgings of the grace-and-favour occupants. Like the plan of 1706 (**cat. 19**), Couse's plan is annotated with letters denoting the extent of grace-and-favour apartments. There is no key so the identity of the owners is lost; however removing occupants and compensating them would have probably required a plan to be made. This is what happened at Whitehall in 1670 when it was thought that that palace might be rebuilt (Simon Thurley, *The Whitehall Palace Plan of 1670*

(London Topographical Society 153, 1998), pp. 16-26). A further reason could be to aid salvage and demolition. Brick and stone from the old palace were used in the foundations and core work of Sir William Chambers's new building, and fireplaces and panelling were sold to builders' merchants.

The drawing is of exceptional quality and detail; rooms are labelled or numbered (the key is incomplete) and the principal-floor rooms have their dimensions written in. The drawing has washes and the gardens are rendered with trees in perspective. The immediate environs are captured and the plan makes it clear that most of the land formerly attached to the palace had been alienated from the Crown.

Couse captured the old palace at the eleventh hour, creating a permanent record of a building that had been maintained by the Office of Works for nearly a century.

BIBLIOGRAPHY

H. M. Colvin, *A Biographical Dictionary of British Architects 1600-1840* (3rd edition, Yale, 1995), pp. 274-5.

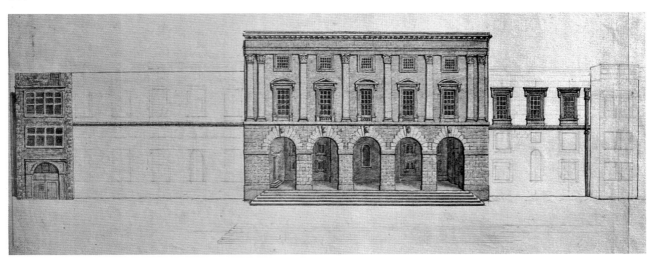

Cat 34.

M. H. Port, 'Kenton Couse', *Oxford Dictionary of National Biography*.

H. M. Colvin, ed., *The History of the King's Works* V (London, 1976).

Catalogue 34

James Basire, *The Gallery at Old Somerset House* (*c.* 1775)

Society of Antiquaries of London Red Portfolios Middlesex, vol. 4, f. 14

19¾in. × 11 in. (50cm × 29cm)

James Basire came from a dynasty of draughtsmen and printmakers and followed his father and grandfather into the profession. In 1755 he was appointed engraver to the Society of Antiquaries and antiquarian or topographical engraving became the mainstay of his career. The view of the south front of Somerset House is still in the Antiquaries' collection and is a meticulous rendering of the front in about 1775. His record is one of a number made at the end of the palace's life and in this case records the part of the palace most admired by architects as being designed by Inigo Jones.

Importantly, this elevation shows, on the far left, one of the last parts of the sixteenth-century palace left unmodernized — the gateway to the kitchens and the casement windows of the kitchens themselves.

BIBLIOGRAPHY

Lucy Peltz, 'Isaac Basire', *Oxford Dictionary of National Biography*.

Catalogue 35

William Moss, *The North Front of Somerset House* (1776)

Ashmolean Musem WA.C.II.III.175b

Pen and ink and watercolour; 7⅓in. × 8⁹⁄₁₀in. (18.4cm × 22.7cm)

Moss was a landscape painter, etcher, architectural draughtsman and minor architect admitted to the Royal Academy Schools in 1774. The Academy was sited in Somerset House, and so the ancient building was perhaps an obvious subject for a 22-year-old student. His careful drawing is the only complete record of the outer court of the palace. The drawing with the addition of some imaginative street life was later turned into a large aquatint engraved by F. Dukes in 1777; a copy of this can be found in the Guildhall Library La.Pr.W2/Som.

The watercolour shows clearly the decayed appearance of the Strand frontage with serious stone erosion to the mouldings and carvings. Only two of the original chimneys seem to survive.

BIBLIOGRAPHY

David Blayney Brown, *Catalogue of the Collection of Drawings, IV: The Earlier British Drawings — British Artists and Foreigners Working in Britain Born before c.1775* (Oxford, 1982), cat. 1444.

H. Colvin, *Biographical Dictionary of Architects 1600-1840* (3rd edition, 1995), p. 670.

Cat 35.

Cat 36.

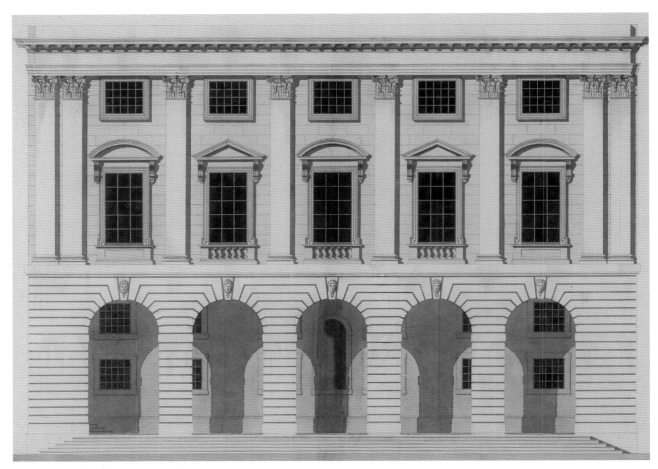

Cat 37.

Catalogue 36

William Moss, *The Outer Courtyard of Somerset House* (1776)

Ashmolean Musem WA.C.II.III.175a

Pen and ink and watercolour; 5⅘in.× 9¹/₁₀in. (14.8cm × 22.9cm)

Moss's second image of Somerset House on the eve of its demolition, with the addition of figures and vehicles, was later turned into a large aquatint engraved by F. Dukes in 1777. A reduction was engraved by W. M. Fellows and published in 1808 for J. T. Smith's *Westminster*, also in the Guildhall at Pr. W2/Som.

This watercolour is particularly important as it is the only one to reliably record the outer court of Somerset House. What Moss shows is much altered from its prime in the seventeenth century. The courtyard is topped, not by a balustrade, but by a plain parapet. Like the Strand elevation there

is much stone decay; the pilasters framing the upper storey of the windows on both the east and west seem to be damaged. In the south-west corner a low wall encloses steps that lead down to the vaults beneath the courtyard.

BIBLIOGRAPHY

David Blayney Brown, *Catalogue of the Collection of Drawings, IV: The Earlier British Drawings — British Artists and Foreigners Working in Britain Born before c.1775* (Oxford, 1982), cat. 1445.

H. Colvin, *Biographical Dictionary of Architects 1600-1840* (3rd edition, Yale, 1995), p. 670.

Catalogue 37

Office of William Chambers, *Elevation of Somerset House to the River*

Government Art Collection 10252

24 in. × 32 in. (62cm × 81.5cm)

Cat 38.

Sir William Chambers was a great admirer of the southern frontispiece of Somerset House which he believed to be by Inigo Jones and John Webb. He had used this part of the building as a theme in his designs for a new palace for George III at Richmond, from about 1770 (David Watkin, *The Architect King. George III and the Culture of the Enlightenment* (London, 2004), pp. 120-1). Therefore it is not surprising that amongst the papers in his office was this record elevation of the façade. Although the Richmond Schemes were never to be built, the southern frontispiece was the inspiration for the central part of the strand façade of New Somerset House.

Catalogue 38

The Demolition of Old Somerset House

Museum of London

8½in.× 9½in. (21.6cm × 24.1cm)

This is the best and most interesting of a small group of drawings showing the demolition of Old Somerset House. The event was obviously of great interest at the time and it is unusual to have produced so many careful records drawn from different angles.

The Museum of London watercolour shows the north elevation of the inner court under demolition. Prominently in the centre is Protector

Cat 39.

Somerset's gatehouse, and either side of it the north walls of the strand range. Workmen are dismantling the west tower and throwing down timber baulks to be sorted. Meanwhile well-dressed gentlemen view the sight.

Architecturally this view is valuable as it shows details of the frieze in the inner court, the treatment of the archway and other features such as the roundel high between the gate towers.

In the right background can be seen the new houses on the Strand and the spire of St Mary-le-Strand.

Catalogue 39

Unknown, *Old Somerset House (in course of demolition).* Early home of the Royal Academy

Arts Journal (1887), p. 399

This view of the demolition of the old palace was taken from Somerset House yard looking east. The chapel would have stood to the right of the view, but this has already been demolished. On the right is the carcass of the kitchens and state apartments beyond. The hall cupola stands over the middle of the ruins and to the left part of the east range of the outer court. The mixture of stone and brick

and casement windows and sashes shows that this was part of the outer court rather than a show front.

Catalogue 40

Unknown, *The ruins of Old Somerset House and Part of the New*

TNA Work 30/267 (contained in Work 30/259)

Pen and wash; 12in. × 11in. (30.5cm × 27.9cm)

This anonymous drawing of the partially demolished palace shows the remains of the great hall from the north. The loggia has been demolished and the great door to what was, in 1775, the guard chamber can be seen in the middle of the range flanked by round-headed niches. The façade is of stone and the casement windows of the upper part of the hall can be seen beneath the cupola of the clock.

In the left foreground are the remains of the eastern return of the south-east corner of the outer court built for Anne of Denmark. The walls of the outer court are revealed to be of brick, and clinging to an interior face is a small section of decorated plaster frieze.

Cat 40.

Cat 41.

It can be seen that the hall range was built up upon round-headed brick vaults and that the emerging west range of Chambers' building is lower than the Tudor palace. This helps to explain Kenton Couse's plan of the basement level of the courtyard (**cat. 33**).

Catalogue 41

Unknown, *The demolition of Somerset House, engraved by Midland*

British Museum Prints and Drawings, Crace Portfolio VI, sheet 13, no. 200

Print; 6in. × 4in. (15.2cm × 10.2cm)

A version of **cat. 40** with the Strand front of Chambers' building to the right was engraved by Midland and first published in the *Gentleman's Magazine* in January 1798. It was subsequently used in 1806 by Pegge to illustrate the Somerset House section of *Curialia* (pl. 5 on p. 90).

BIBLIOGRAPHY

Airs, Malcolm, 'Pomp and Glory: The Influence of Theobalds', in Pauline Croft, ed., *Patronage, Culture and Power. The Early Cecils 1558–1612* (Studies in British Art 8, Yale, 2002)

Airs, Malcolm, *The Tudor and Jacobean Country House. A Building History* (Gloucester, 1995)

Alford, Stephen, *Kingship and Politics in the Reign of Edward VI* (Cambridge, 2002)

Allsopp, Bruce, ed., *Inigo Jones on Palladio, being the notes by Inigo Jones in the Copy of I Quattro Libri dell'architettura de Andrea Palladio, 1601, in the Library of Worcester College Oxford*, 2 vols (Newcastle upon Tyne, 1970)

Androuet Du Cerceau, Jacques, *Exempla arcuum, partim ab ipso inventa, partim ex veterum sumpta monumenta* (Orléans, 1549)

Anglo, Sydney, *Spectacle Pageantry and Early Tudor Policy* (Oxford, 1969)

Avery, Charles, 'The Collector Earl and his Modern Marbles. Thomas Howard and François Dieussart', *Apollo* CLXIII (June 2006)

Bachrach, A. G. H., and Collmer, R. G., ed. and trans., *Lodweijk Huygens: The English Journal 1651–1652* (Leiden, 1982)

Barroll, Leeds, 'The Court of the First Stuart Queen', in Linda Levy Peck, ed., *The Mental World of the Jacobean Court* (Cambridge 1991)

Bathe, Graham, 'The Duke of Somerset's Grand Mansion at The Brails, Great Bedwyn: A Review of the Evidence', *Wiltshire Archaeological and Natural History Magazine* 99 (2006)

Batho, G. R., 'Henry, Ninth Earl of Northumberland and Syon House, Middlesex', *Transactions of the Ancient Monuments Society* n.s. IV (1956)

Batho, G. R., 'Syon House: The First Two Hundred Years, 1431–1632', *Transactions of the London and Middlesex Archaeological Society* n.s. 19 (1958)

Beattie, J. M., *The English Court in the Reign of George I* (Cambridge, 1967)

Beddard, Robert, *A Kingdom Without a King. The Journal of the Provisional Government in the Revolution of 1688* (Oxford, 1988)

Beer, Barrett L., ed., *The Life and Raigne of King Edward the Sixth by John Hayward* (Kent, Ohio and London, 1993)

Beer, E. S., ed., *The Diary of John Evelyn*, 6 vols (Oxford, 1955)

Bellot, H. H. L., *Inner and Middle Temple* (London, 1902)

Birch, T., ed., *The Court and Times of Charles I*, 2 vols (London, 1849)

Bold, John, *John Webb. Architectural Theory and Practice in the Seventeenth Century* (Oxford, 1990)

Brewer, John S., ed., *Dr. Godfrey Goodman, The Court of King James the First*, 2 vols (London, 1839)

Britland, Karen, *Drama at the Courts of Queen Henrietta Maria* (Cambridge, 2006)

Brown, Jonathan and Elliott, John, eds, *The Sale of the Century. Artistic Relations Between Spain and Great Britain, 1604–1655* (Yale, 2002)

Brown, Jonathan, *Kings and Connoisseurs. Collecting Art in Seventeenth-Century Europe* (Yale, 1995)

Bush, M. L., *The Government Policy of Protector Somerset* (London, 1975)

Carlton, Charles, *Charles I. The Personal Monarch* (2nd edition, London, 1995)

Chambers, E. K., *The Elizabethan Stage*, 4 vols (Oxford, 1923)

Clarendon, Earl of (Edward), *The History of the Rebellion and Civil Wars in England*, 6 vols (Oxford, 1888)

Colvin, H. M., *Biographical Dictionary of British Architects* (3rd edition, Yale, 1995)

Colvin, Howard, and Foister, Susan, and Ann Saunders, ed., *The Panorama of London circa 1544* (London Topographical Society 151 in association with the Ashmolean, Oxford, 1996)

Colvin, Howard, ed., *The History of the King's Works*, 6 vols (London, 1963–82)

Corp, Edward, 'Catherine of Braganza and Cultural Politics', in Clarissa Campbell Orr, ed., *Queenship in Britain 1660–1837* (Manchester, 2002)

Croft, Pauline, ed., *Patronage, Culture and Power. The Early Cecils 1558–1612* (Studies in British Art 8, Yale, 2002)

Delavand, M. Louis, Gaucheron, Roger, and Dermenghem, Émile, *Memoires de Cardinal de Richelieu* 5 (Paris, Société de l'Histoire de France, 1907 (31))

Dewar, Mary, *Sir Thomas Smith, A Tudor Intellectual in Office* (London, 1964)

Dunbar, J. G, *Scottish Royal Palaces. The Architecture of the Royal Residences During the Late Medieval and Early Renaissance Periods* (East Linton, 1999)

Fanshawe H. C., ed., *Memoirs of Ann, Lady Fanshawe* (London, 1907)

Finet, Sir John, *Finetti Philoxensis: Som Choice Observations of Sir John Finett, Knight, and Master of Ceremonies to the two Last Kings, Touching the Reception, and Precedence, and the Treatment and Audience, the Punctillios and Contests of Forren Ambassadors in England* (London, 1656)

Firth, C. H., rev. A. J. Hopper, 'Sir Samuel Tuke', *Oxford Dictionary of National Biography* (2004)

Firth, C. H., ed., *The Memoirs of Edmund Ludlow*, 2 vols (Oxford, 1894)

Fisher, Geoffrey, and Newman, John, 'A Fountain Design by Inigo Jones', *Burlington Magazine* 127 (August 1985)

Fisher N. R. R., 'The Queenes Courte in her Councell Chamber at Westminster', *English Historical Review* (1993), pp. 315-17; Maureen M. Meikle, 'Holde her at the Oeconomike rule of the House', pp. 105-10; Lodge, *Illustrations of British History*, pp. 208-14

Furnivall, Frederick J., ed., *Harrison's Description of England in Shakespeare's Youth, being the second and third books of his Description of Britaine and England* (London, 1877)

Gaimster, David, and Gilchrist, Roberta, *The Archaeology of the Reformation* (Society for Post-Medieval Archaeology, 2003)

Girouard, Mark, *Robert Smythson and the Elizabethan Country House* (Yale, 1983)

Girouard, Mark, *Social Life in the English Country House* (Yale, 1978)

Girouard, Mark, 'The Development of Longleat House between 1546 and 1572', *Archaeological Journal* CXVI (1959)

Girouard, Mark, *Life in the French Country House* (London, 2000)

Gunn, S. J., and Lindley, P. G., *Cardinal Wolsey, Church, State and Art* (Cambridge, 1991)

Harris, John, 'The Link between a Roman Second-Century Sculptor, Van Dyck, Inigo Jones and Queen Henrietta Maria', *Burlington Magazine* 115 (August 1973)

Harris, John, and Higgott, Gordon, *Inigo Jones, Complete Architectural Drawings* (London, 1989)

Harris, John, and Tait, A. A., *Catalogue of the Drawings by Inigo Jones, John Webb and Isaac de Caus at Worcester College Oxford* (Oxford, 1979)

Harris, John, *Catalogue of the Drawings Collection of the Royal Institute of British Architects. Inigo Jones and John Webb* (London, 1972)

Harris, Tim, 'London Crowds and the Revolution of 1688', in Eveline Cruikshanks, ed., *By Force or Default? The Revolution of 1688–89* (Edinburgh, 1989)

Harvey, John, *English Medieval Architects, A Biographical Dictionary Down to 1550* (Gloucester, 1984)

Hattendorf, J. B., 'John Robinson', *Oxford Dictionary of National Biography* (2004)

Hearn, Karen, ed., *Dynasties. Painting in Tudor and Jacobean England* (Tate, 1995)

Henderson, Paula, 'The Loggia in Tudor and Early Stuart England: The Adaption and Function of Classical Form', in Lucy Gent, ed., *Albion's Classicism: The Visual Arts in Britain, 1550–1660* (Studies in British Art 2, Yale, 1995)

Hibbard, Caroline, 'Henrietta Maria in the 1630s: Perspectives on the Role of Consort Queens in *Ancien Régime* Courts', in Ian Atherton and Julie Sanders, eds, *The 1630s. Interdisciplinary Essays on Culture and Politics in the Caroline Era* (Manchester, 2006)

Hibbard, Caroline, 'Translating Royalty: Henrietta Maria and the Transition from Princess to Queen', *The Court Historian* 5 (1) (May 2000)

Hibbard, Caroline, 'Somerset House Chapel and the Topography of London Catholicism', in George Gorst and Malcolm Smutts, eds, *The Politics of Court Space in Europe and the Mediterranean, ca. 1500–1750* (Rome, 2009)

Higgott, Gordon, 'Inigo Jones's Theory of Design', *Architectural History* 35 (1992)

Hippeau, M. C., *Mémoires Inédits du comte Leveneur de Tillières* (Paris, 1862)

Howard, Deborah, *The Architectural History of Scotland* (Edinburgh, 1995)

Howard, Maurice, *The Early Tudor Country House. Architecture and Politics 1490–1550* (London, 1987)

Husselby, Gillian, 'Architecture at Burghley House: The Patronage of William Cecil 1553–1598', 3 vols (unpublished PhD Thesis, Warwick, 1996)

Inderwick, F. A., ed., *The Inner Temple: History and Records, 1505–1603* (London, 1896)

Jackson, J. E., 'Wulfhall and the Seymours', *The Wiltshire Archaeological and Natural History Magazine* XV (1875)

James, Susan, 'Edward Seymour, Duke of Somerset? Re-examining a Tudor Portrait', *The British Art Journal* II (2) (Winter 2000/1)

Jervis, Simon, '"Shadows, not substantial things". Furniture in the Commonwealth Inventories', in Arthur MacGregor, ed., *The Late King's Goods* (London and Oxford, 1989)

Jordan, W. K., *The Chronicle and Political Papers of King Edward VI* (New York, Cornell, 1966)

Jordan, W. K., *Edward VI: The Threshold of Power. The Dominance of the Duke of Northumberland* (Harvard, 1970)

Journal of the House of Commons, VII

Keay, Anna, 'The Ceremonies of Charles II Court' (unpublished PhD Thesis, London, 2004)

Keene, Derek, Burns, Arthur, and Saint, Andrew, eds, *St. Paul's. The Cathedral Church of London 604–2004* (Yale, 2004)

King, John Norman, 'Protector Somerset, Patron of the English Renaissance', *The Papers of the Bibliographical Society of America* 70 (1976)

Kingsford, C. L., ed., *A Survey of London by John Stow*, reprinted from the text of 1603, 2 vols (Oxford, 1908)

Knoppers Lunger, Laura, *Constructing Cromwell. Ceremony, Portrait and Print 1645–1661* (Cambridge, 2000)

Knowler, William, ed., *Thomas Wentworth, Earl of Strafford, Letters and Dispatches* (Dublin, 1711)

Knowles, James, '"To Enlight the darksome Night, Pale Cinthia Doth Arise": Anna of Denmark, Elizabeth I and the Images of Royalty', in Clare McManus, ed., *Women and Culture at the Courts of the Stuart Queens* (Basingstoke, 2003)

Larsen, Ruth M., 'Mary Campbell', *Oxford Dictionary of National Biography* (2004)

Latham, Robert, and Matthews, William, eds, *The Diary of Samuel Pepys*, 11 vols (London, 1970–83)

Leech, Peter, 'Musicians in the Catholic Chapel of Catherine of Braganza, 1662–92', *Early Music* (November 2001)

Lindley, David, *The Court Masque* (Manchester, 1984)

Lindley, K. J., 'The Lay Catholics of England in the Reign of Charles I', *Journal of Ecclesiastical History* XXII (3) (1971)

Lobel, Mary D., ed., *The British Atlas of Historic Towns. 3, The City of London from Prehistoric Times to c.1520* (Oxford, 1989)

Lockyer, Roger, *Buckingham. The Life and Political Career of George Villiers, First Duke of Buckingham, 1592–1628,* (London, 1984)

Lodge, E., *Illustrations of British History, Biography and Manners* (London, 1791)

Loomie, Albert J., 'The Destruction of Rubens's "Crucifixion" in the Queen's Chapel, Somerset House', *Burlington Magazine* 140 (October 1998)

MacCulloch, Diarmaid, *The Boy King Edward VI and the Protestant Reformation* (New York, 2001)

MacKechnie, Aonghus, 'James VI's Architects and their Architecture', in Julian Goodare and Michael Lynch, eds, *The Reign of James VI* (East Linton, 2000)

MacKechnie, Aonghus, 'The Royal Palace of Dunfermline', in Richard Fawcett, ed., *Royal Dunfermline* (Society of Antiquaries of Scotland, 2005)

McClure, N. E., ed., 'The Letters of John Chamberlain', *Memoirs of the American Philosophical Society*, 2 vols (1939)

McCullough, Peter E., *Sermons at Court. Politics and Religion in Elizabethan and Jacobean Preaching* (Cambridge, 1998)

McKean, Charles, *The Scottish Chateau. The Country Houses of Renaissance Scotland* (Stroud, 2001)

McKellar, Elizabeth, *The Birth of Modern London* (Manchester, 1999)

McManus, Clare, ed., *Women and Culture at the Courts of the Stuart Queens* (Basingstoke, 2003)

Meikle, Maureen M., '"Holde her at the Oeconomike rule of the House": Anna of Denmark and Scottish Court Finances, 1589–1603', in Elizabeth Ewan and Maureen M. Meikle, eds, *Women in Scotland c.1100–c.1750* (East Linton, 1999)

Merriman, Marcus, 'Italian Military Engineers in Britain in the 1540s', in Sarah Tyacke, ed., *English Map Making, 1500–1650: Historical Essays* (London, 1983)

Merriman, Marcus, 'Sir Richard Lee', *Dictionary of National Biography* (Oxford, 2004)

Millar, Oliver, ed., 'The Inventories and Valuations of the King's Goods 1649–1651', *Walpole Society* 43 (1970–2)

Moryson, Fynes, *An Itinerary*, 4 vols (London, 1617)

Needham, Raymond, and Webster, Alexander, *Somerset House, Past and Present* (London, 1905)

Nichols, J. G., 'The Diary of Henry Machyn', *Camden Society* 42 (1842), p. 37

Nichols, John, The *Progresses and Public Processions of Queen Elizabeth*, 3 vols (London, 1823)

Nichols, John, *The Progresses, Processions and Magnificent Festivities of King James the First*, 4 vols (London, 1828)

Norden, John, *Speculum Britanniae* (London, 1580)

Orrell, John, *The Theatres of Inigo Jones and John Webb* (Cambridge, 1985)

Payne, M. T. W., 'An Inventory of Queen Anna of Denmark's "Ornaments, furniture, householde stuffe, and other parcels" at Denmark House, 1619', *Journal of the History of Collections* 13 (1) (2001)

Pegge, Samuel, *Curialia or an Historical Account of Some Branches of the Royal Household, Part I A Succinct History of Somerset House* (London, 1806)

Pevsner, Nikolaus, 'Old Somerset Place', *The Architectural Review* CXVI (1954)

Pitcher, John, ed., *Samuel Daniel, Hymen's Triumph* (Oxford, Malone Society reprints, 1994)

Pollard, A. F., *England under Protector Somerset; an Essay* (London, 1900)

Porter, Stephen, 'William Crofts', *Oxford Dictionary of National Biography* (2004)

Poulton, Rob and Cook, Alan, with a major contribution from Thurley, Simon, *Excavations at Oatlands Palace 1968–73 and 1983–4* (in press)

Ravelhofer, Barbara, *The Early Stuart Masque. Dance, Costume, and Music* (Oxford, 2006)

Rosser, Gervase, and Thurley, Simon, 'Whitehall Palace and King Street Westminster: The Urban Cost of Princely Magnificence', *London Topographical Record* XXVI (1990)

Rosser, Gervase, *Medieval Westminster 1200–1540* (Oxford, 1989)

Rushworth, John, *Historical Collections Abridg'd and Improved*, 4 vols (London, 1702)

Rye, W. B., ed., *England as seen by Foreigners, in the days of Elizabeth and James the First* (London, 1865)

Salzman, L. F., *Building in England Down to 1540* (Oxford, 1952)

Saunders, Ann, ed., *The Royal Exchange* (London Topographical Society 152, 1997)

Schofield, John, *The London Surveys of Ralph Treswell* (London Topographical Society 135, 1987)

Serre, P. de la, *Histoire de l'Entrée de la Reyne Mere du Roy très Chrétien dans la Grande Bretagne* (London, 1639)

Sharpe, Kevin, *The Personal Rule of Charles I* (Yale, 1992)

Shelby, L. R., *John Rogers. Tudor Military Engineer* (Oxford, 1967)

Sherwood, Roy, *Oliver Cromwell. King in all but Name 1653–1658* (Gloucester, 1997)

Sloane, Barney, and Malcolm, Gordon, *Excavations at the Priory of the Order of the Hospital of St. John of Jerusalem, Clerkenwell, London*, MoLAS monograph 20 (Museum of London, 2004)

Smolenaars, Marja, 'Gerard, John', *Oxford Dictionary of National Biography* (2004)

Smuts, Malcolm R., *Court Culture and the Royalist Tradition in Early Stuart England* (Philadelphia, 1999)

Spalding, Ruth, ed., 'The Diary of Bulstrode Whitelocke 1605–1675', *Records of Social and Economic History* n.s. XIII (Oxford, 1990)

Spiers, W. L., 'The Note Book and Account Book of Nicholas Stone', *Walpole Society* VII (1918–19)

Spraggon, Julie, *Puritan Iconoclasm During the English Civil War* (Woodbridge, 2003)

Starkey, David, *Elizabeth* (London, 2000)

Stone, Lawrence, 'Inigo Jones and the New Exchange', *Archaeological Journal* 114 (1957)

Stow, J., *The Survey of London* (London, 1618)

Strong, Roy, *The Artist and the Garden* (Yale, 2000)

Strong, Roy, *The Renaissance Garden in England* (London, 1998)

Strype, John, ed., *Stow's Survey of London* (London, 1720)

Summerson, John, with a foreword by Sir Howard Colvin, *Inigo Jones* (Yale, 2000)

Summerson, Sir John, *Architecture in Britain 1530–1830* (1953)

Thornton, Peter, *Seventeenth Century Interior Decoration in England, France, and Holland* (Yale, 1983)

Thurley, Simon, 'Cardinal Wolsey's Domestic Building Works', in S. J. Gunn, and P. G. Lindley, eds, *Cardinal Wolsey, Church, State and Art* (Cambridge, 1991)

Thurley, Simon, *The Royal Palaces of Tudor England* (Yale, 1993)

Thurley, Simon, *Whitehall Palace. An Architectural History of the Royal Apartments, 1240–1698* (Yale, 1999)

Thurley, Simon, 'Nonsuch: A Palace Fit for a Prince?' *Country Life*, 11 August 2005

Thurley, Simon, 'The Stuart Kings, Oliver Cromwell and the Chapel Royal 1618–1685', *Architectural History* 45 (2002)

Thurley, Simon, *Hampton Court. A Social and Architectural History* (Yale, 2003)

Thurley, Simon, 'A Country Seat Fit for a King: Charles II, Greenwich and Winchester', in Eveline Cruikshanks, ed., *The Stuart Courts* (Gloucester, 2000)

Thurley, Simon, 'The Politics of Court Space in Early Stuart London', in George Gorst and Malcolm Smutts, eds, *The Politics of Court Space* (forthcoming, 2009).

Toynbee, M., 'The Wedding Journey of King Charles I', *Archaeologia Cantiana* LXIX (1955)

Turquet, Josephine C., 'The Inner Court of Nonsuch Palace' (unpublished PhD Thesis, London, 1983)

Veevers, Erica, *Images of Love and Religion. Henrietta Maria and Court Entertainments* (Cambridge, 1989)

Von Klarwill, Victor, *The Fugger Newsletters* (London, 1926)

Wade, Mara R., *Triumphus Nuptialis Danicus. German Court Culture and Denmark. The 'Great Wedding' of 1634* (Wiesbaden, 1996)

Whinney, M., *Sculpture in Britain 1530–1830* (Harmondsworth, 1964)

White, Michelle Anna, *Henrietta Maria and the English Civil Wars* (Ashgate, 2006)

Whitelocke, Bulstrode, 'Diary of 1605–1675', *Records of Social and Economic History* n.s. XIII (Oxford, 1990)

Willetts, Pamela J., *Catalogue of the Manuscripts in the Society of Antiquaries of London* (London, 2000)

Wood, Duncan, and Munby, Julian, 'The Historical Development of Somerset House: An Archaeological Investigation', *Transactions of the London and Middlesex Archaeological Society* 54 (2003)

Woodward, Jennifer, *The Theatre of Death. The Ritual Management of Royal Funerals in Renaissance England, 1570–1625* (Woodbridge, 1997)

Worsley, Giles, *Inigo Jones and the European Classicist Tradition* (Yale, 2007)

Worsley, Giles, *The British Stable* (Yale, 2004)

INDEX